Henry Beauclerk

Jesus; his life in the very words of the four gospels

Henry Beauclerk

Jesus; his life in the very words of the four gospels

ISBN/EAN: 9783741189012

Manufactured in Europe, USA, Canada, Australia, Japa

Cover: Foto ©ninafisch / pixelio.de

Manufactured and distributed by brebook publishing software (www.brebook.com)

Henry Beauclerk

Jesus; his life in the very words of the four gospels

JESUS

HIS LIFE IN THE VERY WORDS OF THE FOUR GOSPELS

A
DIATESSARON

BY
HENRY BEAUCLERK
Priest of the Society of Jesus

LONDON: BURNS AND OATES, LIMITED.
NEW YORK, CINCINNATI, CHICAGO: BENZIGER BROTHERS.
1896.

[All rights reserved.]

PREFACE.

DIATESSARON, or *Through the Four*, was the title given by the Syrian writer Tatian in the second century, to his *Life of Jesus Christ*, compiled from the four Gospels. The present work embodies the same idea. It professes to set forth the life of our Lord in one connected uniform narrative, from which no *event*, *discourse*, or even *detail*, occurring in any of the four Gospels has been omitted, nevertheless the whole narrative being made up entirely of the words of the inspired writers.

Wherever the same thing is recorded by two or more of the Evangelists, I have chosen that account which is fullest or most circumstantial, and have illustrated and filled out the details of it by extracts from the other narratives.

Reference to the four indexes at the end will prove that, either in the text itself or in the margin, every single verse of the four Gospels has been accounted for.

The marginal references will, it is hoped, enable the reader to see, at a glance, what parts of our Lord's life are narrated by only one, and what by more than one of the Evangelists. They will enable him also to judge whether, in the transposition of words and paragraphs, the sacred text has been treated legitimately, and in no arbitrary manner. As a further aid to such study, the "superiors," Mt. Mk. Lk. Jn., have been inserted in the body of the text, but, it is hoped, of such a pattern as to prove as little distracting as possible to the ordinary reader.

To supply a commentary was beyond the scope of this little work. The notes which I have thought it advisable to add are, for a similar reason, as concise as possible. They are intended mainly to guide those who have opportunities for a fuller study of the matters treated in them; the ordinary devout reader may pass them over without notice. The notes are comparatively few in number; and all of them bear, directly or indirectly, on mere questions of chronology. . . . The chronology of events as herein set down may be in many cases at fault, but I have at least spared no pains, by a diligent study of the best authorities, Catholic as well as Protestant, to guide myself to that order which seemed most satisfactory. It must however be borne in mind, that, with the Scriptural materials at our command, absolute certainty on some points is out of the question.

The book has been divided into six parts:—

Part I.—The Incarnation and Hidden Life.
" II.—From the first to the second Pasch.
" III.—From the second to the third Pasch.
" IV.—From the third to the fourth Pasch.
" V.—The Passion and Death of our Lord.
" VI.—The Resurrection and Ascension; the Descent of the Holy Ghost.

In conclusion, as I have found the revision of a diatessaron almost as difficult a task as its compilation, any corrections suggested to the publishers will be received with gratitude.

HENRY BEAUCLERK, S.J.

Jamaica, Dec. 1895.

CONTENTS.

PART I.
THE INCARNATION AND HIDDEN LIFE.

	PAGE		PAGE
"In the beginning"	1	Flight into Egypt	13
St. Luke to Theophilus	2	Massacre of the Innocents	14
Zachary and Elizabeth	3	Loss and finding	14
Annunciation	4	The Baptist: his preaching and testimony	15
Visitation	5		
Genealogy by St. Matthew	6	Baptism of our Lord	17
St. Joseph's trouble	7	Genealogy by St. Luke	18
The Baptist: his birth	8	Fast and temptations	19
Nativity	10	The Baptist: "Lamb of God"	20
Circumcision	11	First disciples	21
Presentation	11	Philip and Nathanael	21
Epiphany	12	Feast at Cana	22

PART II.
FROM THE FIRST TO THE SECOND PASCH.

Buyers and sellers	24	Simon's wife's mother	33
Nicodemus and Baptism	25	Sermon on the Mount	35
The Baptist: further testimony	26	The draught of fishes	42
The Baptist: imprisoned	27	Simon and companions	43
The woman of Samaria	28	The leper	43
The ruler's son	30	The paralytic	44
Dishonoured at Nazareth	31	Matthew	45
Simon and companions	32	Fasting	45
The unclean devil	33		

PART III.
FROM THE SECOND TO THE THIRD PASCH.

The Probatic Pool	47	The Father and the Son	49
Sabbath-breaking	47	Plots by Pharisees and Herodians	51
Man with withered hand	49		
Persecution	49	Apostles chosen	52

	PAGE		PAGE
Sermon on the Plain	53	The mustard-seed	65
The centurion's servant	55	The leaven	66
The widow of Naim	56	The treasure	66
The Baptist: disciples sent to Jesus	57	The pearl	66
		The seine net	67
The Magdalene	59	Stilling the storm	67
Ministered to by women	60	The legion of devils	68
The blind and dumb devil	60	The daughter of Jairus	69
Beelzebub, prince of devils	60	The woman with issue of blood	69
His Mother and brethren	62	The two blind men	71
Parables	62	The dumb man	71
The sower	62	Dishonoured again at Nazareth	72
The candle	64	Mission of the Twelve, "two and two"	72
The cockle	64		
The seed	65	The Baptist: his martyrdom	76

PART IV.

FROM THE THIRD TO THE FOURTH PASCH.

Five thousand men fed	78	Murmurs and plots	99
Walking on the water	80	The adulteress	102
The Bread from Heaven	82	Light of the world	103
Jewish traditions	82	Dispute with Jews	103
Syrophœnician woman	86	Attempt to stone Him	106
The deaf and dumb man	87	The man born blind	106
Four thousand men fed	88	The Good Shepherd	109
The sign of Jonas	89	Feast of Dedication	110
The leaven of the Pharisees	89	"I and the Father are One"	111
The blind man at Bethsaida	89	Attempt to seize Him	111
"Thou art Peter"	90	Lazarus	111
The Passion predicted	90	Last journey begins	115
Self-denial	91	"The foxes have holes"	116
The Transfiguration	91	Mission of the seventy-two	117
The lunatic boy	93	"Wo to thee, Corozain"	117
Faith	94	The Good Samaritan	119
The Passion again predicted	94	Martha and Mary	120
The didrachma tax	95	Prayer	120
Humility	95	The dumb devil	122
Right zeal	95	"Beelzebub, prince of devils"	122
Scandal	96	Sign of Jonas	123
Fraternal correction	97	"If thy eye be single"	123
Binding and loosing	97	"Wo to you Pharisees"	124
Power of prayer	97	"Wo to you lawyers"	124
Forgiveness	98	Leaven of the Pharisees	125
The wicked servant	98	Confidence in God	125
Feast of Tabernacles	99	Covetousness	126
The world	99	Solicitude	126

CONTENTS.

	PAGE		PAGE
Watchfulness	127	Judas	151
"I am come to cast fire"	128	Mary	151
Wilful blindness	128	Procession of palms	152
Judgments of God	129	Weeps over Jerusalem	154
Good fruits	129	"Unless the grain of wheat die"	155
The infirm woman	130	The voice from Heaven	155
Sabbath-breaking	130	The fig-tree is cursed	156
The Kingdom of God	130	The buyers and sellers	156
On circuit to Jerusalem	130	The fig-tree dried up	157
The narrow gate	131	Faith	157
Warned against Herod	131	Forgiveness	157
Man with the dropsy	132	"By what authority?"	158
Humility	132	The two sons	158
Purity of intention	132	The wicked husbandmen	158
The world before God	133	"The stone which the builders rejected"	159
The true disciple	133		
The lost sheep	134	The marriage-feast	160
The lost groat	135	Tribute to Cæsar	161
The prodigal son	135	The Sadducees	161
The unjust steward	136	The blessed in Heaven	162
Matrimony	138	The resurrection of the dead	162
Dives and Lazarus	138	The dual law of charity	163
Scandals	139	The son of David	163
Forgiveness	139	"Wo to you Scribes and Pharisees"	164
Faith	139		
Duty	139	The widow's mite	166
The ten lepers	140	Belief in Christ	167
The Kingdom of God	140	Persecution	168
The unjust judge	141	Destruction of Jerusalem prophesied	169
The Pharisee and the publican	142		
Farewell to Galilee	142	Antichrists	170
Matrimony	142	End of the world	170
Chastity	143	Last Judgment	171
Humility	143	"Watch ye ... praying"	172
"If thou wilt be perfect"	144	The ten virgins'	173
Riches and poverty	144	The talents	174
"The last shall be first"	145	Last sentence	175
The Passion again predicted	146	The Passion again predicted	176
The sons of Zebedee	147	Caiphas and the chief priests conspire His Death	176
Humility	147		
Approach to Jericho	147	Judas makes his bargain	176
The blind man	148	The Last Supper	177
Zaccheus	148	Washing of feet	178
The nobleman	149	Humility	178
Bartimæus	150	"Is it I, Lord?"	179
"Six days before the Pasch"	151	Judas goes forth	180
Supper at Bethania	151	Last discourse begins	180

	PAGE		PAGE
Peter warned	180	Last discourse continues	182
Strife for pre-eminence	180	The Blessed Sacrament	184
Peter again warned	181	Last discourse continues	184

PART V.
PASSION AND DEATH.

Departure from Cenacle	191	The crowning	203
Peter again warned	191	Mocked and spat upon	203
Agony in the Garden	191	"Ecce homo!"	203
The traitor's kiss	193	"I find no cause"	203
"Whom seek ye?"	193	Condemnation	203
Peter and the sword	193	Via dolorosa	203
"This is your hour"	194	Helped by Simon	204
Deserted by disciples	194	Bewailed by women	204
Bound and led away	194	Wine and myrrh offered	204
Peter's first denial	195	Crucifixion	205
Annas: first trial	195	"Father, forgive them"	205
Peter's second denial	196	The inscription	205
Caiphas: second trial	196	His garments	205
Peter's third denial	197	Mocked and blasphemed	206
Peter's repentance	197	Reproached by the thieves	206
Jesus mocked and spat upon	197	The good thief	206
Sanhedrin: third trial	198	Mary and John	206
Judas hangs himself	198	"My God! My God!"	207
Pilate: first civil trial	199	"I thirst"	207
"I find no cause"	200	"It is consummated"	207
Herod: second civil trial	200	"Father, into Thy hands"	207
Mocked and set at nought	200	Death of Jesus	207
Pilate: third civil trial	201	Nature moved	207
"I find no cause"	201	Mankind in fear	208
Pilate's wife's dream	201	His Side opened	208
"Barabbas or Jesus?"	202	Joseph and Nicodemus	209
"I find no cause"	202	Sepulture	209
Pilate's innocence	202	Guards set	210
The scourging	202		

PART VI.
THE RESURRECTION AND ASCENSION; THE DESCENT OF THE HOLY GHOST.

"Mary Magdalene and the other Mary" leave Bethania about sunset on Saturday, to buy and prepare spices overnight, so as to be ready "to see the sepulchre" as early as possible on Sunday morning	211	The earthquake, and rolling back of the stone by the angel, who, sitting upon it, so terrifies the guard that they "became as dead men," that is, we may infer, are unconscious for some little time	212
"But He, rising early"	211		

	PAGE		PAGE
Arrival of first party of women (as in Matthew, Mark, John); Magdalene, seeing in the distance the stone rolled back, at once concludes the Body has been taken away. She runs off and reports to Peter and John	213	St. Luke's party arrives, and is consoled by two angels .	215
		Apparition on the road to Emmaus	216
		Apparition to Simon Peter .	217
		Apparition to disciples, Thomas being absent . . .	217
		Apparition to disciples, Thomas being present . . .	219
The other two women enter the tomb, and see the angel, now sitting within; after hearing his message they depart in fear, stopping to tell no man by the way, until they come to where the disciples are .	213	Apparition to seven at the Sea of Tiberias	219
		"Feed My lambs;" "Feed My sheep"	221
		Apparition to the five hundred in Galilee	222
		"Going therefore teach ye all nations"	222
They miss Peter and John, who now come, accompanied by Magdalene. The Apostles are comforted by an angel, and depart wondering . .	213	Apparition to James . .	222
		Apparition to the eleven in Jerusalem	222
		Last walk to Mount Olivet .	223
Magdalene lingering at the tomb is accosted by two angels; is the first to whom our Lord appears; she goes to tell His disciples . .	214	Last words and blessing . .	223
		The Ascension . . .	223
		The waiting for the Holy Ghost	224
		Mathias chosen . . .	225
Jesus appears to her companions	215	Descent of the Holy Ghost .	225
		St. Peter's first sermon . .	226
Guards report, and are bribed to silence	215	The Apostles, "going forth, preached everywhere". .	228

"IN THE BEGINNING."

John 1, 1—14.

In the beginning was the Word, and the Word was with God, and the Word was God; the same was in the beginning with God. All things were made by Him, and without Him was made nothing that was made. In Him was life, and the life was the light of men, and the light shineth in darkness, and the darkness did not comprehend it.

There was a man sent from God, whose name was John. This man came for a witness, to give testimony of the light, that all men might believe through him. He was not the light, but was to give testimony of the light.

That was the true light, which enlighteneth every man that cometh into this world. He was in the world, and the world was made by Him, and the world knew Him not. He came unto His own, and His own received Him not. But as many as received Him, He gave them power to be made the sons of God, to them that believe in His name; who are born, not of blood, nor of the will of the flesh, nor of the will of man, but of God.

And the Word was made flesh, and dwelt among us (and we saw His glory, the glory as it were of the only-begotten of the Father), full of grace and truth.

PROLOGUE.

Luke 1, 1—4.

[To Theophilus].

FORASMUCH as many have taken in hand, to set forth in order a narration of the things that have been accomplished among us, according as they have delivered them unto us, who from the beginning were eye-witnesses and ministers of the Word; it seemed good to me also, having diligently attained to all things from the beginning, to write to thee in order, most excellent Theophilus, that thou mayest know the verity of those words in which thou hast been instructed.

Part I.

THE BEGINNING OF THE GOSPEL OF JESUS CHRIST, THE SON OF GOD.

Mark 1, 1.

THERE was in the days of Herod the King of Judea a certain priest named Zachary, of the course of Abia, and his wife was of the daughters of Aaron and her name Elizabeth. And they were both just before God, walking in all the commandments and justifications of the Lord without blame. And they had no son, for that Elizabeth was barren, and they both were well advanced in years.

Luke 1, 5-56.

And it came to pass, when he executed the priestly function in the order of his course before God, according to the custom of the priestly office, it was his lot to offer incense, going into the Temple of the Lord; and all the multitude of the people was praying without, at the hour of incense.

8.

And there appeared to him an Angel of the Lord, standing at the right side of the altar of incense. And Zachary seeing him, was troubled, and fear fell upon him. But the Angel said to him: "Fear not, Zachary, for thy prayer is heard, and thy wife Elizabeth shall bear thee a son, and thou shalt call his name John; and thou shalt have joy and gladness, and many shall rejoice in his nativity. For he shall be great before the Lord, and shall drink no wine or strong drink, and he shall be filled with the Holy Ghost even from his mother's womb. And he shall convert many of the children of Israel to the Lord their God. And he shall go before Him in the spirit and power of Elias, that he may turn the hearts of the fathers unto the children, and the incredulous to the wisdom of the just, to prepare unto the Lord a perfect people."

18. And Zachary said to the Angel: "Whereby shall I know this, for I am an old man and my wife is advanced in years?" And the Angel answering said to him: "I am Gabriel, who stand before God, and am sent to speak to thee, and to bring thee these good tidings. And behold thou shalt be dumb, and shalt not be able to speak until the day when these things shall come to pass, because thou hast not believed my words, which shall be fulfilled in their time."

21. And the people were waiting for Zachary; and they wondered that he tarried so long in the Temple. And when he came out he could not speak to them, and they understood that he had seen a vision in the Temple. And he made signs to them and remained dumb. And it came to pass, after the days of his office were accomplished, he departed to his own house.

24. And after those days Elizabeth his wife conceived, and hid herself five months, saying: "Thus hath the Lord dealt with me, in the days wherein He hath had regard to take away my reproach among men."

26. And in the sixth month, the Angel Gabriel was sent from God into a city of Galilee, called Nazareth, to a virgin espoused to a man whose name was Joseph, of the house of David; and the virgin's name was Mary.

28. And the Angel being come in, said unto her:

PART I. THE BEGINNING OF THE GOSPEL.

"Hail, full of grace, the Lord is with thee; blessed art thou among women." Who having heard was troubled at his saying, and thought with herself what manner of salutation this should be. And the Angel said to her: "Fear not, Mary, for thou hast found grace with God. Behold, thou shalt conceive in thy womb, and shalt bring forth a Son, and thou shalt call His name Jesus. He shall be great, and shall be called the Son of the Most High, and the Lord God shall give unto Him the throne of David His Father; and He shall reign in the house of Jacob for ever; and of His Kingdom there shall be no end."

And Mary said to the Angel: "How shall this be done, because I know not man?" And the Angel answering, said to her: "The Holy Ghost shall come upon thee, and the power of the Most High shall overshadow thee; and therefore also the Holy, which shall be born of thee, shall be called the Son of God. And behold thy cousin Elizabeth, she also hath conceived a son in her old age; and this is the sixth month with her that is called barren, because no word shall be impossible with God."

And Mary said: "Behold the handmaid of the Lord, be it done to me according to thy word." And the Angel departed from her.

And Mary rising up in those days, went into the hill country with haste, into a city of Juda. And she entered into the house of Zachary and saluted Elizabeth. And it came to pass, that when Elizabeth heard the salutation of Mary, the infant leaped in her womb. And Elizabeth was filled with the Holy Ghost, and she cried out with a loud voice and said: "Blessed art thou among women, and blessed is the fruit of thy womb. And whence is this to me, that the mother of my Lord should come to me? For behold, as soon as the voice of thy salutation sounded in my ears, the infant in my womb leaped for joy. And blessed art thou that hast believed, because those things shall be accomplished that were spoken to thee by the Lord."

46. And Mary said: "My soul doth magnify the Lord, and my spirit hath rejoiced in God my Saviour, because He hath regarded the humility of His handmaid; for behold from henceforth all generations shall call me blessed. Because He that is mighty hath done great things to me, and holy is His name. And His mercy is from generation unto generations, to them that fear Him. He hath showed might in His arm; He hath scattered the proud in the conceit of their heart. He hath put down the mighty from their seat and hath exalted the humble. He hath filled the hungry with good things, and the rich He hath sent empty away. He hath received Israel His servant, being mindful of His mercy; as He spoke to our fathers, to Abraham and to his seed for ever."

56. And Mary abode with her about three months, and she returned to her own house.

. . . . .

Matt. 1, 1-25. The book of the generation of Jesus Christ, the Son of David, the son of Abraham: Abraham begot Isaac, and Isaac begot Jacob. And Jacob begot Judas and his brethren. And Judas begot Phares and Zara of Thamar. And Phares begot Esron. And Esron begot Aram. And Aram begot Aminadab. And Aminadab begot Naasson. And Naasson begot Salmon. And Salmon begot Booz of Rahab. And Booz begot Obed of Ruth.

And Obed begot Jesse. And Jesse begot David the King.

And David the King begot Solomon, of her that 6. had been the wife of Urias. And Solomon begot Roboam. And Roboam begot Abia. And Abia begot Asa. And Asa begot Josaphat. And Josaphat begot Joram. And Joram begot Ozias. And Ozias begot Joatham. And Joatham begot Achaz. And Achaz begot Ezechias. And Ezechias begot Manasses. And Manasses begot Amon. And Amon begot Josias. And Josias begot Jechonias and his brethren in the transmigration of Babylon.

And after the transmigration of Babylon Jecho- 12. nias begot Salathiel. And Salathiel begot Zorobabel. And Zorobabel begot Abiud. And Abiud begot Eliacim. And Eliacim begot Azor. And Azor begot Sadoc. And Sadoc begot Achim. And Achim begot Eliud. And Eliud begot Eleazar. And Eleazar begot Mathan. And Mathan begot Jacob. And Jacob begot Joseph, the husband of Mary, of whom was born Jesus, Who is called Christ.

So all the generations from Abraham to David 17. are fourteen generations. And from David to the transmigration of Babylon are fourteen generations. And from the transmigration of Babylon to Christ are fourteen generations.

Now the generation of Christ was in this wise: 18. When as His mother Mary was espoused to Joseph, before they came together, she was found with child of the Holy Ghost. Whereupon Joseph her husband, being a just man, and not willing publicly to expose her, was minded to put her away privately.

But while he thought on these things, behold 20.

the Angel of the Lord appeared to him in his sleep, saying: "Joseph, son of David, fear not to take unto thee Mary thy wife, for that which is conceived in her is of the Holy Ghost. And she shall bring forth a son, and thou shalt call His name Jesus; for He shall save His people from their sins."

22. Now all this was done, that it might be fulfilled which the Lord spoke by the prophet, saying: Behold a virgin shall be with child, and bring forth a son, and they shall call His name Emmanuel, which being interpreted, is God with us. And Joseph, rising up from sleep, did as the Angel of the Lord had commanded him, and took unto him his wife; and he knew her not till she brought forth her first-born Son; and he called His name Jesus.

Luke 1, 57-80. Now Elizabeth's full time of being delivered was come, and she brought forth a son. And her neighbours and kinsfolk heard that the Lord had showed His great mercy towards her, and they congratulated with her.

59. And it came to pass that on the eighth day they came to circumcise the child, and they called him by his father's name, Zachary. And his mother answering said: "Not so, but he shall be called John." And they said to her: "There is none of thy kindred which is called by this name." And they made signs to his father, how he would have him called. And demanding a writing-table he wrote, saying: "John is his name."

64. And they all wondered; and immediately his mouth was opened, and his tongue loosed, and he spoke blessing God. And fear came upon all their neighbours; and all these things were noised abroad over all the hill country of Judea. And all

they that had heard them, laid them up in their hearts saying: "What an one think ye shall this child be?" For the hand of the Lord was with him.

And Zachary his father was filled with the Holy 67. Ghost, and he prophesied, saying: "Blessed be the Lord God of Israel, because He has visited and wrought the redemption of His people; and hath raised up an horn of salvation to us, in the house of David His servant. As He spoke by the mouth of His holy prophets, who are from the beginning; salvation from our enemies, and from the hand of all that hate us; to perform mercy to our fathers, and to remember His holy testament; the oath which He swore to Abraham our father; that He would grant to us, that being delivered from the hand of our enemies, we may serve Him without fear, in holiness and justice before Him all our days. And thou, child, shalt be called the prophet of the Highest, for thou shalt go before the face of the Lord to prepare His ways, to give knowledge of salvation to His people, unto the remission of their sins, through the bowels of the mercy of our God, in which the Orient from on high hath visited us; to enlighten them that sit in darkness and in the shadow of death; to direct our feet into the way of peace."

And the child grew, and was strengthened in 80. spirit, and was in the deserts until the day of his manifestation to Israel.

And it came to pass that in those days there Luke 2, 1-39. went out a decree from Cæsar Augustus, that the whole world should be enrolled. This enrolling was first made by Cyrinus, the Governor of Syria. And all went to be enrolled, every one into his own city. And Joseph also went up from Galilee, out of the city of Nazareth into Judea, to the city of David which is called Bethlehem, because he was of the house and family of David, to be enrolled with Mary his espoused wife who was with child.

6. And it came to pass, that when they were there, her days were accomplished that she should be delivered. And she brought forth her first-born Son, and wrapped Him up in swaddling clothes, and laid Him in a manger, because there was no room for them in the inn.

8. And there were in the same country shepherds watching, and keeping the night-watches over their flocks. And behold an Angel of the Lord stood by them, and the brightness of God shone round about them, and they feared with a great fear. And the Angel said to them: "Fear not; for behold, I bring you good tidings of great joy, that shall be to all the people; for this day is born to you a Saviour, who is Christ the Lord, in the city of David. And this shall be a sign unto you. You shall find the Infant wrapped in swaddling clothes, and laid in a manger." And suddenly, there was with the Angel a multitude of the heavenly army, praising God and saying: "Glory to God in the highest, and on earth, peace to men of good-will."

15. And it came to pass, after the Angels departed from them into heaven, the shepherds said one to another: "Let us go over to Bethlehem, and let us see this word that is come to pass, which the Lord hath showed to us." And they came with haste, and they found Mary and Joseph, and the Infant lying in the manger. And seeing, they understood of the word that had been spoken to them concerning this Child; and all that heard wondered, and at those things that were told them by the shepherds. But Mary kept all these words, pondering them in her heart. And the shepherds returned, glorifying and praising God for all the things they had heard and seen, as it was told unto them.

And after eight days were accomplished that the child should be circumcised, His name was called Jesus, which was called by the Angel, before He was conceived in the womb.

And after the days of her purification, according to the law of Moses, were accomplished, they carried Him to Jerusalem to present Him to the Lord, as it is written in the law of the Lord: *Every male opening the womb shall be called holy to the Lord;* and to offer a sacrifice, according as it is written in the law of the Lord, a pair of turtle-doves or two young pigeons.

And behold there was a man in Jerusalem named Simeon, and this man was just and devout, waiting for the consolation of Israel; and the Holy Ghost was in him. And he had received an answer from the Holy Ghost, that he should not see death before he had seen the Christ of the Lord. And he came by the Spirit into the Temple. And when His parents brought in the Child Jesus, to do for Him according to the custom of the law, he also took Him into his arms and blessed God and said: "Now Thou dost dismiss Thy servant, O Lord, according to Thy word, in peace; because my eyes have seen Thy salvation, which Thou hast prepared before the face of all peoples; a light to the revelation of the Gentiles, and the glory of Thy people Israel."

And His father and mother were wondering at

those things which were spoken concerning Him. And Simeon blessed them, and said to Mary His mother: "Behold this Child is set for the fall, and for the resurrection of many in Israel, and for a sign which shall be contradicted; and thy own soul a sword shall pierce, that out of many hearts thoughts may be revealed."

36. And there was one Anna, a prophetess, the daughter of Phanuel, of the tribe of Aser; she was far advanced in years, and had lived with her husband seven years from her virginity; and she was a widow until fourscore and four years; who departed not from the Temple, by fastings and prayers serving night and day. Now she at the same hour coming in, confessed to the Lord, and spoke of Him to all that looked for the redemption of Israel.

39. And after they had performed all things according to the law of the Lord [and after all, to be now narrated by St. Matthew, had occurred], they returned into Galilee, to their city Nazareth.[1]

Matt. 2, 1-23. When Jesus therefore was born in Bethlehem of Juda in the days of King Herod, behold there came wise men from the East to Jerusalem, saying:

---

[1] Compare Fillion, Fouard, and others. A case closely parallel to this hiatus of St. Luke occurs in his twenty-fourth chapter, from which, but for the guidance of the other Evangelists, we should be led to conclude that the Ascension took place on the day of the Resurrection.

Another recognized view, however, is that the Holy Family did return to Nazareth, as St. Luke might seem to imply, *immediately* after the Presentation, but only to gather together their little property in order to take up a more permanent abode in Bethlehem. That St. Joseph had fixed on Bethlehem as their future home—perhaps the more fully to carry out the prophecy of Micheas v. 2—we learn from Matt. ii. 22, for, on his return from Egypt, he would have settled in Judea but for his fear of Archelaus.

"Where is He that is born King of the Jews? for we have seen His star in the East and are come to adore Him." And King Herod hearing this was troubled, and all Jerusalem with him; and assembling together all the chief priests and scribes of the people, he inquired of them where Christ should be born. But they said to him: "In Bethlehem of Juda. For so it is written by the prophet: *And thou Bethlehem, the land of Juda, art not the least among the princes of Juda; for out of thee shall come forth the captain that shall rule my people Israel.*

Then Herod, privately calling the wise men, 7. learned diligently of them the time of the star which appeared to them; and sending them into Bethlehem, said: "Go and diligently inquire after the Child; and when you have found Him, bring me word again, that I also may come and adore Him."

Who having heard the King went their way; 9. and behold the star which they had seen in the East went before them until it came and stood over where the Child was. And seeing the star, they rejoiced with exceeding great joy. And entering into the house, they found the Child with Mary His mother, and falling down they adored Him; and opening their treasures, they offered Him gifts, gold, frankincense, and myrrh. And having received an answer in sleep that they should not return to Herod, they went back another way into their own country.

And after they were departed, behold an Angel 13. of the Lord appeared in sleep to Joseph, saying: "Arise, and take the Child and His mother, and fly into Egypt; and be there until I shall tell thee. For it will come to pass, that Herod will seek the

Child to destroy Him." Who arose, and took the Child and His mother by night, and retired into Egypt; and he was there until the death of Herod; that it might be fulfilled which the Lord spoke by the prophet, saying: *Out of Egypt have I called My Son.*

16. Then Herod, perceiving that he was deluded by the wise men, was exceeding angry, and sending, killed all the men-children that were in Bethlehem and in all the borders thereof, from two years and under, according to the time which he had diligently inquired of the wise men.

17. Then was fulfilled that which was spoken by Jeremias the prophet saying: *A voice in Rama was heard, lamentation and great mourning; Rachel bewailing her children, and would not be comforted, because they are not.*

19. But when Herod was dead, behold an Angel of the Lord appeared in sleep to Joseph in Egypt, saying: "Arise and take the Child and His mother, and go into the land of Israel; for they are dead that sought the life of the Child." Who arose, and took the Child and His mother, and came into the land of Israel. But hearing that Archelaus reigned in Judea, in the room of Herod his father, he was afraid to go thither, and being warned in sleep, retired into the quarters of Galilee.

23. And coming he dwelt in a city called Nazareth, that it might be fulfilled which was said by the prophets, that He shall be called a Nazarite.

Luke 2, 40-52. And the Child grew and waxed strong, full of wisdom, and the grace of God was in Him. And His parents went every year to Jerusalem at the solemn day of the Pasch. And when He was twelve years old, they going up into Jerusalem according to the custom of the feast, and having

PART I.   THE BEGINNING OF THE GOSPEL.   15

fulfilled the days, when they returned, the Child Jesus remained in Jerusalem, and His parents knew it not. And thinking that He was in the company, they came a day's journey, and sought Him among their kinsfolk and acquaintance. And not finding Him they returned into Jerusalem seeking Him.

And it came to pass, that after three days they 46 found Him in the Temple, sitting in the midst of the doctors, hearing them and asking them questions. And all that heard Him were astonished at His wisdom and His answers. And seeing Him they wondered. And His mother said to Him: "Son, why hast Thou done so to us? behold Thy father and I have sought Thee sorrowing." And He said to them: "How is it that you sought Me? Did you not know that I must be about My Father's business?" And they understood not the word that He spoke unto them.

And He went down with them, and came to 51. Nazareth, and was subject to them. And His mother kept all these words in her heart. And Jesus advanced in wisdom and age and grace with God and men.

Now in the fifteenth year of the reign of Tiberius Luke 3, 1-2. Cæsar, Pontius Pilate being Governor of Judea, and Herod being Tetrarch of Galilee, and Philip his brother Tetrarch of Iturea and the country of Trachonitis, and Lysanias Tetrarch of Abilina, under the High Priests Annas and Caiaphas; the word of the Lord was made unto John the son of Zachary in the desert.

ᴸᵏAnd he came into all the country about the Matt. 3 1-3. Jordan preaching the baptism of penance for the Mark 1, 9-4. remission of sins, as it was written in the book Luke 3, 3-6.

of the sayings of Isaias the prophet: ᴹᴷ*Behold I send My angel before Thy face, who shall prepare the way before Thee;* ᴸᴷ*A voice of one crying in the wilderness: Prepare ye the way of the Lord, make straight His paths; every valley shall be filled, and every mountain and hill shall be brought low, and the crooked shall be made straight and the rough ways plain; and all flesh shall see the salvation of God.*

Matt. 3, 4-6.
Mark 1, 5-6.

ᴹᵀAnd the same John had his garment of camel's hair, and a leathern girdle about his loins, and his meat was locusts and wild honey. Then went out to him Jerusalem and all Judea and all the country about Jordan, and were baptized by him in the Jordan, confessing their sins.

Matt. 3, 7-10.
Luke 3, 7-9.

ᴹᵀAnd seeing many of the Pharisees and Sadducees coming to his baptism, he said to them: "Ye brood of vipers, who hath showed you to flee from the wrath to come? Bring forth therefore fruits worthy of penance, and think not to say within yourselves: We have Abraham for our father. For I tell you that God is able of these stones to raise up children to Abraham. For now the axe is laid to the root of the trees. Every tree therefore that doth not yield good fruit shall be cut down and cast into the fire."

Luke 3, 10-15.

And the people asked him saying: "What then shall we do? And he answering said to them: "He that hath two coats, let him give to him that hath none; and he that hath meat, let him do in like manner."

12. And the publicans also came to be baptized, and said to him: "Master, what shall we do?" But he said to them: "Do nothing more than that which is appointed you."

14. And the soldiers also asked him saying: "And

PART I. THE BEGINNING OF THE GOSPEL. 17

what shall we do?" And he said to them: "Do violence to no man; neither calumniate any man; and be content with your pay."

And as the people was of opinion, and all were thinking in their hearts of John, that perhaps he might be the Christ, John answered saying unto all: ^{MT}"I indeed baptize you with water unto penance, but He that shall come after me is mightier than I, whose shoes I am not worthy to bear, ^{MK}the latchet of whose shoes I am not worthy to stoop down and loose. I have baptized you with water, but He shall baptize you with the Holy Ghost ^{LK}and with fire.

^{MT}"Whose fan is in His hand, and He will thoroughly cleanse His floor, and gather His wheat into the barn, but the chaff He will burn with unquenchable fire."

^{LK}And many other things exhorting, did he preach to the people.

^{MT}Then cometh Jesus, from ^{MK}Nazareth of ^{MT}Galilee, to the Jordan unto John, to be baptized by him.

^{MT}But John stayed Him, saying: "I ought to be baptized by Thee, and comest Thou to me?" And Jesus answering, said to Him: "Suffer it to be so now, for so it becometh us to fulfil all justice." Then he suffered Him.

^{MT}And Jesus being baptized, forthwith came out of the water; and lo! the heavens were opened to Him; and He saw the Spirit of God descending ^{LK}in a bodily shape as a dove, and ^{MK}remaining upon Him. And there came a voice from heaven: "Thou art My beloved Son; in Thee I am well pleased."

John beareth witness of Him, and crieth out saying: "This was He of Whom I spoke: He

Matt. 3, 11.
Mark 1, 7, 8.
Luke 3, 16.

Matt. 3, 12.
Luke 3, 17.

Luke 3, 18.

Matt. 3, 13.
Mark 1, 9.
Luke 3, 21.

Matt. 3, 14, 15.

Matt. 3, 16, 17.
Mark 1, 10, 11.
Luke 3, 21, 22.

John 1, 15—18.

C

that shall come after me, is preferred before me, because He was before me; and of His fulness we all have received, and grace for grace. For the law was given by Moses; grace and truth came by Jesus Christ. No man has seen God at any time; the only begotten Son, Who is in the bosom of the Father, Who hath declared Him."

Luke 3. 23—38.
And Jesus Himself was beginning about the age of thirty years, being (as it was supposed) the son of Joseph, who was of Heli, who was of Mathat, who was of Levi, who was of Melchi, who was of Janne, who was of Joseph, who was of Mathathias, who was of Amos, who was of Nahum, who was of Hesli, who was of Nagge, who was of Makath, who was of Mathathias, who was of Semei, who was of Joseph, who was of Juda, who was of Joanna, who was of Reza, who was of Zorobabel, who was of Salathiel, who was of Neri, who was of Melchi, who was of Addi, who was of Cosan, who was of Helmadan, who was of Her, who was of Jesus, who was of Eliezer, who was of Jorim, who was of Mathat, who was of Levi, who was of Simeon, who was of Judas, who was of Joseph, who was of Jona, who was of Eliakim, who was of Melea, who was of Menna, who was of Mathatha, who was of Nathan, who was of David, who was of Jesse, who was of Obed, who was of Booz, who was of Salmon, who was of Naasson, who was of Aminadab, who was of Aram, who was of Esron, who was of Phares, who was of Judas, who was of Jacob, who was of Isaac, who was of Abraham, who was of Thares, who was of Nachor, who was of Sarug, who was of Ragau, who was of Phaleg, who was of Heber, who was of Sale, who was of Cainan, who was of Arphaxad, who was of Sem, who was of Noe, who was of Lamech, who was of Mathusale, who was of

PART I. THE BEGINNING OF THE GOSPEL. 19

Henoch, who was of Jared, who was of Malaleel, who was of Cainan, who was of Henos, who was of Seth, who was of Adam, who was of God.

^{LK}And Jesus being full of the Holy Ghost, returned from the Jordan, ^{MK}and immediately the Spirit drove Him out into the desert. And He was in the desert forty days and forty nights, and was tempted by Satan; and He was with beasts. ^{LK}And He ate nothing in those days; and when they were ended, He was hungry. Matt. 4, 1, 2. Mark 1, 12, 13. Luke 4, 1, 2.

^{MT}And the tempter coming said to him: "If Thou be the Son of God, command that these stones be made bread." Who answered and said: "It is written: *Not in bread alone doth man live, but in every word that proceedeth from the mouth of God.*" Matt. 4, 3—11. Luke 4, 3—13.

Then the devil took Him up into the holy city, and set Him upon the pinnacle of the temple, and said to Him: "If Thou be the Son of God, cast Thyself down, for it is written: *That He hath given His angels charge over Thee, and in their hands shall they bear Thee up, lest perhaps Thou dash Thy foot against a stone.*" Jesus said to him: "It is written again: *Thou shalt not tempt the Lord thy God.*"

Again the devil took Him up into a very high mountain, and showed Him all the kingdoms of the world and the glory of them ^{LK}in a moment of time, and he said to Him: "To Thee will I give all this power, and the glory of them; for to me they are delivered, and to whom I will I give them. If Thou therefore wilt adore before me, all shall be Thine." ^{MT}Then Jesus saith to him: "Begone Satan! for it is written: *The Lord thy God shalt thou adore, and Him only shalt thou serve.*" ᴸᴷAnd all the temptation being ended, the devil departed from Him for a time; ᴹᵀand behold, Angels came and ministered to Him.

<small>Matt. 4, 11.
Mark 1, 13.</small>

<small>John 1, 19—51.</small> And this is the testimony of John, when the Jews sent from Jerusalem priests and Levites to him to ask him: "Who art thou?" And he confessed and did not deny; and he confessed: "I am not the Christ."

21. And they asked him: "What then? Art thou Elias?" And he said: "I am not." "Art thou the prophet?" and he answered: "No." And they said therefore unto him: "Who art thou, that we may give an answer to them that sent us? what sayest thou of thyself?" He said: "*I am the voice of one crying in the wilderness: Make straight the way of the Lord*, as said the prophet Isaias."

24. And they that were sent were of the Pharisees. And they asked him and said to him: "Why then dost thou baptize, if thou be not Christ, nor Elias, nor the prophet?" John answered them saying: "I baptize with water; but there hath stood One in the midst of you, whom you know not. The same is He that shall come after me, Who is preferred before me, the latchet of whose shoe I am not worthy to loose." These things were done in Bethania beyond the Jordan, where John was baptizing.

29 The next day, John saw Jesus coming to him, and he said: "Behold the Lamb of God! behold Him Who taketh away the sin of the world! This is He of Whom I said: "After me there cometh a Man, Who is preferred before me, because He was before me. And I knew Him not; but that He may be made manifest in Israel, therefore am I come, baptizing with water."

PART I. THE BEGINNING OF THE GOSPEL.

And John gave testimony saying: "I saw the Spirit coming down as a dove from heaven, and He remained upon Him, and I knew Him not; but He Who sent me to baptize with water said to me: He upon whom thou shalt see the Spirit descending and remaining upon Him, He it is that baptizeth with the Holy Ghost. And I saw; and I gave testimony that this is the Son of God." 32.

The next day again John stood, and two of his disciples, and beholding Jesus walking, he saith: "Behold! the Lamb of God." 35.

And the two disciples heard him speak, and they followed Jesus. And Jesus turning, and seeing them following Him, saith to them: "What seek you?" Who said to Him: "Rabbi (which is to say, being interpreted, Master), where dwellest Thou?" He saith to them: "Come and see." They came and saw where He abode, and they staid with Him that day; now it was about the tenth hour. 37.

And Andrew, the brother of Simon Peter was one of the two who had heard of John, and followed Him. He findeth first his brother Simon and saith to him: "We have found the Messias," which is, being interpreted, the Christ. And he brought him to Jesus. And Jesus looking upon him said: "Thou art Simon, the son of Jona; thou shalt be called Cephas," which is, interpreted, Peter. 40.

On the following day He would go forth into Galilee; and He findeth Philip. And Jesus saith to him: "Follow Me." Now Philip was of Bethsaida [from][1] the city of Andrew and Peter. 43.

[1] See the Rev. E. Greswell, Dissertation XXXII., "On the village of Martha and Mary." He calls in question the correctness here, both of the Rheims and the Authorized Versions, on the score that, translated direct from the Vulgate of St. Jerome, they do not give us the full force of the Greek. The Greek text

Philip findeth Nathanael, and saith to him: "We have found Him of Whom Moses in the law and the prophets did write, Jesus, the son of Joseph, of Nazareth." And Nathanael said to him: "Can anything of good come from Nazareth?" Philip saith to him: "Come and see."

47. Jesus saw Nathanael coming to Him, and He saith of him: "Behold an Israelite indeed, in whom there is no guile." Nathanael saith to Him: "Whence knowest Thou me?" Jesus answered and said to him: "Before that Philip called thee, when thou wast under the fig-tree, I saw thee. Nathanael answered Him and said: "Rabbi, Thou art the Son of God; Thou art the King of Israel." Jesus answered and said to him: "Because I said unto thee: I saw thee under the fig-tree, thou believest; greater things than these shalt thou see." And He saith to him: "Amen, Amen, I say to you, you shall see the heaven opened, and the angels of God ascending and descending upon the Son of Man."

John 2, 1—12. And the third day there was a marriage in Cana

---

now current has, *ἐκ τῆς πόλεως* (*from* the city), which in Latin should read *ex civitate*, not as St. Jerome has it, *civitate* alone, as if in apposition to Bethsaida.

Greswell's view is confirmed by the recently published Revised Version, which has adopted the translation: "*from* the city of," as given in the text. He moreover proves that the force of the Greek prepositions *ἀπό* and *ἐκ* when they are used, as here, in close juxtaposition, and before two towns, is such as entirely to preclude the translation: "of Bethsaida, the city."

Lastly, from the texts, Matt. viii. 5, 14; Mark i. 21, 29; Luke iv. 31, 38, we may as legitimately conclude that Capharnaum was the *birthplace* of Andrew and Peter, as that Bethsaida was.

The important bearing of this note will be seen when we have, on precisely similar grounds, to side with Mr. Greswell in his rejection of Bethania as the birthplace or even the permanent dwelling-place of Martha and Mary.

of Galilee; and the mother of Jesus was there. And Jesus also was invited, and His disciples, to the marriage. And the wine failing, the mother of Jesus saith to Him: "They have no wine." And Jesus saith to her: "Woman, what is to me and to thee? my hour is not yet come." His mother saith to the waiters: "Whatsoever He shall say to you, do ye."

Now there were set there six water-pots of stone, 6. according to the manner of the purifying of the Jews, containing two or three measures apiece. Jesus saith to them: "Fill the water-pots with water;" and they filled them to the brim. And Jesus saith to them: "Draw out now, and carry to the chief steward of the feast;" and they carried it.

And when the chief steward had tasted the 9. water made wine, and knew not whence it was, but the waiters knew, who had drawn the water, the chief steward calleth the bridegroom, and saith to him: "Every man at first setteth forth good wine, and when men have well drunk, then that which is worse; but thou hast kept the good wine until now."

This beginning of miracles did Jesus in Cana of 11. Galilee, and manifested His glory; and His disciples believed in Him. After this He went down to Capharnaum, He and His mother, and His brethren, and His disciples; and they remained there not many days.

Part II.

FROM THE FIRST TO THE SECOND PASCH.

John 2, 13—25. AND the Pasch of the Jews was at hand, and Jesus went up to Jerusalem. And He found in the temple them that sold oxen and sheep and doves, and the changers of money sitting. And when He had made as it were a scourge of little cords, He drove them all out of the temple—the sheep also and the oxen; and the money of the changers He poured out, and the tables He overthrew. And to them that sold doves He said: "Take these things hence, and make not the house of My Father a house of traffic." And His disciples remembered that it was written: *The zeal of Thy house hath eaten Me up.*

18. The Jews therefore answered, and said to Him: "What sign doth Thou show unto us, seeing Thou dost these things?" Jesus answered, and said to them: "Destroy this temple, and in three days I will raise it up." The Jews then said: "Six and forty years was this temple in building, and wilt Thou raise it up in three days?" But He spoke of the temple of His Body. When therefore He had risen from the dead, His disciples remembered that He had said this, and they believed the Scripture, and the word that Jesus had said.

23. Now when He was at Jerusalem at the Pasch upon the festival-day, many believed in His name, seeing His signs which He did. But Jesus did not trust Himself unto them, for that He knew all men, and because He needed not that any should give testimony of man; for He knew what was in man.

And there was a man of the Pharisees named John 3. 1—36. Nicodemus, a ruler of the Jews. This man came to Jesus by night and said to Him: "Rabbi, we know that Thou art come a teacher from God, for no man can do these signs which Thou dost, unless God be with him."

Jesus answered, and said to him: "Amen, 3. amen, I say to thee, except a man be born again, he cannot see the Kingdom of God." Nicodemus saith to Him: "How can a man be born when he is old? Can he enter a second time into his mother's womb, and be born again?" Jesus answered: "Amen, amen, I say to thee, unless a man be born again of water and the Holy Ghost, he cannot enter into the Kingdom of God. That which is born of the flesh is flesh, and that which is born of the Spirit is spirit. Wonder not that I said to thee: You must be born again. The Spirit breatheth where He will, and thou hearest His voice; but thou knowest not whence He cometh nor whither He goeth; so is every one that is born of the Spirit."

Nicodemus answered, and said to Him: "How 9. can these things be done?" Jesus answered and said to him: "Art thou a master in Israel and knowest not these things? Amen, amen, I say to thee, that We speak what We know, and We testify what We have seen, and you receive not Our testimony. If I have spoken to you earthly 12. things and you believe not, how will you believe if I shall speak to you heavenly things?

13. "And no man hath ascended into Heaven, but He that descended from Heaven, the Son of Man Who is in Heaven. And as Moses lifted up the serpent in the desert, so must the Son of Man be lifted up, that whosoever believeth in Him may not perish, but may have life everlasting. For God so loved the world as to give His only-begotten Son, that whosoever believeth in Him may not perish, but may have life everlasting. For God sent not His Son into the world to judge the world, but that the world may be saved by Him. He that believeth in Him is not judged; but he that doth not believe is already judged, because he believeth not in the name of the only-begotten Son of God.

19. "And this is the judgment, because the light has come into the world; and men loved darkness rather than light, for their works were evil. For every one that doth evil hateth the light, and cometh not to the light, that his works may not be reproved. But he that doth truth cometh to the light, that his works may be made manifest, because they are done in God."

22. After these things, Jesus and His disciples came into the land of Judea, and there He abode with them and baptized. And John also was baptizing in Ennon near Salim, because there was much water there, and they came and were baptized. For John was not yet cast into prison.

25. And there arose a question between some of John's disciples and the Jews, concerning purification; and they came to John and said to him: "Rabbi, He Who was with thee beyond the Jordan to Whom thou gavest testimony, behold He baptizeth and all men come to Him." John answered and said: "A man cannot receive any-

thing unless it be given him from Heaven. You yourselves do bear me witness that I said: I am not the Christ, but that I am sent before Him. He that hath the bride is the bridegroom, but the friend of the bridegroom, who standeth and heareth him, rejoiceth with joy because of the bridegroom's voice. This my joy therefore is fulfilled. He must increase; but I must decrease. He Who cometh from above is above all. He who is of the earth, of the earth he is, and of the earth he speaketh. He Who cometh from Heaven is above all. And what He hath seen and heard, that He testifieth, and no man receiveth His testimony. He who hath received His testimony hath set to his seal that God is true. For he whom God hath sent, speaketh the words of God; for God doth not give the Spirit by measure. The Father loveth the Son, and He hath given all things into His hand. He who believeth in the Son, hath life everlasting; but he who believeth not the Son, shall not see life, but the wrath of God abideth on him."

When Jesus therefore understood that the Pharisees had heard that Jesus maketh more disciples, and baptizeth more than John (though Jesus Himself did not baptize but His disciples), He left Judea. *John 4, 1—3.*

But Herod the Tetrarch, when he was reproved by him [John] for Herodias, his brother's wife, and for all the evils which Herod had done, he added this also above all, and shut up John in prison. *Luke 3, 19, 20.*

^{MT}And when Jesus had heard that John was delivered up, He retired into Galilee. *Matt. 4, 12. Mark 1, 14.*

And He was of necessity to pass through Samaria. He cometh therefore to a city of Samaria which is called Sichar, near the piece *John 4, 4—42.*

of ground which Jacob gave to his son Joseph. Now Jacob's well was there. Jesus therefore being wearied with his journey sat thus on the well. It was about the sixth hour.

7. There cometh a woman of Samaria to draw water. Jesus saith to her: "Give Me to drink;" for His disciples had gone into the city to buy meats. Then that Samaritan woman saith to Him: "How dost Thou, being a Jew, ask of me to drink, who am a Samaritan woman?" For the Jews do not communicate with the Samaritans.

10. Jesus answered and said to her: "If thou didst know the gift of God, and Who He is that saith to thee: Give Me to drink, thou perhaps wouldst have asked of Him, and He would have given thee living water." The woman said to Him: "Sir, Thou hast nothing wherein to draw, and the well is deep; from whence then hast Thou living water? Art Thou greater than our father Jacob, who gave us the well, and drank thereof himself, and his children, and his cattle?"

13. Jesus answered and said to her: "Whosoever drinketh of this water shall thirst again, but he that shall drink of the water that I shall give him, shall not thirst for ever, but the water that I shall give him shall become in him a fountain of water springing up into life everlasting." The woman saith to Him: "Sir, give me this water, that I may not thirst, nor come hither to draw."

16. Jesus saith to her: "Go, call thy husband and come hither." The woman answered and said: "I have no husband." Jesus said to her: "Thou hast said well: I have no husband; for thou hast had five husbands, and he whom thou now hast, is not thy husband; this thou hast said truly."

19. The woman saith to Him: "Sir, I perceive that

Thou art a prophet. Our fathers adored on this mountain, and you say, that at Jerusalem is the place where men must adore." Jesus saith to her: "Woman, believe Me, that the hour cometh when you shall, neither on this mountain nor in Jerusalem, adore the Father. You adore that which you know not, we adore that which we know, for salvation is of the Jews. But the hour cometh, and now is, when the true adorers shall adore the Father in spirit and in truth. For the Father also seeketh such to adore Him. God is a Spirit, and they that adore Him must adore Him in spirit and in truth."

The woman saith to Him: "I know that the Messias cometh (Who is called Christ); therefore, when He is come, He will tell us all things." Jesus saith to her: "I am He Who am speaking with thee." And immediately His disciples came; and they wondered that He talked with the woman. Yet no man said: What seekest Thou? or why talkest Thou with her?

The woman therefore left her water-pot, and went her way into the city, and saith to the men there: "Come and see a Man Who has told me all things whatsoever I have done. Is not He the Christ?" They went therefore out of the city and came unto Him.

In the meantime the disciples prayed Him, saying: "Rabbi, eat." But He said to them: "I have meat to eat which you know not." The disciples said therefore one to another: "Hath any man brought Him to eat?" Jesus said to them: "My meat is to do the will of Him that sent Me, that I may perfect His work. Do not you say, there are yet four months and then the harvest cometh? Behold! I say to thee, lift up your eyes, and see the countries, for they are white already to harvest. And he that reapeth, receiveth wages and gathereth fruit unto life everlasting, that both he that soweth, and he that reapeth, may rejoice together. For in this is the saying true: that it is one man that soweth, and it is another that reapeth. I have sent you to reap that, in which you did not labour; others have laboured, and you have entered into their labours."

39. Now of that city many of the Samaritans believed in Him for the word of the woman giving testimony: He told me all things whatsoever I have done. So when the Samaritans were come to Him, they desired Him that He would tarry there. And He abode there two days. And many more believed in Him because of His own word. And they said to the woman: "We now believe, not for thy saying, for we ourselves have heard Him, and know that this is indeed the Saviour of the world."

[Luke 4, 14.]
[John 4, 43—54.]
^{JN}Now after two days He departed thence and went into Galilee. For Jesus Himself gave testimony, that a prophet hath no honour in his own country. And when He was come into Galilee, the Galilæans received Him, having seen all the things which He had done in Jerusalem on the festival-day; for they also went to the festival-day.

46. He came again therefore into Cana of Galilee, where He made the water wine. And there was a certain ruler whose son was sick at Capharnaum. He having heard that Jesus was come from Judea into Galilee, went to Him, and prayed Him to come down, and heal his son, for he was at the point of death. Jesus therefore said to him: "Unless you see signs and wonders you believe not." The ruler saith to Him: "Lord, come

down before that my son die." Jesus saith to him: "Go thy way, thy son liveth." The man believed the word which Jesus said to him, and went his way. And as he was going down, his servants met him, and they brought him word that his son lived. He asked therefore of them the hour wherein he grew better, and they said to him: "Yesterday at the seventh hour the fever left him." The father therefore knew that it was at the same hour that Jesus said to him: Thy son liveth; and himself believed, and his whole house. This is again the second miracle that Jesus did when He was come out of Judea into Galilee. And the fame of Him went out through the whole country. And He taught in their synagogues and was magnified by all. And He came to Nazareth, where He was brought up, and He went into the synagogue, according to His custom, on the Sabbath-day; and He rose up to read; and the book of Isaias the prophet was delivered unto Him. And as He unfolded the book, He found the place where it was written: *The spirit of the Lord is upon Me, wherefore He hath anointed Me to preach the Gospel to the poor; He hath sent Me to heal the contrite of heart, to preach deliverance to the captives, and sight to the blind, to set at liberty them that are bruised, to preach the acceptable year of the Lord, and the day of reward.*

And when He had folded the book, He restored it to the minister, and sat down. And the eyes of all in the Synagogue were fixed on Him. And He began to say to them: "This day is fulfilled this Scripture in your ears." And all gave testimony to Him, and they wondered at the words of grace that proceeded from His mouth, and they said: "Is not this the son of Joseph?" And He said to them: "Doubtless you will say to Me this similitude: Physician, heal Thyself; as great things as we have heard done in Capharnaum, do also here in Thy own country." And He said: "Amen, I say to you, that no prophet is accepted in his own country. In truth I say to you, there were many widows in the days of Elias in Israel, when heaven was shut up three years and six months, when there was a great famine throughout all the earth, and to none of them was Elias sent, but to Sarepta of Sidon, a widow woman. And there were many lepers in Israel in the time of Eliseus the prophet, and none of them was cleansed but Naaman the Syrian."

28. And all they in the Synagogue hearing these things were filled with anger. And they rose up and thrust Him out of the city; and they brought Him to the brow of the hill, whereon their city was built, that they might cast Him down headlong. But He passing through the midst of them went His way.

Matt. 4, 13—16. And leaving the city of Nazareth, He came and dwelt in Capharnaum on the sea coast, in the borders of Zabulon and Nepthalim, that it might be fulfilled which was said by Isaias the prophet: *The land of Zabulon, and the land of Nephthalim, the way of the sea beyond the Jordan, Galilee of the Gentiles; the people that sat in darkness saw great light, and to them that sat in the region of the shadow of death, light is sprung up.*

Matt. 4, 17—22.
Mark 1, 14—20. ᴹᵀFrom that time Jesus began to preach ᴹᴷthe Gospel of the Kingdom of God, . . . saying: "The time is accomplished, and the Kingdom of God is at hand; repent and believe the Gospel."

And passing by the sea of Galilee, He saw Simon and Andrew his brother casting nets into the sea (for they were fishermen). And Jesus said to them: "Come after Me, and I will make you to become fishers of men." And immediately leaving their nets they followed Him. And going on from thence a little further, He saw James the son of Zebedee, and John his brother, who also were mending their nets in the ship; and forthwith He called them. And leaving their father Zebedee in the ship with his hired men, they followed Him.

^{MK}And they entered into Capharnaum, ^{LK}a city of Galilee, ^{MK}and forthwith upon the Sabbath-days, going into the synagogue He taught them. And they were astonished at His doctrine, for He was teaching them as one having power, and not as the Scribes. ^{LK}And in the synagogue there was a man who had an unclean devil, and he cried out with a loud voice, saying: "Let us alone; what have we to do with Thee, Jesus of Nazareth? Art Thou come to destroy us? I know Thee, Who Thou art, the Holy One of God." And Jesus rebuked him, saying: "Hold thy peace, and go out of him."

Mark 1, 21—28.
Luke 4, 31—37.

And when the devil had thrown him into the midst, ^{MK}tearing him, and crying with a loud voice, ^{LK}he went out of him, and hurt him not at all. ^{MK}And they were all amazed, ^{LK}and there came fear upon all, ^{MK}insomuch that they questioned among themselves saying: "What thing is this? what is this new doctrine? for with power He commandeth even the unclean spirits, and they obey Him." And the fame of Him was spread forthwith through all the country of Galilee.

^{MK}And immediately going out of the synagogue, they came into the house of Simon and Andrew, with James and John. And Simon's wife's mother lay in a fit of a fever, and forthwith they tell Him

Matt. 8, 14—17.
Mark 1, 29—34.
Luke 4, 38—41.

of her. And coming to her, He lifted her up, taking her by the hand; ^{LK}and standing over her, He commanded the fever, ^{MK}and immediately the fever left her, and she ministered unto them.

And when it was evening, after sunset, they brought all to Him that were ill, and that were possessed with devils. And all the city was gathered together at the door, and He healed many that were troubled of divers diseases, ^{MT}that it might be fulfilled which was spoken by Isaias the prophet, saying: *He took our infirmities, and bore our diseases.*

Mark 1, 35—38.
Luke 4, 42, 43.

^{LK}And devils went out of many, crying out and saying: "Thou art the Son of God." And rebuking them He suffered them not to speak, for they knew that He was Christ.

^{MK}And rising very early, going out He went into a desert place, and there He prayed. And Simon, and they that were with him, followed after Him, and when they found Him they said to Him: "All seek for Thee." ^{LK}And the multitudes besought Him and they stayed Him, that He would not depart from them. ^{MK}And He saith to them: "Let us go into the neighbouring towns and cities, that I may preach there also ^{LK}the Kingdom of God, ^{MK}for to this purpose am I come."

Matt. 4, 23.
Mark 1, 39.
Luke 4, 44.

^{MT}And Jesus went about all Galilee, teaching in their synagogues, and preaching the Gospel of the Kingdom, and healing all manner of sickness and every infirmity among the people.

Matt. 4, 24, 25.

And His fame went throughout all Syria, and they presented to Him all sick people that were taken with divers diseases and torments, and such as were possessed by devils; and lunatics, and those that had the palsy, and He healed them. And much people followed Him from Galilee, and from Decapolis, and from Jerusalem, and from Judea, and from beyond the Jordan.

And seeing the multitudes, He went up into a mountain, and when He had sat down, His disciples came to Him, and opening His mouth He taught them saying: "Blessed are the poor in spirit, for theirs is the Kingdom of Heaven; blessed are the meek, for they shall possess the land; blessed are they that mourn, for they shall be comforted; blessed are they that hunger and thirst after justice, for they shall have their fill; blessed are the merciful, for they shall obtain mercy; blessed are the clean of heart, for they shall see God; blessed are the peace-makers, for they shall be called the children of God; blessed are they that suffer persecution for justice sake, for theirs is the Kingdom of Heaven; blessed are ye, when men shall revile you and persecute you and shall say all manner of evil against you untruly for My sake; be glad and rejoice, for your reward is very great in Heaven, for so they persecuted the prophets that were before you. *Matt. 5, 1—48.*

"You are the salt of the earth, but if the salt have lost its savour, wherewith shall it be salted? It is good for nothing any more, but to be cast out and to be trodden upon by men. You are the light of the world. A city seated on a mountain cannot be hid. Neither do men light a candle and put it under a bushel, but upon a candlestick, that it may shine to all that are in the house. So let your light shine before men, that they may see your good works, and glorify your Father Who is in Heaven. *13.*

"Do not think that I am come to destroy the law or the prophets; I am not come to destroy, but to fulfil. For amen I say unto you, till heaven and *17.*

earth pass, one jot or one tittle shall not pass from
the law, till all be fulfilled. He therefore that shall
break one of these least commandments, and shall
so teach men, shall be called the least in the
Kingdom of Heaven; but he that shall do and
teach, he shall be called great in the Kingdom of
Heaven. For I tell you, that unless your justice
abound more than that of the Scribes and Pharisees, you shall not enter into the Kingdom of
Heaven.

21. "You have heard that it was said to them of old:
Thou shalt not kill; and whosoever shall kill, shall
be guilty of the Judgment. But I say to you, that
whosoever is angry with his brother, shall be guilty
of the Judgment; and whosoever shall say to his
brother: Raca, shall be guilty of the Council; and
whosoever shall say: Thou fool, shall be guilty of
Hell fire. If therefore thou offer thy gift at the
altar, and there shalt remember that thy brother
hath anything against thee, leave there thy offering
before the altar, and go first to be reconciled to thy
brother, and then coming thou shalt offer thy gift.
Be at an agreement with thy adversary betimes,
whilst thou art in the way with him, lest perhaps
the adversary deliver thee to the judge, and the
judge deliver thee to the officer, and thou be cast
into prison; amen I say to thee, thou shalt not go
out from thence, till thou repay the last farthing.

27. "You have heard that it was said to them of old:
Thou shalt not commit adultery. But I say unto
you, that whosoever shall look after a woman to
lust after her, hath already committed adultery with
her in his heart. And if thy right eye scandalize
thee, pluck it out and cast it from thee, for it is
expedient for thee that one of thy members should
perish, rather than that thy whole body should be

cast into Hell. And if thy right hand scandalize thee, cut it off, and cast it from thee, for it is expedient for thee that one of thy members should perish, rather than that thy whole body go into Hell.

"And it hath been said: Whosoever shall put away his wife, let him give her a bill of divorce. But I say to you, that whosoever shall put away his wife, excepting the cause of fornication, maketh her to commit adultery; and he that shall marry her that is put away committeth adultery.

"Again, you have heard that it was said to them of old: Thou shalt not forswear thyself, but thou shalt perform thy oaths to the Lord. But I say to you, not to swear at all, neither by Heaven, for it is the throne of God; nor by the earth, for it is His footstool; nor by Jerusalem, for it is the city of the great King. Neither shalt thou swear by thy head, because thou canst not make one hair white or black. But let your speech be: Yea, yea; No, no; and that which is over and above these is of evil.

"You have heard that it hath been said: An eye for an eye; a tooth for a tooth. But I say to you not to resist evil, but if one strike thee on thy right cheek, turn to him the other also. And if a man contend with thee in judgment, and take away thy coat, let go thy cloak also unto him. And whosoever shall force thee one mile, go with him other two. Give to him that asketh of thee, and from him that would borrow of thee, turn not away.

"You have heard that it hath been said: Thou shalt love thy neighbour, and hate thy enemy. But I say to you, love your enemies, do good to them that hate you, and pray for them that persecute and calumniate you, that you may be the children of your Father Who is in Heaven, Who maketh His sun to rise upon the good and bad, and raineth upon the just and the unjust. For if you love them that love you, what reward shall you have? do not even the publicans this? And if you salute your brethren only, what do you more? do not also the heathens this? Be you therefore perfect, as also your heavenly Father is perfect.

Matt. 6, 1—34.

"Take heed that you do not your justice before men, to be seen by them, otherwise you shall not have a reward of your Father Who is in Heaven. Therefore, when thou dost an almsdeed, sound not a trumpet before thee, as the hypocrites do in the synagogues and in the streets, that they may be honoured by men. Amen I say to you they have received their reward. But when thou dost alms, let not thy left hand know what thy right hand doth, that thy alms may be in secret, and thy Father Who seeth in secret will repay thee.

6. "And when ye pray, you shall not be as the hypocrites, that love to stand and pray in the synagogues and corners of the streets, that they may be seen by men. Amen I say to you, they have received their reward. But thou, when thou shalt pray, enter into thy chamber, and having shut the door, pray to thy Father in secret, and thy Father who seeth in secret will repay thee. And when you are praying, speak not much as the heathens; for they think that in their much speaking they may be heard. Be not you therefore like to them, for your Father knoweth what is needful for you before you ask Him. Thus therefore shall you pray: Our Father Who art in Heaven, hallowed be Thy name; Thy Kingdom come; Thy will be done on earth as it is in Heaven. Give us this day our supersubstantial

bread, and forgive us our debts as we also forgive our debtors; and lead us not into temptation; but deliver us from evil, Amen. For if you will forgive men their offences, your heavenly Father will forgive you also your offences. But if you will not forgive men, neither will your Father forgive you your offences.

"And when you fast, be not as the hypocrites, 15. sad; for they disfigure their faces, that they may appear unto men to fast. Amen I say to you, they have received their reward. But thou, when thou fastest, anoint thy head and wash thy face, that thou appear not to men to fast, but to thy Father Who is in secret, and thy Father Who seeth in secret will repay thee.

"Lay not up to yourselves treasures on earth, 19. where the rust and moth consume, and where thieves break through and steal. But lay up to yourselves treasures in Heaven, where neither the rust nor moth doth consume, and where thieves do not break through nor steal. For where thy treasure is, there is thy heart also.

"The light of thy body is thy eye. If thy eye be 22. single, thy whole body shall be lightsome. But if thy eye be evil, thy whole body shall be darksome. If then the light that is in thee be darkness, the darkness itself how great shall it be!

"No man can serve two masters; for either he 24. will hate the one and love the other, or he will sustain the one and despise the other. You cannot serve God and mammon. Therefore I say to you, be not solicitous for your life, what you shall eat, nor for your body, what you shall put on. Is not the life more than the meat, and the body more than the raiment? Behold the birds of the air, for they neither sow, nor do they reap, nor gather into barns; and your heavenly Father feedeth them. Are not you of much more value than they? And which of you by taking thought can add to his stature one cubit? And for raiment, why are you solicitous? Consider the lilies of the field, how they grow; they labour not, neither do they spin; but I say to you, that not even Solomon in all his glory was arrayed as one of these. And if the grass of the field, which is to-day and to-morrow is cast into the oven, God doth so clothe, how much more you, O ye of little faith! Be not solicitous therefore saying: What shall we eat, or what shall we drink, or wherewith shall we be clothed? For after all these things do the heathens seek. For your Father knoweth that you have need of all these things. Seek ye therefore first the Kingdom of God and His justice, and all these things shall be added unto you. Be not therefore solicitous for to-morrow, for the morrow will be solicitous for itself. Sufficient for the day is the evil thereof.

Matt. 7, 1—29.

"Judge not, that you may not be judged; for with what judgment you judge, you shall be judged, and with what measure you mete, it shall be measured to you again. And why seest thou 'the mote that is in thy brother's eye, and seest not the beam that is in thy own eye? Or how sayest thou to thy brother: 'Let me cast the mote out of thy eye,' and behold a beam is in thy own eye? Thou hypocrite, cast out first the beam out of thy own eye, and then shalt thou see to cast out the mote out of thy brother's eye.

6. "Give not that which is holy to dogs, neither cast ye your pearls before swine, lest perhaps they trample them under their feet, and turning upon you they tear you.

"Ask and it shall be given you, seek and you shall find, knock and it shall be opened to you. For every one that asketh receiveth, and he that seeketh findeth, and to him that knocketh it shall be opened. Or what man is there among you, of whom if his son shall ask bread, will he reach him a stone? Or if he shall ask him a fish, will he reach him a serpent? If you then being evil, know how to give good gifts to your children, how much more will your Father Who is in Heaven give good gifts to them that ask Him? All things therefore whatsoever ye would that men should do to you, do you also to them, for this is the law and the prophets.

"Enter ye in at the narrow gate, for wide is the gate and broad is the way that leadeth to destruction, and many there are who go in thereat. How narrow is the gate and strait is the way that leadeth to life, and few there are that find it!

"Beware of false prophets, who come to you in the clothing of sheep, but inwardly they are ravening wolves. By their fruits you shall know them. Do men gather grapes of thorns, or figs of thistles? Even so every good tree bringeth forth good fruit and the evil tree bringeth forth evil fruit. A good tree cannot bring forth evil fruit, neither can an evil tree bring forth good fruit. Every tree that bringeth not forth good fruit shall be cut down, and shall be cast into the fire. Wherefore by their fruits ye shall know them.

"Not every one that sayeth to Me: Lord! Lord! shall enter into the Kingdom of Heaven, but he that doth the will of My Father Who is in Heaven, he shall enter into the Kingdom of Heaven. Many will say to Me in that day: Lord, Lord, have not we prophesied in Thy name, and cast out devils in

Thy name, and done many miracles in Thy name?
And then will I profess unto them: I never knew
you; depart from Me, you that work iniquity.
Every one therefore that heareth these My words
and doth them, shall be likened to a wise man that
built his house upon a rock. And the rain fell, and
the floods came, and the winds blew, and they beat
upon that house, and it fell not, for it was founded
upon a rock. And every one that heareth these
My words and doth them not, shall be like a
foolish man, that built his house upon the sand.
And the rain fell, and the floods came, and the
winds blew, and they beat upon that house, and it
fell, and great was the fall thereof."

28. And it came to pass when Jesus had fully ended
these words, the people were in admiration at His
doctrine; for He was teaching them as one having
power, and not as their Scribes and Pharisees.

Matt. 8, 1. And when He was come down from the
mountain great multitudes followed Him.

Luke 5, 1—12. And it came to pass, that when the multitudes
pressed upon Him to hear the word of God, He
stood by the lake of Genesareth. And He saw
two ships standing by the lake, but the fishermen
were gone out of them and were washing their
nets. And going into one of the ships that was
Simon's, He desired him to draw back a little
from the land, and sitting He taught the multitudes out of the ship.

4. Now when He had ceased to speak He said
to Simon: "Launch out into the deep, and let
down your nets for a draught." And Simon
answering said to Him: "Master, we have laboured
all the night, and have taken nothing, but at Thy
word I will let down the net." And when they
had done this, they enclosed a very great multitude

PART II.   TO THE SECOND PASCH.   43

of fishes, and their net broke. And they beckoned to their partners that were in the other ship, that they should come and help them. And they came and filled both the ships, so that they were almost sinking. Which when Simon Peter saw, he fell down at Jesus' knees, saying: "Depart from me, for I am a sinful man, O Lord."ᴸ For he was wholly astonished and all that were with him, at the draught of the fishes which they had taken, and so were also James and John, the sons of Zebedee, who were Simon's partners. And Jesus saith to Simon: "Fear not, from henceforth thou shalt catch men." And having brought their ships to land, leaving all things they followed Him.¹

ᴸᴷAnd it came to pass when He was in a certain city, behold a man full of leprosy, who seeing Jesus and falling on his face, besought Him, saying: "Lord, if Thou wilt, Thou canst make me clean." ᴹᴷAnd Jesus having compassion on him, stretched forth His hand, and touching him, saith to him: "I will, be thou made clean." And when He had spoken, immediately the leprosy departed from him, and he was made clean. And He strictly charged him, and forthwith sent him away; and He saith to him: "See thou tell no one, but go, show thyself to the high priest, and offer for thy cleansing the things that Moses commanded for a testimony to them."

ᴹᴷBut he being gone out began to publish and to blaze abroad the word; so that He could not openly go into the city, but was without in desert

<small>Matt. 8, 2—4.
Mark 1, 40—44.
Luke 5, 12—14.</small>

<small>Mark 1, 45.
Luke 5, 15, 16.</small>

---

¹ Father Coleridge and others consider that there is ample evidence, furnished by difference of circumstance and detail, to establish the fact of a second and final call by our Lord to these four fishermen, distinct from that recorded by St. Matt. iv. 18, and by St. Mark i. 16. (See p. 33.)

places, and they flocked to Him from all sides, ^{LK}and He retired into the desert and prayed.

Mark 2, 1, 2.   And again He entered into Capharnaum after some days, and it was heard that He was in the house, and many came together, so that there was no room, no, not even at the door: and He spoke to them the word.

Luke 5, 17.   And it came to pass ... as He sat teaching, that there were also Pharisees and doctors of the law sitting by, that were come out of every town of Galilee and Judea and Jerusalem, and the power of the Lord was to heal them.

Matt. 9, 2.
Mark 2, 3.
Luke 5, 18.   ^{MT}And behold they brought to Him one sick of the palsy, lying in a bed, ^{MK}who was carried by four; ^{LK}and they sought means to bring him in, and to lay him before Him.

Mark 2, 4.
Luke 5, 19.   ^{LK}And when they could not find by what way they might bring him in, because of the multitude, they went up upon the roof, and let him down through the tiles with his bed, in the midst, before Jesus.

Matt. 9, 2—8.
Mark 2, 5—12.
Luke 5, 20—26.   ^{MK}And when Jesus had seen their faith, He saith to the sick of the palsy: "Son, thy sins are forgiven thee." And there were some of the Scribes sitting there, and thinking in their hearts: Why doth this Man speak thus? He blasphemeth. Who can forgive sins but God only? Which Jesus presently knowing in His Spirit that they so thought within themselves, saith to them: "Why think you these things in your hearts? Which is easier, to say to the sick of the palsy: Thy sins are forgiven thee; or to say: Arise, take up thy bed and walk? But that you may know that the Son of Man hath power on earth to forgive sins" (He saith to the sick of the palsy): "I say to thee, arise, take up thy bed, and go into thy house." ^{LK}And immediately rising up before them, he took

up the bed on which he lay, and he went away to his own house glorifying God. And all were astonished, and they glorified God. And they were filled with fear, saying: "We have seen wonderful things to-day."

^{MK}And He went forth again to the seaside, and all the multitude came to Him, and He taught them. Mark 2, 13.

^{MT}And when Jesus passed on from thence, He saw a man sitting in the custom-house named Matthew—^{LK}a publican, ^{MK}Levi, the son of Alpheus —^{MT}and He saith to him: "Follow Me." ^{LK}And leaving all things he rose up and followed Him. Matt. 9, 9—13.
Mark 2, 14—17.
Luke 5, 27—32.

^{LK}And Levi made Him a great feast in his own house. ^{MK}And it came to pass that as He sat at meat ... many publicans and sinners sat down together with Jesus and His disciples; for they were many who also followed Him. And the Scribes and Pharisees seeing that He ate with publicans and sinners, said to His disciples: "Why doth your Master eat and drink with publicans and sinners?" ^{MT}Jesus hearing this said: "They that are in health need not a physician, but they that are ill. Go then, and learn what this meaneth: *I will have mercy and not sacrifice;* for I am not come to call the just, but sinners."

^{MK}And the disciples of John, and the Pharisees, used to fast; and they come and say to Him: "Why do the disciples of John and of the Pharisees fast ^{LK}often, and make prayers, ^{MK}but Thy disciples do not fast?" And Jesus saith to them: "Can the children of the marriage fast, as long as the bridegroom is with them? As long as they have the bridegroom with them, they cannot fast. But the days will come when the bridegroom shall be taken away from them, and then they shall fast Matt. 9, 14—17.
Mark 2, 18—22.
Luke 5, 33—39.

in those days." ^{Lk}And He spoke also a similitude to them, that no man putteth a piece from a new garment upon an old garment, otherwise he both rendeth the new, and the piece taken from the new agreeth not with the old. And no man putteth new wine into old bottles, otherwise the new wine will break the bottles, and it will be spilled, and the bottles will be lost. But new wine must be put into new bottles, and both are preserved. And no man drinking old, hath presently a mind to new, for he saith: The old is better.

Part III.

FROM THE SECOND TO THE THIRD PASCH.

AFTER these things was a festival-day of the Jews, John 5. 1—15. and Jesus went up to Jerusalem. Now there is at Jerusalem a pond called Probatica, which in Hebrew is called Bethsaida, having five porches. In these lay a great multitude of sick, of blind, of lame, of withered, waiting for the moving of the water. And an angel of the Lord descended at certain times into the pond, and the water was moved. And he that went down first into the pond after the motion of the water, was made whole of whatsoever infirmity he lay under. And there was a certain man there that had been eight and thirty years under his infirmity. Him when Jesus had seen lying and knew that he had been now a long time, He saith to him: "Wilt thou be made whole?" The infirm man answered Him: "Sir, I have no man, when the water is troubled, to put me into the pond; for whilst I am coming, another goeth down before me." Jesus saith to him: "Arise, take up thy bed and walk." And immediately the man was made whole and he took up his bed and walked. And it was the Sabbath that day. The Jews therefore said to him that was healed: "It is the Sabbath; it is not lawful for thee to take up thy bed." He answered them: "He that made me whole, He said to me, 'Take up thy bed and walk.'" They asked him therefore, "Who is that man who said to thee, 'Take up thy bed and walk?'" But he that was healed knew not who it was, for Jesus went aside from the multitude standing in the place. Afterwards Jesus findeth him in the Temple and saith to him: "Behold thou art made whole, sin no more, lest some worse thing happen to thee." The man went his way and told the Jews that it was Jesus Who made him whole.

<small>Matt. 12, 1—4.
Mark 2, 23—26.
Luke 6, 1—4.</small>
^{LK}And it came to pass on the second first Sabbath, that as He went through the corn-fields, His disciples ^{MT}being hungry ^{MK}began to go forward and to pluck the ears of corn, ^{LK}rubbing them in their hands. And some of the Pharisees said to them: "Why do you that which is not lawful on the Sabbath-days?" And Jesus answering them, said: "Have you not read so much as this, what David did when himself was hungry and they that were with him: How he went into the house of God and took and eat the bread of proposition, and gave to them that were with him, which is not lawful to eat, but only for the priests?

<small>Matt. 12, 5—7.</small>
"Or have ye not read in the law, that on the Sabbath-days, the priests in the Temple break the Sabbath, and are without blame? But I tell you that there is here a greater than the Temple. And if you knew what this meaneth; *I will have mercy and not sacrifice*, you would never have condemned the innocent."

<small>Mark 2, 27.</small>
And He said to them: "The Sabbath was made for man, and not man for the Sabbath."

<small>Matt. 12, 8—13.
Mark 2, 28.</small>
^{LK}And He said to them: "The Son of Man is Lord also of the Sabbath."

<small>Mark 3, 1—5.
Luke 6, 5—10.</small>
And it came to pass also on another Sabbath, that He entered into the synagogue and taught.

And there was a man whose right hand was withered. And the Scribes and Pharisees watched if he would heal on the Sabbath, that they might find an accusation against Him.

^{LK}But He knew their thoughts, and said to the man who had the withered hand: "Arise, and stand forth in the midst." And rising he stood forth. Then Jesus said to them: "I ask you if it be lawful on the Sabbath-days to do good or to do evil, to save life or to destroy?" ^{MK}But they held their peace.

^{MT}But He said to them: "What man shall there be among you that hath one sheep, and if the same fall into a pit on the Sabbath-day, will he not take hold on it and lift it up? How much better is a man than a sheep? Therefore it is lawful to do a good deed on the Sabbath-day." ^{MK}And looking round about on them with anger, being grieved for the blindness of their hearts, He saith to the man: "Stretch forth thy hand." And he stretched it forth, and his hand was restored unto him.

Therefore did the Jews persecute Jesus, because He did these things on the Sabbath. But Jesus answered them: "My Father worketh until now, and I work." Hereupon therefore the Jews sought the more to kill Him, because He did not only break the Sabbath, but also said that God was His Father, making Himself equal to God. Then Jesus answered and said to them: "Amen, amen, I say unto you, the Son cannot do anything of Himself, but what He seeth the Father doing, or what things soever He doth, these the Son also doth in like manner. For the Father loveth the Son and showeth Him all things which Himself doth, and greater works than these will He show

John 5, 16—47.

Him, that you may wonder. For as the Father raiseth up the dead and giveth life, so the Son also giveth life to whom He will. For neither does the Father judge any man, but hath given all judgment to the Son, that all men may honour the Son as they honour the Father. He who honoureth not the Son, honoureth not the Father Who sent Him. Amen, amen, I say unto you, that he who heareth My word, and believeth Him that sent Me, hath life everlasting and cometh not into judgment, but is passed from death to life. Amen, amen, I say unto you, that the hour cometh and now is, when the dead shall hear the voice of the Son of God, and they that hear shall live. For as the Father hath life in Himself, so He hath given to the Son also to have life in Himself. And He hath given Him power to do judgment, because He is the Son of Man. Wonder not at this, for the hour cometh when all that are in the graves shall hear the voice of the Son of God. And they that have done good things, shall come forth unto the resurrection of life, but they that have done evil, unto the resurrection of judgment. I cannot of Myself do anything. As I hear, so I judge, and My judgment is just, because I seek not My own will, but the will of Him Who sent Me. If I bear witness to Myself My witness is not true. There is another that beareth witness of Me, and I know that the witness which He witnesseth of Me is true. You sent to John and he gave testimony of the truth. But I receive not testimony from man; but I say these things that you may be saved. He was a burning and a shining light, and you were willing for a time to rejoice in his light. But I have a greater testimony than that of John, for the works which the Father hath given me to perfect, the works themselves which I do, give testimony of Me, that the Father hath sent Me. And the Father Himself Who hath sent Me, hath given testimony of Me. Neither have you heard His voice at any time nor seen His shape. And you have not His word abiding in you, for Whom He hath sent, Him you believe not. Search the Scriptures, for you think in them to have life everlasting, and the same are they that give testimony of Me. And you will not come to Me that you may have life. I receive not glory from men, but I know you, that you have not the love of God in you. I am come in the name of My Father, and you receive Me not; if another shall come in his own name him you will receive. How can you believe, who receive glory one from another, and the glory which is from God alone you do not seek? Think not that I will accuse you to the Father. There is one that accuseth you, Moses, in whom you trust. For if you did believe Moses, you would perhaps believe Me also, for He wrote of Me. But if you do not believe his writings, how shall you believe My words?"

And the Pharisees ᴸᴷwere filled with madness, and they talked one with another, what they might do to Jesus, [and] ᴹᴷgoing out immediately, made a consultation with the Herodians against Him, how they might destroy Him. _{Matt. 12, 14.} _{Mark 3, 6.} _{Luke 6, 11.}

ᴹᵀBut Jesus knowing it, retired from thence ᴹᴷwith His disciples to the sea; ᴹᵀand many followed Him, and He healed them all. And He charged them that they should not make Him known. _{Matt. 12, 15, 16.} _{Mark 3, 7.}

And a great multitude followed Him from Galilee and from Jerusalem and Idumea, and from beyond the Jordan; and they about Tyre _{Mark 3, 7—12.}

and Sidon, a great multitude, hearing the things which He did, came to Him.

And He spoke to His disciples that a small ship should wait on Him because of the multitude, lest they should throng Him. For He healed many, so that they pressed upon Him for to touch Him, as many as had evils. And the unclean spirits, when they saw Him, fell down before Him, and they cried, saying, "Thou art the Son of God." And He strictly charged them that they should not make Him known.

Matt. 12, 17—21.

That it might be fulfilled which was spoken by Isaias the Prophet, saying: *Behold, My servant whom I have chosen, My beloved in whom My Soul hath been well pleased. I will put My Spirit upon Him, and He shall show judgment to the Gentiles. He shall not contend, nor cry out, neither shall any man hear His voice in the streets. The bruised reed He shall not break, and smoking flax He shall not extinguish, till He send forth judgment unto victory. And in His Name the Gentiles shall hope.*

Mark 3, 13—19.
Luke 6, 12—16.

LKAnd it came to pass in those days that He went out into a mountain to pray, and He passed the whole night in the prayer of God. And when day was come, He called unto Him His disciples; MKwhom He would Himself, and they came to Him. And He made that twelve should be with Him, and that He might send them to preach, LK(whom also He named Apostles), Simon whom He surnamed Peter, and Andrew his brother, MKand James the son of Zebedee, and John the brother of James, and He called them Boanerges, which is, the sons of thunder; LKPhilip and Bartholomew, Matthew and Thomas, James the son of Alpheus, and Simon MKthe Cananean, LKwho is called Zelotes, and Jude the brother of James, and Judas Iscariot, who was the traitor. ^{Mk}And He gave them power to heal sicknesses and to cast out devils.

And coming down with them, He stood in a plain place, and the company of His disciples, and a very great multitude of people from all Judea and Jerusalem and the sea-coast both of Tyre and Sidon, who were come to hear Him and to be healed of their diseases. And they that were troubled with unclean spirits were cured. And all the multitude sought to touch Him, for virtue went out from Him and healed all. And He, lifting up His eyes on His disciples, said: "Blessed are ye poor, for yours is the Kingdom of God; blessed are ye that hunger now, for you shall be filled; blessed are ye that weep now, for you shall laugh; blessed shall you be when men shall hate you, and when they shall separate you, and shall reproach you, and cast out your name as evil for the Son of Man's sake. Be glad in that day and rejoice, for behold your reward is great in Heaven. For according to these things did their fathers to the prophets.

Luke 6, 17—49.

"But wo to you that are rich, for you have your consolation. Wo to you that are filled, for you shall hunger. Wo to you that now laugh, for you shall mourn and weep. Wo to you when men shall bless you, for according to these things did their fathers to the false prophets. But I say to you that hear, love your enemies, do good to them that hate you. Bless them that curse you, and pray for them that calumniate you. And to him that striketh thee on the one cheek, offer also the other. And him that taketh away from thee thy cloak, forbid not to take thy coat also.

24.

"Give to every one that asketh thee, and of him

30.

that taketh away thy goods, ask them not again. And as you would that men should do to you, do you also to them in like manner. And if you love them that love you, what thanks are to you? for sinners also love those that love them. And if you do good to them who do good to you, what thanks are to you? for sinners also do this? And if ye lend to them of whom you hope to receive, what thanks are to you? for sinners also lend to sinners, for to receive as much. But love ye your enemies, do good and lend, hoping for nothing thereby, and your reward shall be great and you shall be the sons of the Highest, for He is kind to the unthankful, and to the evil. Be ye therefore merciful as your Father also is merciful.

37. "Judge not, and you shall not be judged. Condemn not, and you shall not be condemned. Forgive, and you shall be forgiven. Give, and it shall be given to you, good measure, and pressed down and shaken together and running over, shall be given into your bosom. For with the same measure that you shall mete withal, it shall be measured to you again."

39. And He spoke also to them a similitude: "Can the blind lead the blind? do they not both fall into the ditch? The disciple is not above his master, but every one shall be perfect, if he be as his master. And why seest thou the mote in thy brother's eye, but the beam that is in thy own eye thou considerest not? Or how canst thou say to thy brother: 'Brother, let me pull the mote out of thy eye,' when thou thyself seest not the beam in thy own eye? Hypocrite, cast first the beam out of thy own eye, and then shalt thou see clearly to take out the mote from thy brother's eye.

"For there is no good tree that bringeth forth

evil fruit, nor an evil tree that bringeth forth good fruit. For every tree is known by its fruit. For men do not gather figs from thorns, nor from a bramble bush do they gather the grape. A good man, out of the good treasure of his heart, bringeth forth that which is good, and an evil man, out of the evil treasure, bringeth forth that which is evil. For out of the abundance of the heart, the mouth speaketh.

"And why call you Me, Lord, Lord, and do not the things which I say? Every one that cometh to Me and heareth My words, and doth them, I will show you to whom he is like. He is like to a man building a house, who digged deep, and laid the foundation upon a rock, and when a flood came, the stream beat vehemently upon that house, and it could not shake it, for it was founded on a rock. But he that heareth and doth not, is like to a man building his house upon the earth without a foundation, against which the stream beat vehemently, and immediately it fell and the ruin of that house was great." ^{46.}

^{LK}And when He had finished all His words in the hearing of the people, He entered into Capharnaum. The servant of a certain centurion, who was dear to him, being sick, was ready to die. And when he had heard of Jesus he sent to Him the ancients of the Jews, desiring Him to come and heal his servant. And when they came to Jesus they besought Him earnestly, saying to Him, "He is worthy that Thou shouldst do this for him, for he loveth our nation and he hath built us a synagogue." And Jesus went with them. And when He was now not far from the house, the centurion sent his friends to Him, saying: "Lord, trouble not Thyself, for I am not worthy that Thou

<small>Matt. 8, 5—10. Luke 7, 1—9.</small>

shouldst enter under my roof. For which cause neither did I think myself worthy to come to Thee: but say the word and my servant shall be healed. For I also am a man subject to authority, having under me soldiers; and I say to one: Go! and he goeth; and to another: Come! and he cometh; and to my servant: Do this! and he doth it." Which Jesus hearing, marvelled, and turning about to the multitude that followed Him, He said: "Amen I say to you, I have not found so great faith, not even in Israel.

Matt. 8, 11—13.

"And I say to you that many shall come from the east and the west, and shall sit down with Abraham, and Isaac, and Jacob, in the Kingdom of Heaven. But the children of the Kingdom shall be cast out into the exterior darkness: there shall be weeping and gnashing of teeth."

And Jesus said to [the friends of] the centurion:[1] "Go, and as thou hast believed, so be it done to thee." And the servant was healed at the same hour.

Luke 7, 10.

And they who were sent, being returned to the house, found the servant whole, who had been sick.

Mark 3, 20, 21.

And they came to a house, and the multitude cometh together again, so that they could not so much as eat bread. And when His friends had heard of it, they went out to lay hold on Him, for they said: "He is become mad."

Luke 7, 11—18.

And it came to pass afterwards, that He went into a certain city that is called Naim, and there went with Him His disciples and a great multitude.

---

[1] ["The friends of."] It is quite in keeping with St. Matthew's terseness of style, to represent the centurion as coming himself, and not, as St. Luke has it, making his request through his servants and friends.

And when He came nigh to the gate of the city, behold a dead man was carried out, the only son of his mother, and she was a widow, and a great multitude of the city was with her. Whom when the Lord had seen, being moved with mercy towards her, He said to her: "Weep not." And He came near and touched the bier. And they that carried it stood still. And He said: "Young man, I say to thee, Arise." And he that was dead sat up and began to speak. And He gave him to his mother. And there came a fear on them all and they glorified God, saying: "A great Prophet is risen up among us, and God hath visited His people." And this rumour of Him went forth throughout all Judea, and throughout all the country round about. And John's disciples told him of all these things.

^{MT}Now when John had heard in prison the works of Christ ^{LK}[he] called to him two of his disciples and sent them to Jesus, saying: "Art Thou He that art to come, or look we for another?" And when the men were come unto Him they said: "John the Baptist hath sent us to Thee, saying: Art Thou He that art to come, or look we for another?" (And in that same hour He cured many of their diseases, and hurts, and evil spirits, and to many that were blind He gave sight.) And answering, He said to them: "Go and relate to John what you have heard and seen: the blind see, the lame walk, the lepers are made clean, the deaf hear, the dead rise again, to the poor the Gospel is preached, and blessed is he whosoever shall not be scandalized in Me."

And when the messengers of John were departed, He began to speak to the multitudes concerning John. "What went you out into the desert to

Matt. 11, 2—11.
Luke 7, 19—28.

see? a reed shaken with the wind? But what went you out to see? a man clothed in soft garments? Behold, they that are in costly apparel, and live delicately, are in the houses of kings? But what went you out to see? A Prophet? Yea, I say to you, and more than a Prophet; this is he of whom it is written: *Behold, I send My angel before Thy face, who shall prepare Thy way before Thee.* For I say to you, amongst those that are born of women, there is not a greater Prophet than John the Baptist. But he that is the lesser in the Kingdom of God, is greater than he.

<small>Matt. 11, 12—15.</small>

ᴹᵀ"And from the days of John the Baptist until now, the Kingdom of Heaven suffereth violence, and the violent bear it away. For all the Prophets and the law prophesied until John. And if you will receive it, he is Elias that is to come. He that hath ears to hear, let him hear."

<small>Luke 7, 29, 30.</small>

And all the people hearing, and the publicans, justified God, being baptized with John's baptism. But the Pharisees and the lawyers despised the counsel of God against themselves, being not baptized by him.

<small>Matt. 11, 16—19. Luke 7, 31—35.</small>

ᴸᴷAnd the Lord said: "Whereunto then shall I liken the men of this generation? and to what are they like? They are like to children sitting in the market-place and speaking one to another and saying: 'We have piped to you and you have not danced, we have mourned and you have not wept.' For John the Baptist came, neither eating bread, nor drinking wine, and you say: He hath a devil. The Son of Man is come eating and drinking, and you say: 'Behold a man that is a glutton and a wine drinker, a friend of publicans and sinners;' and wisdom is justified by all her children."

<small>Luke 7, 36—50.</small>

And one of the Pharisees desired Him to eat

with him. And He went into the house of the Pharisee and sat down to meat. And behold, a woman that was in the city, a sinner, when she knew that He sat at meat in the Pharisee's house, brought an alabaster box of ointment, and standing behind at His feet, she began to wash His feet with tears, and wipe them with the hairs of her head, and kissed His feet, and anointed them with the ointment. And the Pharisee who had invited Him, seeing it, spoke within himself saying: "This man, if He were a prophet, would know surely who and what manner of woman this is that toucheth Him, that she is a sinner." And Jesus answering, said to him: "Simon, I have somewhat to say to thee." But he said: "Master, say it." "A certain creditor had two debtors; the one owed five hundred pence and the other fifty. And whereas they had not wherewith to pay, he forgave them both. Which therefore of the two loveth Him most?" Simon answering said: "I suppose that he to whom he forgave most." And He said to him, "Thou hast judged rightly."

And turning to the woman, He said unto Simon: "Dost thou see this woman? I entered into thy house; thou gavest Me no water for My feet; but she with tears hath washed My feet, and with her hairs hath wiped them. Thou gavest Me no kiss, but she, since she came in, hath not ceased to kiss My feet. My head with oil thou didst not anoint, but she with ointment hath anointed My feet. Wherefore I say to thee, many sins are forgiven her, because she hath loved much. But to whom less is forgiven, he loveth less." And He said to her, "Thy sins are forgiven thee."

And they that sat at meat with Him began to say within themselves: "Who is this that forgiveth sins also?" And He said to the woman: "Thy faith hath made thee safe, go in peace."

Luke 8, 1—3. And it came to pass afterwards that He travelled through the cities and towns, preaching and evangelizing the Kingdom of God, and the Twelve with Him, and certain women who had been healed of evil spirits and infirmities, Mary who is called Magdalene, out of whom seven devils were gone forth, and Joanna, the wife of Chusa Herod's steward, and Susanna, and many others who ministered unto Him of their substance.

Matt. 12, 22, 23. Then was offered to Him one possessed with a devil, blind and dumb, and He healed him, so that he spoke and saw. And all the multitude were amazed and said, "Is not this the Son of David?"

Matt. 12, 24—26.
Mark 3, 22—26. ᴹᵀBut the Pharisees ᴹᴷand the Scribes who were come down from Jerusalem, said: "He hath Beelzebub, and by the prince of devils He casteth out devils." And after He had called them together, He said to them in parables: "How can Satan cast out Satan? And if a kingdom be divided against itself, that kingdom cannot stand: and if a house be divided against itself, that house cannot stand. And if Satan be risen up against himself, he is divided, and cannot stand, but hath an end.

Matt. 12, 27, 28. "And if I by Beelzebub cast out devils, by whom do your children cast them out? Therefore they shall be your judges. But if I, by the Spirit of God, cast out devils, then is the Kingdom of God come upon you.

Matt. 12, 29.
Mark 3, 27. ᴹᵀ"Or how can any one enter into the house of the strong, and rifle his goods, unless he first bind the strong? and then he will rifle his house.

Matt. 12, 30. "He that is not with Me is against Me, and He that gathereth not with Me scattereth.

M[" "Therefore I say to you, every sin and blasphemy shall be forgiven men, but the blasphemy of the Spirit shall not be forgiven. And whosoever shall speak a word against the Son of Man, it shall be forgiven him, but he that shall speak against the Holy Ghost, it shall not be forgiven him, neither in this world nor in the world to come." Matt. 12, 31, 32. Mark 3, 28, 29.

Because they said: He hath an unclean spirit. "Either make the tree good and its fruit good, or make the tree evil and its fruit evil. For by the fruit the tree is known. O generation of vipers, how can you speak good things, whereas you are evil? for out of the abundance of the heart the mouth speaketh. A good man out of a good treasure bringeth forth good things, and an evil man out of an evil treasure bringeth forth evil things. But I say unto you, that every idle word that men shall speak, they shall render an account for in the day of judgment. For by thy words thou shalt be justified, and by thy words thou shalt be condemned." Mark 3, 30. Matt. 12, 33—45.

Then some of the Scribes and Pharisees answered Him saying: "Master, we would see a sign from Thee." Who answering said to them: "An evil and adulterous generation seeketh a sign, and a sign shall not be given it, but the sign of Jonas the Prophet. For as Jonas was in the whale's belly three days and three nights, so shall the Son of Man be in the heart of the earth three days and three nights. 38.

"The men of Ninive shall rise in judgment with this generation, and shall condemn it, because they did penance at the preaching of Jonas, and behold a greater than Jonas here. The Queen of the south shall rise in judgment 41.

with this generation and shall condemn it, because she came from the ends of the earth to hear the wisdom of Solomon, and behold a greater than Solomon here.

43. "And when an unclean spirit is gone out of a man, he walketh through dry places, seeking rest, and findeth none. Then he saith, I will return into my house, from whence I came out. And coming, he findeth it empty, swept, and garnished. Then he goeth and taketh with him seven other spirits more wicked than himself, and they enter in and dwell there, and the last state of that man is made worse than the first. So shall it be also to this wicked generation."

Matt. 12, 46—50.
Mark 3, 31—35.
Luke 8, 19—21.

^{MT}As He was yet speaking to the multitudes, behold His Mother and His brethren stood without, seeking to speak to Him. And one said unto Him: "Behold, Thy Mother and Thy brethren stand without seeking Thee." But He answering him that told Him, said: "Who is My Mother, and who are My brethren?" And stretching forth His hand towards His disciples, He said: "Behold, My Mother and My brethren. For whosoever shall do the will of My Father that is in Heaven, he is My brother and sister and mother."

Matt. 13, 1—9.
Mark 4, 1—9.
Luke 8, 4—8.

^{MK}And again He began to teach by the seaside, and a great multitude was gathered together unto Him, so that He went up into a ship and sat in the sea; and all the multitude was upon the land by the seaside. And He taught them many things in parables, and said unto them in His doctrine: "Hear ye! Behold, the sower went out to sow, and whilst He soweth, some fell by the wayside, and the birds of the air came and ate it up. And other some fell among stony ground, where it had

not much earth, and it shot up immediately, because it had no depth of earth. And when the sun was risen it was scorched, and because it had no root it withered away. And some fell among thorns, and the thorns grew up and choked it, and it yielded no fruit. And some fell upon good ground, and brought forth fruit that grew up and increased and yielded, one thirty, another sixty, and another a hundred." And He said: "He that hath ears to hear, let him hear."

^{MT}And His disciples came and said to Him: "Why speakest Thou to them in parables?" Who answered and said to them: "Because to you it is given to know the mysteries of the Kingdom of Heaven, but to them it is not given. For he that hath, to him shall be given, and he shall abound; but he that hath not, from him shall be taken away that also which he hath. Therefore, do I speak to them in parables, because seeing they see not, and hearing they hear not, neither do they understand. And the prophecy of Isaias is fulfilled in them, who saith: *By hearing you shall hear, and shall not understand; and seeing you shall see, and shall not perceive. For the heart of this people is grown gross, and with their ears they have been dull of hearing, and their eyes they have shut, lest at any time they should see with their eyes, and hear with their ears, and understand with their heart, and be converted and I should heal them.* But blessed are your eyes because they see, and your ears because they hear. For Amen I say to you, many prophets and just men have desired to see the things that you see, and have not seen them, and to hear the things that you hear, and have not heard them."

And He saith to them: "Are you ignorant

Matt. 13, 10—17.
Mark 4, 10—12.
Luke 8, 9, 10.

Mark 4, 13.

of this parable? and how shall you know all parables?

Matt. 13, 18—23.
Mark 4, 14—20.
Luke 8, 11—15.

^{MT}" Hear you therefore the parable of the sower. When any one heareth the word of the Kingdom, and understandeth it not, there cometh the wicked one, and catcheth away that which was sown in his heart; this is he that receiveth the seed by the wayside. And he that receiveth the seed on stony ground, this is he that heareth the word, and immediately receiveth it with joy. Yet hath he not root in himself, but is only for a time, and when there ariseth tribulation and persecution because of the word, he is presently scandalized. And he that receiveth the seed among thorns, is he that heareth the word, and the care of this world, and the deceitfulness of riches, ^{MK}and the lusts after other things, [these] ^{MT}choke up the word, and he becometh fruitless. But he that receiveth the seed upon good ground, this is he that heareth the word, and understandeth, and beareth fruit, and yieldeth, the one a hundred-fold, another sixty, and another thirty."

Mark 4, 21—25.
Luke 8, 16—18.

^{MK}And He said to them: "Doth a candle come in to be put under a bushel or under a bed? and not to be set on a candlestick? For there is nothing hid which shall not be made manifest, neither was it made secret, but that it may come abroad. If any man hath ears to hear, let him hear."

And He said to them: "Take heed what you hear. In what measure you shall mete, it shall be measured to you again, and more shall be given to you. For he that hath, to him shall be given, and he that hath not, that also which he ^{LK}thinketh he hath, ^{MK}shall be taken from him.

Matt. 13, 24—30.

Another parable He proposed to them [the

people] saying: "The Kingdom of Heaven is likened to a man that sowed good seed in his field. But while men were asleep, his enemy came and oversowed cockle among the wheat, and went his way. And when the blade was sprung up, and had brought forth fruit, then appeared also the cockle. And the servants of the good man of the house coming, said to him: 'Sir, didst thou not sow good seed in thy field? whence then hath it cockle?' And he said to them: 'An enemy hath done this.' And the servants said to him: 'Wilt thou that we go and gather it up?' And he said: 'No! lest perhaps gathering up the cockle, you root up the wheat also together with it. Suffer both to grow until the harvest, and in the time of the harvest, I will say to the reapers: Gather up first the cockle and bind it into bundles to burn, but the wheat, gather ye into my barn.'"

And He said, "So is the Kingdom of God as if a man should cast seed into the earth, and should sleep and rise, night and day; and the seed should spring and grow up whilst he knoweth not. For the earth of itself bringeth forth fruit, first the blade, then the ear, afterwards the full corn in the ear. And when the fruit is brought forth, immediately he putteth in the sickle, because the harvest is come." *Mark 4 26—29.*

^{MK}And He said: "To what shall we liken the Kingdom of God? or to what parable shall we compare it? It is as a grain of mustard seed, which when it is sown in the earth is less than all the seeds that are in the earth. And when it is sown it groweth up, and becometh greater than all herbs, and shooteth out great branches, so that the birds of the air may dwell under the shadow thereof." *Matt. 13, 31, 32.- Mark 4, 30—32.*

F

Matt. 13, 33.

Another parable He spoke to them: "The Kingdom of Heaven is like to leaven, which a woman took and hid in three measures of meal until the whole was leavened."

Matt. 13, 34, 35.
Mark 4, 33, 34.

^{MT}All these things Jesus spoke in parables to the multitudes, and without parables He did not speak to them. That it might be fulfilled which was spoken by the Prophet, saying: *I will open My mouth in parables; I will utter things hidden from the foundation of the world.* ^{MK}But apart, He explained all things to His disciples.

Matt. 13, 36—53.

^{MT}Then having sent away the multitudes, He came into the house, and His disciples came to Him, saying: "Expound to us the parable of the cockle of the field." Who made answer and said to them: "He that soweth the good seed is the Son of Man, and the field is the world; and the good seed are the children of the Kingdom, and the cockle are the children of the wicked one; and the enemy that sowed them is the devil. But the harvest is the end of the world, and the reapers are the angels. Even as cockle therefore is gathered up and burnt with fire, so shall it be at the end of the world. The Son of Man shall send His angels, and they shall gather out of His Kingdom all scandals, and them that work iniquity, and shall cast them into the furnace of fire; there shall be weeping and gnashing of teeth. Then shall the just shine as the sun, in the Kingdom of their Father. He that hath ears to hear, let him hear.

44. "The Kingdom of Heaven is like unto a treasure hidden in a field, which a man having found, hid it, and for joy thereof, goeth and selleth all that he hath and buyeth that field.

45. "Again, the Kingdom of Heaven is like to a

merchant seeking good pearls; who when he had found one pearl of great price, went his way and sold all that he had and bought it.

"Again, the Kingdom of Heaven is like to a net cast into the sea, and gathering together of all kind of fishes, which when it was filled they drew out, and sitting by the shore, they chose out the good into vessels, but the bad they cast forth. So shall it be at the end of the world. The angels shall go out and shall separate the wicked from among the just, and shall cast them into the furnace of fire; there shall be weeping and gnashing of teeth. Have ye understood all these things?" They say to him: "Yea." He said unto them: "Therefore every scribe instructed in the Kingdom of Heaven, is like to a man that is a householder, who bringeth forth out of his treasure new things and old."

And it came to pass when Jesus had finished these parables He passed from thence.

^{MT}And Jesus seeing great multitudes about Him, ^{MK}when evening was come, ^{MT}gave orders to pass over the water. . . . ^{MK}And sending away the multitude, they take Him, even as He was, in the ship, and there were other ships with Him. And there arose a great storm of wind, and the waves beat into the ship, so that the ship was filled. And He was in the hinder part of the ship sleeping upon a pillow, and they awake Him and say to Him: "Master, doth it not concern Thee that we perish?" And rising up He rebuked the wind, and said to the sea: "Peace, be still." And the wind ceased, and there was made a great calm. And He said to them: "Why are you fearful? Have you not faith yet?" And they feared exceedingly, and they said one to another: "Who

47.

53.

Matt. 8, 18.
Matt. 8, 23—27.
Mark 4, 35—40.
Luke 8, 22—25.

is this (thinkest thou), that both wind and sea obey Him?"

^{Matt. 8, 28.}
^{Mark 5, 1—3.}
^{Luke 8, 26, 27.}

^{MK}And they came over the strait of the sea into the country of the Gerasenes, ^{LK}which is over against Galilee. ^{MK}And as He went out of the ship, immediately there met Him out of the monuments a man with an unclean spirit,¹ who had his dwelling in the tombs, ^{LK}and he wore no clothes, ^{MK}and no man now could bind him not even with chains.

^{Mark 5, 4, 5.}
^{Luke 8, 29.}

^{MK}For having been bound with fetters and chains, he had burst the chains and broken the fetters in pieces, and no one could tame him. And he was always day and night in the monuments and in the mountains, crying and cutting himself with stones.

^{Matt. 8, 29.}
^{Mark 5, 6, 7.}
^{Luke 8, 28.}

^{MK}And seeing Jesus afar off, he ran and adored Him. And crying out with a loud voice he said: "What have I to do with Thee, Jesus, the Son of the Most High God? I adjure Thee by God, that Thou torment me not."

^{Mark 5, 8—10.}
^{Luke 8, 29—31.}

^{MK}For He said unto him: "Go out of the man, thou unclean spirit." And He asked him: "What is thy name?" And he saith to Him: "My name is Legion, for we are many." And he besought Him much, that He would not drive Him away out of the country.

^{Matt. 8, 30—34.}
^{Mark 5, 11—17.}
^{Luke 8, 32—37.}

^{MK}And there was there near the mountain a great herd of swine, feeding. And the spirits besought Him, saying: ^{MT}"If Thou cast us out hence, ^{MK}send us into the swine, that we may enter into them." And Jesus immediately gave them leave. ^{MT}And He said to them: "Go." ^{MK}And the unclean spirits going out, entered into the swine, and the herd with great violence was carried headlong into the sea, being about two thousand, and were stifled

¹ St. Matthew says *two* men.

in the sea. And they that fed them fled, and told it in the city and in the fields. And they went out to see what was done. And they came to Jesus, ᴸᴷand found the man out of whom the devils were departed sitting at His feet, clothed and in his right mind, and they were afraid. ᴹᴷAnd they that had seen it, told them in what manner he had been dealt with who had the devil, ᴸᴷhow he had been healed from the legion, ᴹᴷand concerning the swine. And they began to pray Him that He would depart from their coasts.

ᴹᴷAnd when He went up into the ship, he that had been troubled with the devil, began to beseech him that he might be with Him. And He admitted him not, but saith to him: "Go into thy house, to thy friends, and tell them how great things the Lord had done for thee, and hath had mercy on thee." And he went his way, and began to publish in Decapolis how great things Jesus had done for him, and all men wondered. *(Mark 5, 18—20. Luke 8, 38, 39.)*

ᴹᴷAnd when Jesus had passed again in the ship over the strait, a great multitude assembled together unto Him, ᴸᴷfor they were all waiting for Him. *(Matt. 9, 1. Mark 5, 21. Luke 8, 40.)*

And behold there came a man, whose name was Jairus, and he was a ruler of the Synagogue, and he fell down at the feet of Jesus, beseeching Him that He would come into his house, for he had an only daughter, almost twelve years old, and she was dying. ᴹᴷAnd he besought Him much, saying: "My daughter is at the point of death; come, lay Thy hand upon her, that she may be safe and may live." And He went with him, and a great multitude followed Him, and they thronged Him. *(Matt. 9, 18—21. Mark 5, 22—28. Luke 8, 41—44.)*

ᴸᴷAnd there was a certain woman, having an issue of blood twelve years, who had bestowed all her substance on physicians, and could not be healed by any, ᴹᴷand had suffered many things from many physicians, and had spent all that she had, and was nothing the better, but rather the worse, when she had heard of Jesus, came in the crowd behind Him, and touched His garment. For she said: "If I shall touch but His garment I shall be whole."

<small>Mark 5, 29—33.
Luke 8, 44—47.</small>

ᴹᴷAnd forthwith the fountain of her blood was dried up, and she felt in her body that she was healed of the evil. And immediately Jesus, knowing in Himself the virtue that had proceeded from Him, turning to the multitude, said: "Who hath touched my garments?" ᴸᴷAnd all denying, Peter and they that were with him said: "Master, the multitude throng and press Thee, and dost Thou say: Who touched Me?" And Jesus said: "Somebody hath touched Me, for I know that virtue hath gone out from Me." ᴹᴷBut the woman fearing and trembling, knowing what was done in her, [and] seeing she was not hid, ᴹᴷcame and fell down before Him, and told Him all the truth, ᴸᴷand declared before all the people for what cause she had touched Him, and how she was immediately cured.

<small>Matt. 9, 22.
Mark 5, 34.
Luke 8, 48.</small>

ᴹᵀBut Jesus ... seeing her, said: "Be of good heart, daughter, thy faith hath made thee whole; ᴸᴷgo thy way in peace." ᴹᵀAnd the woman was made whole from that hour.

<small>Mark 5, 35—38.
Luke 8, 49, 50.</small>

ᴹᴷWhile He was yet speaking, some came from the ruler of the Synagogue's house, saying: "Thy daughter is dead, why dost thou trouble the Master any farther?" But Jesus, having heard the word that was spoken, saith to the ruler of the Synagogue: "Fear not, only believe." And He admitted not any man to follow Him, but

Peter, James, and John the brother of James. And they come to the house of the ruler of the Synagogue; and He seeth a tumult and people weeping and wailing much.

^{MK}And going in He saith to them: "Why make you this ado and weep? the damsel is not dead but sleepeth." And they laughed Him to scorn. But He having put them all out, taketh the father and the mother of the damsel, and them that were with Him, and entereth in where the damsel was lying. And taking the damsel by the hand He saith to her: "Talitha cumi," which is, being interpreted: "Damsel, I say to thee, arise." ^{LK}And her spirit returned, ^{MK}and immediately the damsel rose up, and walked; and she was twelve years old. And they were astonished with a great astonishment. And He charged them strictly that no man should know it, and commanded that something should be given her to eat. Matt. 9, 23—26. Mark 5, 39—43. Luke 8, 51—56.

And as Jesus passed from thence there followed Him two blind men, crying out and saying: "Have mercy on us, O Son of David." And when He was come to the house, the blind men came to Him. And Jesus saith to them: "Do you believe that I can do this unto you?" They say to Him: "Yea, Lord." Then he touched their eyes, saying: "According to your faith, be it done unto you." And their eyes were opened; and Jesus strictly charged them, saying: "See that no man know this." But they going out spread His fame abroad in all that country. Matt. 9, 27—34.

And when they were gone out, behold they brought Him a dumb man possessed with a devil. And after the devil was cast out, the dumb man spoke, and the multitude wondered, saying: "Never was the like seen in Israel." But the Pharisees 32.

said: "By the prince of devils He casteth out devils."

^{MK}And going out from thence, He went into His own country, and His disciples followed Him. And when the sabbath was come, He began to teach in the synagogue: and many hearing Him were in admiration at His doctrine, saying: "How came this Man by all these things? and what wisdom is this which is given to Him, and such miracles as are wrought by His hands? Is not this the carpenter, the son of Mary, the brother of James, and Joseph, and Jude and Simon? Are not also His sisters here with us?" And they were scandalized in regard of Him. And Jesus said to them: "A prophet is not without honour save in his own country, and in his own house, and among his own kindred." And He could not do many miracles there, only that He cured a few that were sick, laying His hands upon them, and He wondered because of their unbelief. And He went through the villages, ^{MT}cities and towns, teaching in their synagogues and preaching the Gospel of the kingdom, and healing every disease and every infirmity.

And seeing the multitudes He had compassion on them, because they were distressed and lying like sheep that have no shepherd. Then He saith to His disciples: "The harvest indeed is great, but the labourers are few. Pray ye therefore the Lord of the harvest, that He send forth labourers into His harvest."

^{MT}And having called His twelve disciples together He gave them power over unclean spirits, to cast them out, and to heal all manner of diseases and all manner of infirmities. ^{LK}And He sent them, ^{MK}two and two, ^{LK}to preach the Kingdom of God, and to cure the sick.

PART III.   TO THE THIRD PASCH.   73

And the names of the twelve Apostles are these: Matt. 10, 2—8. the first Simon, who is called Peter, and Andrew his brother; James the son of Zebedee, and John his brother, Philip and Bartholomew; Thomas, and Matthew the publican; James the son of Alphœus, and Thaddeus; Simon the Cananean, and Judas Iscariot who also betrayed Him. These twelve Jesus sent, commanding them saying: "Go ye not into the way of the Gentiles, and into the cities of the Samaritans enter ye not. But go ye rather to the lost sheep of the house of Israel. And going preach, saying, The Kingdom of Heaven is at hand. Heal the sick, raise the dead, cleanse the lepers, cast out devils; freely have you received, freely give."

^{MK}And He commanded them that they should take nothing for the journey, but a staff only. ^{MT}"Do not possess gold, nor silver, nor money in your purses, nor scrip for your journey, ^{LK}nor bread, ^{MT}nor two coats, nor shoes, ^{MK}but to be shod with sandals, ^{MT}nor a staff, for the workman is worthy of his hire. And into whatsoever town you shall enter, inquire who in it is worthy; and there abide till you go thence. Matt. 10, 9—11.
Mark 6, 8—10.
Luke 9, 3, 4.

^{MT}"And when you come into the house, salute it, saying: Peace be to this house. And if that house be worthy, your peace shall come upon it; but if it be not worthy, your peace shall return to you. Matt. 10, 12, 13.

"And whosoever shall not receive you nor hear your words, going forth out of that house or city, shake off ^{LK}even the dust from your feet, for a testimony against them. Amen I say to you, it shall be more tolerable for the land of Sodom and Gomorrha in the Day of Judgment than for that city. Matt. 10, 14.
Mark 6, 11.
Luke 9, 5.

Matt. 10, 15—42.

"Behold I send you as sheep in the midst of 16.

wolves. Be ye therefore wise as serpents and simple as doves. But beware of men, for they will deliver you up in councils, and they will scourge you in their synagogues; and you shall be brought before governors and before kings for My sake, for a testimony to them and to the Gentiles. But when they shall deliver you up, take no thought how or what to speak, for it shall be given you in that hour what to speak. For it is not you that speak, but the Spirit of your Father that speaketh in you. The brother also shall deliver up the brother to death, and the father the son, and the children shall rise up against their parents, and shall put them to death. And you shall be hated by all men for My Name's sake, but he that shall persevere unto the end, he shall be saved. And when they shall persecute you in this city, flee into another. Amen I say to you, you shall not finish all the cities of Israel till the Son of Man come.

24. "The disciple is not above the Master, nor the servant above his lord. It is enough for the disciple that he be as his master, and the servant as his lord. If they have called the good man of the house Beelzebub, how much more them of his household? Therefore fear them not. For nothing is covered that shall not be revealed, nor hid that shall not be known. That which I tell you in the dark, speak ye in the light, and that which you hear in the ear, preach ye upon the housetops. And fear ye not them that kill the body, and are not able to kill the soul, but rather fear Him that can destroy both body and soul into Hell. Are not two sparrows sold for a farthing? and not one of them shall fall to the ground without your Father. But the very hairs of your head are all

numbered. Fear not therefore, better are you than many sparrows. Every one therefore that shall confess Me before men, I will also confess him before My Father Who is in Heaven. But he that shall deny Me before men, I will also deny him before My Father Who is in Heaven.

"Do not think that I came to send peace upon earth. I came not to send peace but the sword. For I came to set a man at variance against his father, and the daughter against her mother, and the daughter-in-law against her mother-in-law. And a man's enemies shall be they of his own household. He that loveth father or mother more than Me, is not worthy of Me; and he that loveth son or daughter more than Me, is not worthy of Me. And he that taketh not up his cross and followeth Me, is not worthy of Me. He that findeth his life shall lose it, and he that shall lose his life for Me, shall find it. He that receiveth you receiveth Me, and he that receiveth Me receiveth Him that sent Me. He that receiveth a prophet in the name of a prophet, shall receive the reward of a prophet; and he that receiveth a just man in the name of a just man, shall receive the reward of a just man. And whosoever shall give to drink to one of these little ones a cup of cold water only, in the name of a disciple, Amen I say to you, he shall not lose his reward." 34.

And it came to pass when Jesus had made an end of commanding His twelve disciples, He passed from thence to teach and preach in their cities. Matt. 11, 1.

^{MK}And going forth they preached that men should do penance, and they cast out many devils and anointed with oil many that were sick, and healed them. Mark 6, 12, 13–Luke 9, 6.

^{MT}At that time Herod the Tetrarch heard the fame of Jesus ^{MK}(for His Name was made manifest) and he said: "John the Baptist is risen again from the dead, and therefore mighty works show forth themselves in him."

^{MK}And others said, "It is Elias." But others said: "It is a prophet, as one of the prophets." Which Herod hearing said: ^{LK}"John I have beheaded, but Who is this of Whom I hear such things? And he sought to see Him."

^{MK}For Herod himself had sent and apprehended John and bound him in prison for the sake of Herodias, the wife of Philip his brother, because he had married her. For John said to Herod: "It is not lawful for thee to have thy brother's wife."

Now Herodias laid snares for him and was desirous to put him to death, and could not; for Herod feared John, knowing him to be a just and holy man; and kept him, and when he heard him, did many things; and he heard him willingly.

21. And when a convenient day was come, Herod made a supper for his birthday, for the princes and tribunes, and chief men of Galilee. And when the daughter of the same Herodias had come in and had danced, and pleased Herod and them that were at table with him, the king said to the damsel: "Ask of me what thou wilt and I will give it thee." And he swore to her: "Whatsoever thou shalt ask, I will give thee, though it be the half of my kingdom." Who when she was gone out, said to her mother: "What shall I ask?" But she said: "The head of John the Baptist."

25. And when she was come in immediately in haste to the King, she asked saying: "I will that forthwith thou give me in a dish the head of John the

Baptist." And the King was struck sad; yet because of his oath, and because of them that were with him at table, he would not displease her. But sending an executioner he commanded that his head should be brought in a dish. And he beheaded him in prison and brought his head in a dish, and gave it to the damsel, and the damsel gave it to her mother. Which his disciples hearing came and took his body and laid it in a tomb ^{MT}and came and told Jesus. Which when Jesus had heard, He retired from thence by a boat, into a desert place apart, and the multitudes having heard of it, followed Him on foot out of the cities.[1]

Matt. 14, 13.

---

[1] This retiring to a desert place is identical with that to be next recorded; a motive for which, St. Matthew here discloses.

Part IV.

FROM THE THIRD TO THE FOURTH PASCH.

<small>Matt. 14, 13—21.
Mark 6, 30—44.
Luke 9, 10—17.
John 6, 1—13.</small>

^{MK}And the Apostles coming together unto Jesus, related to Him all things that they had done and taught. And He said to them: "Come apart into a desert place and rest a little." For there were many coming and going, and they had not so much as time to eat. And going up into a ship, ^{JN}Jesus went over the Sea of Galilee, which is that of Tiberias, ^{LK}and taking them, He went aside into a desert place apart, which belonged to Bethsaida. ^{JN}And a great multitude followed Him, because they saw the miracles which He did on them that were diseased. ^{MK}And they saw them going away, and many knew, and they ran flocking thither on foot from all the cities, and were there before them.

^{JN}Jesus therefore went up into a mountain, and there He sat with His disciples. Now the Pasch, the festival-day of the Jews, was near at hand. When Jesus therefore had lifted up His eyes, and seen that a very great multitude cometh to Him, He said to Philip: "Whence shall we buy bread that these may eat?" And this He said to try him, for He Himself knew what He would do. Philip answered: "Two hundred pennyworth of bread is not sufficient for them, that every one may take a little."

^{LK}And He received them, and spoke to them of the Kingdom of God, and healed them who had need of healing.

^{MK}And when the day was now far spent, His disciples came to Him, saying: "This is a desert place, and the hour is now past; send them away, that going into the next villages and towns they may buy themselves bread." And He answering, said to them: ^{MT}"They have no need to go; give you them to eat." ^{MK}And they said to Him: "Let us go and buy bread for two hundred pence, and we will give them to eat." And He saith to them: "How many loaves have you? go and see." And when they knew, ^{JN}one of His disciples, Andrew, the brother of Simon Peter, saith to Him: "There is a boy here that hath five barley loaves and two fishes, but what are these among so many?" ^{MT}He said to them: "Bring them hither to Me."

^{MK}And He commanded them that they should make them all sit down by companies upon the green grass. And they sat down in ranks, by hundreds and by fifties. And when He had taken the five loaves and the two fishes, looking up to Heaven He blessed and broke the loaves, and gave to His disciples to set before them; and the two fishes He divided among them all. And they all did eat and were filled.

^{JN}And when they were filled, He said to His disciples: "Gather up the fragments that remain, lest they be lost." They gathered up therefore, and filled twelve baskets with the fragments of the five barley loaves ^{MK}and of the fishes, ^{JN}which remained over and above to them that had eaten. And the number of them that did eat was five thousand men, besides women and children.

Matt. 14, 22—36.
Mark 6, 45—56.
John 6, 14—21.

^{MK}And immediately He obliged His disciples to go up into the ship that they might go before Him over the water to Bethsaida, whilst He dismissed the people.¹ ^{JN}Now those men, when they had seen what a miracle Jesus had done, said: "This is of a truth the prophet that is to come into the world." Jesus therefore, when He knew that they would come to take Him by force and make Him King, fled again into the mountain Himself alone.

And when evening was come His disciples went down to the sea. And when they had gone up into a ship, they went over the sea to Capharnaum, and it was now dark, and Jesus was not come unto them. And the sea rose by reason of a great wind that blew. When they had rowed therefore about five-and-twenty or thirty furlongs, they saw Jesus walking upon the sea and drawing nigh to the ship, and they were afraid; ^{MK}and He would have passed by them.

But they seeing Him walking upon the sea, thought it was an apparition, and they cried out; for they all saw Him, and were troubled. And immediately He spoke with them and said to them: "Have a good heart; it is I, fear ye not." ^{MT}And Peter making answer said: "Lord, if it be Thou, bid me come to Thee upon the waters." And He said: "Come." And Peter, going down out of the boat, walked upon the water to come to Jesus. But seeing the wind strong, he was afraid, and when he began to sink he cried out, saying: "Lord, save me." And immediately Jesus, stretching forth His hand, took hold of him and said to

¹ If we take this to mean, that our Lord obliged His disciples to go down the mountain *towards* the boat, so as to embark without Him, St. Mark will harmonize with St. John, who says presently, that "His disciples went down to the sea" *after* Jesus had fled into the mountain.

him: "O thou of little faith, why didst thou doubt?"

And when they were come up into the boat the wind ceased; ^{MK}and they were far more astonished within themselves. For they understood not concerning the loaves, for their heart was blinded. ^{MT}And they that were in the boat came and adored Him, saying: "Indeed Thou art the Son of God." ^{JN}And presently the ship was at the land to which they were going.

^{MK}And when they had passed over, they came into the land of Genesareth and set to the shore.

And when they were gone out of the ship, immediately they knew Him. And running through that whole country they began to carry about in beds those that were sick where they heard Jesus was. And whithersoever He entered, into towns or into villages or cities, they laid the sick in the streets and besought Him that they might touch but the hem of His garment, and as many as touched Him were made whole.

The next day the multitude, that stood on the other side of the sea, saw that there was no other ship there but one, and that Jesus had not entered into the ship with His disciples, but that His disciples were gone away alone; but other ships came in from Tiberias, nigh unto the place where they had eaten the bread, the Lord giving thanks. When therefore the multitude saw that Jesus was not there nor His disciples they took shipping, and came to Capharnaum seeking for Jesus.

John 6, 22—72.

And when they had found Him on the other 25. side of the sea they said to Him: "Rabbi, when camest Thou hither?" Jesus answered them and said: "Amen, Amen, I say to you, you seek Me, not because you have seen miracles, but because

G

you did eat of the loaves and were filled. Labour not for the meat which perisheth, but for that which endureth unto life everlasting, which the Son of Man will give you. For Him hath God the Father sealed."

28. They said therefore unto Him: "What shall we do that we may work the works of God?" Jesus answered and said to them: "This is the work of God, that you believe in Him Whom He hath sent." They said therefore to Him: "What sign therefore dost Thou show? that we may see and may believe Thee: what dost Thou work? Our fathers did eat manna in the desert, as it is written: *He gave them bread from heaven to eat.*" Then Jesus said to them: "Amen, Amen, I say to you, Moses gave you not bread from heaven, but My Father giveth you the true bread from heaven. For the bread of God is that which cometh down from heaven and giveth life to the world." They said therefore unto Him: "Lord, give us always this bread."

35. And Jesus said to them: "I am the bread of life, he that cometh to Me shall not hunger, and he that believeth in Me shall never thirst. But I said unto you, that you also have seen Me and you believe not. All that the Father giveth to Me shall come to Me, and him that cometh to Me I will not cast out. Because I came down from Heaven, not to do My own will, but the will of Him that sent Me. Now this is the will of the Father Who sent Me, that of all He hath given Me I should lose nothing, but should raise it up again in the last day. And this is the will of My Father that sent Me, that every one who seeth the Son, and believeth in Him, may have life everlasting, and I will raise him up in the last day."

The Jews therefore murmured at Him because 41.
He had said: I am the living bread, which came
down from Heaven. And they said: "Is not this
Jesus, the son of Joseph, Whose father and mother
we know? How then saith He: I came down
from Heaven?" Jesus therefore answered and
said to them: "Murmur not among yourselves.
No man can come to Me, except the Father, Who
hath sent Me, draw him, and I will raise him up in
the last day. It is written in the Prophets: *And
they shall all be taught of God.* Everyone that
hath heard of the Father, and hath learned, cometh
to Me. Not that any man hath seen the Father,
but He Who is of God, He hath seen the Father.
Amen, Amen, I say unto you, he that believeth in
Me hath everlasting life. I am the bread of life.
Your fathers did eat manna in the desert and are
dead. This is the bread which cometh down from
heaven, that if any man eat of it he may not die.
I am the living bread which came down from
Heaven. If any man eat of this bread he shall
live for ever; and the bread that I will give is My
flesh for the life of the world."

The Jews therefore strove among themselves, 53.
saying: "How shall this Man give us His flesh to
eat?" Then Jesus said to them: "Amen, amen,
I say unto you, except you eat the flesh of the Son
of Man and drink His blood you shall not have
life in you. He that eateth My flesh and drinketh
My blood hath everlasting life, and I will raise
him up in the last day. For My flesh is meat
indeed and My blood is drink indeed. He that
eateth My flesh and drinketh My blood abideth in
Me and I in him. As the living Father hath sent
Me and I live by the Father, so he that eateth Me,
the same also shall live by Me. This is the bread

that came down from Heaven. Not as your fathers did eat manna and are dead. He that eateth this bread shall live for ever."

60. These things He said, teaching in the Synagogue in Capharnaum. Many therefore of His disciples hearing it said: "This is a hard saying, and who can hear it? But Jesus, knowing in Himself that His disciples murmured at this, said to them: "Doth this scandalize you? If then you shall see the Son of Man ascend up where He was before? It is the spirit that quickeneth, the flesh profiteth nothing. The words that I have spoken to you are spirit and life. But there are some of you that believe not." For Jesus knew from the beginning who they were that did not believe, and who he was that would betray Him. And He said: "Therefore did I say to you, that no man can come to Me, unless it be given him by My Father."

67. After this many of His disciples went back, and walked no more with Him. Then Jesus said to the twelve: "Will you also go away?" And Simon Peter answered Him: "Lord, to whom shall we go? Thou hast the words of eternal life. And we have believed and have known that Thou art the Christ, the Son of God." Jesus answered them: "Have not I chosen you twelve, and one of you is a devil?" Now He meant Judas Iscariot, the son of Simon, for this same was about to betray Him, whereas he was one of the twelve.

Matt. 15, 1.
Mark 7, 1.

^{MK}And there assembled together unto Him the Pharisees and some of the Scribes, coming from Jerusalem.

Mark 7, 2—4.

And when they had seen some of His disciples eat bread with common, that is, with unwashed hands, they found fault. For the Pharisees and all the Jews eat not without often washing their hands, holding the tradition of the ancients, and when they come from the market, unless they be washed, they eat not, and many other things there are that have been delivered to them to observe, the washing of cups, and of pots, and of brazen vessels, and of beds.

ᴹᴷAnd the Pharisees and Scribes asked Him: "Why do not Thy disciples walk according to the tradition of the ancients, but they eat bread with common hands." But He answering, said to them: "Well did Isaias prophesy of you hypocrites as it is written: *This people honoureth Me with their lips, but their heart is far from Me. And in vain do they worship Me, teaching doctrines and precepts of men;* for leaving the commandment of God, you hold the tradition of men, the washing of pots and of cups, and many other things you do like to these." And He said to them: "Well do you make void the commandment of God, that you may keep your own tradition. For Moses said: 'Honour thy father and thy mother, and he that shall curse his father or mother, dying let him die.' But you say: 'If a man shall say to his father or mother, Corban (which is a gift), whatsoever is from me shall profit thee.' And further you suffer him not to do anything for his father or mother, making void the Word of God by your own tradition which you have given forth. And many other such like things you do."

Matt. 15, 2—11.
Mark 7, 5—16.

ᴹᵀAnd having called together the multitudes unto Him, He said to them: "Hear ye and understand. Not that which goeth into the mouth defileth a man, but what cometh out of the mouth, this defileth a man. ᴹᴷIf any one have ears to hear, let him hear."

Matt. 15, 12—14. Then came His disciples and said to Him: "Dost Thou know that the Pharisees, when they heard this word, were scandalized?" But He answering, said: "Every plant, which My Heavenly Father hath not planted, shall be rooted up. Let them alone, they are blind, and leaders of the blind. And if the blind lead the blind, both fall into the pit."

Matt. 15, 15—28.
Mark 7, 17—30. ᴹᵀAnd when He was come into the house from the multitude, His disciples asked Him the parable. And He saith to them: "So are you also without knowledge. Understand you not that everything from without, entering into a man, cannot defile him? Because it entereth not into his heart, but goeth into the belly, and goeth out into the privy, purging all meats. ᴹᵀBut the things which proceed out of the mouth, come forth from the heart, and those things defile a man. For from the heart come forth evil thoughts, murders, adulteries, fornications, thefts, false testimonies, ᴹᵀcovetousness, wickedness, deceit, lasciviousness, an evil eye, blasphemy, pride, foolishness. ᴹᵀThese are the things which defile a man; but to eat with unwashed hands, doth not defile a man."

And rising from thence He went into the coasts of Tyre and Sidon. And entering into a house, He would that no man should know it, but He could not be hid. ᴹᵀAnd behold a woman of Canaan who came out of those coasts, crying out, said to Him: "Have mercy on me, O Lord, Thou Son of David, my daughter is grievously troubled by a devil." Who answered her not a word. And His disciples came and besought Him, saying: "Send her away, for she crieth after us." For the woman was a Gentile, a Syrophœnician born.

PART IV.   TO THE FOURTH PASCH.   87

And she besought Him that He would cast forth the devil out of her daughter. ^{MT}And He answering, said: "I was not sent but to the sheep that are lost of the house of Israel." But she came and adored Him, saying: "Lord, help me." Who answering said: ^{MK}"Suffer first the children to be filled, for it is not good to take the bread from the children, and cast it to the dogs." But she answered and said to Him: "Yea, Lord, for the whelps also eat under the table, of the crumbs of the children." ^{MT}Then Jesus answering, said to her: "O woman, great is thy faith, be it done to thee as thou wilt; ^{MK}for this saying, go thy way, the devil is gone out of thy daughter." And when she was come into her house, she found the girl lying upon the bed, and that the devil was gone out. ^{MT}And her daughter was cured from that hour.

And again, going out of the coasts of Tyre, He came by Sidon to the Sea of Galilee, through the midst of the coasts of Decapolis. And they bring to him one deaf and dumb, and they besought Him that He would lay His hand upon him. And taking him from the multitude apart, He put His fingers into his ears, and spitting, He touched his tongue, and looking up to Heaven He groaned and said to him, "Ephpheta," which is, "Be thou opened." And immediately his ears were opened and the string of his tongue was loosed and he spoke right. And He charged them that they should tell no man. But the more He charged them, so much the more a great deal did they publish it. And so much the more did they wonder, saying: "He hath done all things well, He hath made both the deaf to hear and the dumb to speak."   *Mark 7, 31—37.*

And when Jesus had passed away from thence,   *Matt. 15, 29—31.*

He came nigh the Sea of Galilee and going up into a mountain He sat there. And there came to Him great multitudes having with them the dumb, the blind, the lame, the maimed, and many others, and they cast them down at His feet, and He healed them. So that the multitudes marvelled seeing the dumb speak, the lame walk, the blind see, and they glorified the God of Israel.

Matt. 15, 32—39.
Mark 8, 1—10.

^{MT}And Jesus, ^{MK}in those days again when there was a great multitude, and had nothing to eat, calling His disciples together, He saith to them: "I have compassion on the multitude, for behold they have now been with Me three days, and have not what to eat; and if I send them away fasting to their home, they will faint in the way, for some of them came from afar off. ^{MT}And the disciples say unto Him: "Whence then shall we have so many loaves in the desert as to fill so great a multitude?" And Jesus said to them: "How many loaves have you?" But they said: "Seven, and a few little fishes." And He commanded the multitude to sit down upon the ground. And taking the loaves and the fishes, and giving thanks, He brake and gave to His disciples, and the disciples gave to the people. And they did all eat and were filled. And they took up seven baskets-full of what remained of the fragments. And they that did eat were four thousand men, besides children and women. And having dismissed the multitude He went up into a boat and came into the coasts of Magedan (or) ^{MK}into the parts of Dalmanutha.

Matt. 16, 1—10.
Mark 8, 11—21.

And there came to Him Pharisees and Sadducees tempting, and they asked Him to show them a sign from Heaven. ^{MK}And sighing deeply in spirit, He saith, "Why doth this generation ask a sign?

Amen, I say to you, a sign shall not be given to this generation. ^{MT}When it is evening you say, It will be fine weather, for the sky is red; and in the morning: To-day there will be a storm, for the sky is red and lowering. You know then how to discern the face of the sky, and can you not know the signs of the times? A wicked and adulterous generation seeketh after a sign, and a sign shall not be given it, but the sign of Jonas the prophet. ^{MK}And leaving them, He went up again into the ship and passed to the other side of the water. And they forgot to take bread, and they had but one loaf with them in the ship. And He charged them, saying: "Take heed and beware of the leaven of the Pharisees, and the leaven of Herod." And they reasoned among themselves, saying: "Because we have no bread." Which Jesus knowing, saith to them: "Why do you reason, because you have no bread? do you not yet know or understand? have you still your heart blinded? having eyes see you not? and having ears hear you not? neither do you remember? When I broke the five loaves among five thousand, how many baskets full of fragments took you up?" They say to Him: "Twelve." When also the seven loaves among four thousand, how many baskets of fragments took you up?" And they say to Him: "Seven." And He said to them: "Why do you not understand, that it was not concerning bread I said to you: Beware of the leaven of the Pharisees and Sadducees?" Then they understood that He said, not only that they should beware of the leaven of bread, but of the doctrine of the Pharisees and Sadducees. [Matt. 16, 11, 12.]

And they came to Bethsaida, and they brought to Him a blind man, and they besought Him that [Mark 8, 22—26.]

He would touch him. And taking the blind man by the hand, He led him out of the town, and spitting upon his eyes, laying His hands on him, He asked him if he saw anything. And looking up he said: "I see men, as it were trees walking." After that again, He laid His hands upon his eyes and he began to see, and was restored, so that he saw all things clearly. And He sent him into his house, saying: "Go into thy house, and if thou enter into the town tell nobody."

Matt. 16, 13—16.
Mark 8, 27—29.
Luke 9, 18—20.

^{MT}And Jesus came into the quarters of Cæsarea Philippi. And ^{LK}it came to pass, as He was alone praying, His disciples also were with Him, and He asked them saying: "Who do the people say ^{MT}that the Son of Man is?" But they said: "Some John the Baptist, and other some Elias, and others Jeremias or one of the prophets." Jesus saith to them: "But who do you say that I am?" Simon Peter answered and said: "Thou art Christ, the Son of the living God."

Matt. 16, 17—19.

And Jesus answering said to him: "Blessed art thou, Simon Bar-jona, because flesh and blood hath not revealed it to thee, but My Father Who is in Heaven. And I say to thee, that thou art Peter, and upon this rock I will build My Church, and the gates of Hell shall not prevail against it. And I will give to thee the keys of the Kingdom of Heaven. And whatsoever thou shalt bind upon earth, it shall be bound also in Heaven, and whatsoever thou shalt loose on earth, it shall be loosed also in Heaven."

Matt. 16, 20, 21.
Mark 8, 30—32.
Luke 9, 21, 22.

^{MT}Then He commanded His disciples that they should tell no man that He was Jesus the Christ.

^{MT}And from that time Jesus began to show to His disciples that He must go to Jerusalem, and suffer many things from the ancients and scribes

and chief priests, and be put to death, and the third day rise again. ᴹᴷAnd He spoke the word openly. ᴹᵀAnd Peter taking Him, began to rebuke Him, saying: "Lord, be it far from Thee, this shall not be unto Thee." ᴹᴷWho turning about, and seeing His disciples, ᴹᵀsaid to Peter: "Go behind Me, Satan, thou art a scandal unto Me, because thou savourest not the things that are of God, but the things that are of men." Matt. 16, 22, 23.
Mark 8, 32, 33.

ᴹᴷAnd calling the multitude together with His disciples, He said to them: "If any man will come after Me, let him deny himself, and take up his cross ᴸᴷdaily ᴹᴷand follow Me. For whosoever will save his life shall lose it, and whosoever will lose his life for My sake and the Gospel, shall save it. For what shall it profit a man if he gain the whole world and suffer the loss of his soul? Or what shall a man give in exchange for his soul? For He that shall be ashamed of Me and of My words in this adulterous and sinful generation, the Son of Man also will be ashamed of him, when He shall come in the glory of His Father with the holy angels; ᴹᵀand then will He render to every man according to his works. Amen I say to you, there are some standing here that shall not taste death till they see the Son of Man coming in His Kingdom." Matt. 16, 24—28.
Mark 8, 34—39.
Luke 9, 23—27.

ᴸᴷAnd it came to pass about eight days after these words, that He took Peter and James and John, ᴹᴷand leadeth them up into a high mountain apart by themselves, ᴸᴷto pray. And whilst He prayed ᴹᵀHe was transfigured before them; and His face did shine as the sun, ᴹᴷand His garments became shining and exceeding white as snow, so as no fuller on earth can make white. ᴸᴷAnd behold two men were talking with Him. And they were Matt. 17, 1—3.
Mark 9, 1—3.
Luke 9, 28—30.

Luke 9, 31, 32.	Moses and Elias, appearing in majesty, and they spoke of His decease that He should accomplish in Jerusalem. But Peter, and they that were with him, were heavy with sleep. And waking, they saw His glory, and the two men that stood with Him.
Matt. 17, 4—8. Mark 9, 4—7. Luke 9, 33—36.	^{LK}And it came to pass that, as they were departing from Him, Peter saith to Jesus: "Master, it is good for us to be here, and let us make three tabernacles, one for Thee, and one for Moses, and one for Elias," not knowing what he said, ^{MK}for they were struck with fear. ^{MT}And as he was yet speaking, behold a bright cloud overshadowed them; and lo! a voice out of the cloud, saying: "This is My beloved Son, in Whom I am well pleased; hear ye Him." And the disciples hearing, fell upon their face and were very much afraid. And Jesus came and touched them and said to them: "Arise and fear not." And they, lifting up their eyes, saw no one but only Jesus.
Matt. 17, 9. Mark 9, 8.	^{MK}And as they came down from the mountain, He charged them not to tell any man what they had seen till the Son of Man shall be risen again from the dead.
Luke 9, 36.	And they held their peace, and told no man in those days any of these things which they had seen.
Mark 9, 9.	And they kept the word to themselves, questioning together what that should mean: When He shall be risen from the dead.
Matt. 17, 10—13. Mark 9, 10—12.	^{MT}And His disciples asked Him, saying: "Why then do the Scribes say that Elias must come first?" But He answering said to them: "Elias indeed shall come and restore all things. But I say to you, that Elias is already come, and they knew him not, but have done unto him whatso-

ever they would. So also the Son of Man shall suffer from them, ^{MK}and be despised." ^{MT}Then the disciples understood that He had spoken to them of John the Baptist.

And it came to pass, the day following, when they came down from the mountain, there met Him a great multitude. Luke 9, 37.

And coming to His disciples, He saw a great multitude about them, and the Scribes disputing with them. And presently all the people, seeing Jesus, were astonished and struck with fear, and running they saluted Him, and He asked them: "What do you question among you?" Mark 9, 13—15.

^{LK}And behold a man among the crowd, ^{MT}falling down on his knees before Him, ^{LK}cried out, saying: "Master, I beseech Thee look upon my son, because he is my only one; ^{MT}Lord, have pity upon my son, for he is a lunatic, and suffereth much; for he falleth often into the fire, and often into the water, ^{LK}and lo! a ^{MK}dumb ^{LK}spirit seizeth him, and he suddenly crieth out, and he throweth him down, and teareth him, so that he foameth; and bruising him, he hardly departeth from him. And I desired Thy disciples to cast him out, and they could not." Then Jesus answered and said: ^{MT}"O unbelieving and perverse generation, how long shall I be with you? How long shall I suffer you? Bring him unto Me." And they brought him. Matt. 17, 14—16. Mark 9, 16—19. Luke 9, 38—41.

^{LK}And as he was coming to Him, ^{MK}and when he had seen Him, immediately the spirit troubled him, and being thrown down upon the ground, he rolled about foaming. Mark 9, 19. Luke 9, 42.

And He asked his father: "How long time is it since this hath happened unto him?" But he said: "From his infancy. And oftentimes hath Mark 9, 20—23.

he cast him into the fire and into waters to destroy him; but if Thou canst do anything, help us, having compassion on us." And Jesus saith to him: "If thou canst believe, all things are possible to him that believeth." And immediately the father of the boy, crying out with tears, said: "I do believe, Lord, help my unbelief."

[Matt. 17, 17.
Luke 9, 43.
Mark 9, 24—26.]

^{MK}And when Jesus saw the multitude running together, He threatened the unclean spirit, saying to him: "Deaf and dumb spirit, I command thee, go out of him and enter not any more into him." And crying out and greatly tearing him, he went out of him, and he became as dead, so that many said: "He is dead." But Jesus taking him by the hand lifted him up, ^{LK}and restored him to his father; ^{MT}and the child was cured from that hour.

Matt. 17, 18.
Mark 9, 27.

^{MK}And when He was come into the house, ^{MT}then came the disciples to Jesus secretly and said: "Why could not we cast him out?"

Matt. 17, 19.

Jesus said to them: "Because of your unbelief. For amen I say to you, if you have faith as a grain of mustard seed, you shall say to this mountain: Remove from hence hither, and it shall remove, and nothing shall be impossible to you."

Matt. 17, 20.
Mark 9, 28.

^{MK}And He said to them: "This kind can go out by nothing but by prayer and fasting."

Luke 9, 44.

And all were astonished at the mighty power of God.

Mark 9, 29.
John 7, 1.

^{MK}And departing from thence they passed through Galilee, and He would not that any man should know it: ^{JN}for He would not walk in Judea because the Jews sought to kill Him.

Matt. 17, 21, 22.
Mark 9, 30, 31.
Luke 9, 44, 45.

^{MT}And when they abode together in Galilee, Jesus said to them: "The Son of Man shall be betrayed into the hands of men, and they shall kill Him, and the third day He shall rise again."

PART IV.   TO THE FOURTH PASCH.   95

ᴸᴷBut they understood not this word, and it was hid from them, so that they perceived it not. And they were afraid to ask Him concerning this word. ᴹᵀAnd they were troubled exceedingly.

ᴹᵀAnd when they were come to Capharnaum, they that received the didrachmas, came to Peter and said to him: "Doth not your Master pay the didrachma?" He said: "Yes." And when he was come into the house, Jesus prevented him, saying: "What is thy opinion, Simon? The kings of the earth, of whom do they receive tribute or custom? of their own children or of strangers?" And he said: "Of strangers." Jesus said to him: "Then the children are free. But that we may not scandalize them, go to the sea, and cast in a hook, and that fish which shall first come up, take, and when thou hast opened its mouth, thou shalt find a stater; take that, and give it to them for Me and for thee."

_{Mark 9, 32.}
_{Matt. 17, 23—26.}

ᴹᴷ . . . And when they were in the house, He asked them: "What did you treat of in the way?" But they held their peace, for in the way they had disputed among themselves which of them should be greater.¹ ᴸᴷBut Jesus, seeing the thoughts of their hearts, ᴹᴷsitting down, He called the twelve, and said to them: "If any man desire to be first, he shall be the last of all and the minister of all." ᴹᵀAnd Jesus, calling unto him a little child, set him in the midst of them; ᴹᴷwhom when He had embraced, He saith to them: ᴹᵀ"Amen I say to you, unless you be converted, and become as little

_{Matt. 18, 1, 2.}
_{Mark 9, 32—35.}
_{Luke 9, 46—48.}

_{Matt. 18, 3, 4.}

---

¹ *St. Matthew* says: The disciples came to Jesus, saying: "Who, thinkest Thou, is the greater in the *Kingdom of Heaven?*" The occasion *may* be distinct from the present one, when they were ashamed to acknowledge their dispute as to which should be, simply, *greater*.

children, you shall not enter into the Kingdom of Heaven. Whosoever, therefore, shall humble himself as this little child, he is the greater in the Kingdom of Heaven.

<small>Matt. 18, 5.
Mark 9, 36.
Luke 9, 48.</small>
^{MT}"And he that shall receive one such little child in My name, receiveth Me; ^{MK}and whosoever shall receive Me, receiveth not Me, but Him that sent Me."

<small>Mark 9, 37—39.
Luke 9, 49, 50.</small>
^{MK}John answered Him, saying: "Master, we saw one casting out devils in Thy name, who followed not us, and we forbade him." But Jesus said: "Do not forbid him. For there is no man that doth a miracle in My name, and can soon speak ill of Me. For he that is not against you, is for you."

<small>Mark 9, 40.</small>
"For whosoever shall give you to drink a cup of water in My name, because you belong to Christ, amen, I say to you, he shall not lose his reward.

<small>Matt. 18, 6.
Mark 9, 41.</small>
^{MT}"But he that shall scandalize one of these little ones that believe in Me, it were better for him that a mill-stone should be hanged about his neck, and that he should be drowned in the depth of the sea.

<small>Matt. 18, 7.</small>
"Wo to the world because of scandals. For it must needs be that scandals come, but nevertheless wo to that man by whom the scandal cometh.

<small>Matt. 18, 8, 9.
Mark 9, 42—47.</small>
^{MK}"And if thy hand scandalize thee, cut it off; it is better for thee to enter into life maimed, than having two hands to go into Hell, into unquenchable fire, where their worm dieth not, and the fire is not extinguished.

"And if thy foot scandalize thee, cut it off; it is better for thee to enter lame into life everlasting, than having two feet to be cast into the Hell of unquenchable fire; where their worm dieth not, and the fire is not extinguished. And if thy eye scandalize thee, pluck it out; it is better for thee with one eye to enter into the Kingdom of God, than having two eyes to be cast into the Hell of fire, where their worm dieth not, and the fire is not extinguished.

"For every one shall be salted with fire, and every victim shall be salted with salt. Salt is good; but if the salt become unsavoury, wherewith will you season it? Have salt in you, and have peace among you. Mark 9, 48, 49.

"See that you despise not one of these little ones, for I say to you, that their angels in Heaven always see the face of My Father Who is in Heaven. For the Son of Man is come to save that which was lost. What think you? If a man have a hundred sheep, and one of them should go astray, doth he not leave the ninety-nine in the mountains, and goeth to seek that which is gone astray? And if it so be that he find it, Amen, I say to you, he rejoiceth more for that than for the ninety-nine that went not astray. Even so it is not the will of your Father Who is in Heaven, that one of these little ones should perish. Matt. 18, 10—35.

"But if thy brother shall offend against thee, go and rebuke him between thee and him alone. If he shall hear thee, thou shalt gain thy brother. And if he will not hear thee, take with thee one or two more, that in the mouth of two or three witnesses, every word may stand. And if he will not hear them, tell the Church. And if he will not hear the Church, let him be to thee as the heathen and publican. 15.

"Amen, I say to you, whatsoever you shall bind upon earth shall be bound also in Heaven; and whatsoever you shall loose upon earth, shall be loosed also in Heaven. Again I say to you, that if two of you shall consent upon earth concerning 18.

H

anything, whatsoever they shall ask it shall be done to them by My Father Who is in Heaven. For where there are two or three gathered together in My name, there am I in the midst of them."

21. Then came Peter unto Him and said: "Lord, how often shall my brother offend against me, and I forgive him? till seven times?" Jesus saith to him: "I say not to thee, till seven times, but till seventy times seven times. Therefore is the Kingdom of Heaven likened to a king, who would take an account of his servants. And when he had begun to take the account, one was brought to him that owed him ten thousand talents. And as he had not wherewith to pay it, his lord commanded that he should be sold, and his wife and children, and all that he had, and payment to be made. But that servant falling down, besought him, saying: Have patience with me, and I will pay thee all. And the lord of that servant being moved with pity, let him go, and forgave him the debt. But when that servant was gone out, he found one of his fellow-servants that owed him a hundred pence, and laying hold of him, he throttled him, saying: Pay what thou owest. And his fellow-servant falling down, besought him, saying: Have patience with me, and I will pay thee all. And he would not, but went and cast him into prison, till he paid the debt. Now his fellow-servants seeing what was done, were very much grieved, and they came and told their lord all that was done. Then his lord called him and said to him: Thou wicked servant, I forgave thee all the debt, because thou besoughtest me. Shouldst thou then not have had compassion also on thy fellow-servant, even as I had compassion on thee? And his lord being angry, delivered him to the torturers until he paid

all the debt. So also shall My Heavenly Father do to you, if you forgive not every one his brother from your hearts."

Now the Jews' feast of Tabernacles was at hand.[1] And His brethren said to Him: "Pass from hence, and go into Judea, that Thy disciples also may see Thy works which Thou dost. For there is no man that doth anything in secret, and he himself seeketh to be known openly. If Thou do these things, manifest Thyself to the world." For neither did His brethren believe in Him.

Then Jesus said to them: "My time is not yet come; but your time is always ready. The world cannot hate you, but Me it hateth, because I give testimony of it, that the works thereof are evil. Go you up to this festival-day; but I go not up to this festival-day, because My time is not accomplished." When He had said these things He Himself stayed in Galilee. But after His brethren were gone up, then He also went up to the feast, not openly, but as it were in secret.[2] The Jews therefore sought Him on the festival-day, and said: "Where is He?" And there was much murmuring among the multitude concerning Him. For some said: "He is a good Man." And others said: "No, but He seduceth the people." Yet no man spoke openly of Him for fear of the Jews.

Now about the midst of the feast, Jesus went up into the Temple and taught. And the Jews wondered, saying: "How doth this Man know

John 7, 2—53.

6.

14.

---

[1] September.
[2] Coleridge and Greswell are here opposed to Patrizi, Cornely, and others. The latter consider this journey, "as it were in secret," to be identical with that chronicled by St. Luke (ix. 51, p. 115), although the words used by the Evangelist in that place give no indication at all of secrecy, while at the same time they do most forcibly convey the idea of a *last* journey.

letters, having never learned?" Jesus answered them and said: "My doctrine is not Mine, but His that sent Me. If any man will do the will of Him, he shall know of the doctrine, whether it be of God, or whether I speak of Myself. He that speaketh of himself seeketh his own glory; but he that seeketh the glory of him that sent him, he is true, and there is no injustice in him. Did not Moses give you the law, and yet none of you keepeth the law? Why seek you to kill Me?" The multitude answered and said: "Thou hast a devil. Who seeketh to kill Thee?" Jesus answered and said to them: "One work I have done, and you all wonder. Therefore Moses gave you circumcision (not because it is of Moses, but of the fathers); and on the Sabbath-day you circumcise a man. If a man receive circumcision on the Sabbath-day, that the law of Moses may not be broken, are you angry at Me because I have healed the whole man on the Sabbath-day? Judge not according to the appearance, but judge just judgment."

25. Some therefore of Jerusalem said: "Is not this He Whom they seek to kill? And behold He speaketh openly, and they say nothing to Him. Have the rulers known for a truth that this is the Christ? But we know this Man, whence He is; but when the Christ cometh, no man knoweth whence He is."

28. Jesus therefore cried out in the Temple, teaching and saying: "You both know Me and you know whence I am, and I am not come of Myself, but He that sent Me is true, Whom you know not. I know Him, because I am from Him, and He hath sent Me." They sought therefore to apprehend Him, and no man laid hands on Him,

because His hour was not yet come. But of the people many believed in Him, and said: "When the Christ cometh, shall He do more miracles than these which this Man doth?" The Pharisees heard the people murmuring these things concerning Him, and the rulers and Pharisees sent ministers to apprehend Him.

33. Jesus therefore said to them: "Yet a little while I am with you, and then I go to Him that sent Me. You shall seek Me and shall not find Me, and where I am thither you cannot come." The Jews therefore said amongst themselves: "Whither will He go that we shall not find Him? Will He go unto the dispersed among the Gentiles, and teach the Gentiles? What is this saying that He hath said: You shall seek Me and shall not find Me, and where I am you cannot come."

37. And on the last and great day of the festivity, Jesus stood and cried, saying: "If any man thirst, let him come to Me and drink. He that believeth in Me, as the Scripture saith: *Out of his belly shall flow rivers of living water.*" Now this He said of the Spirit which they should receive who believed in Him, for as yet the Spirit was not given, because Jesus was not yet glorified.

40. Of that multitude, therefore, when they had heard these words of His, some said: "This is the Prophet indeed." Others said: "This is the Christ." But some said: "Doth the Christ come out of Galilee? Doth not the Scripture say that Christ cometh of the seed of David, and from Bethlehem the town where David was?" So there arose a dissension among the people because of Him. And some of them would have apprehended Him, but no man laid hands upon Him.

45. The ministers therefore came to the chief priests

and the Pharisees. And they said to them: "Why have you not brought Him?" The ministers answered: "Never did man speak like this Man." The Pharisees therefore answered them: "Are you also seduced? Hath any one of the rulers believed in Him or of the Pharisees? But this multitude that knoweth not the law are accursed." Nicodemus said to them—he that came to Him by night who was one of them—"Doth our law judge any man unless it first hear him and know what he doth?" They answered and said to him: "Art thou also a Galilæan? Search the Scriptures, and see that out of Galilee a prophet riseth not." And every man returned to his own house; and Jesus went unto Mount Olivet.

John 8, 1—59.

And early in the morning He came again into the Temple, and all the people came to Him; and sitting down, He taught them. And the Scribes and Pharisees bring unto Him a woman taken in adultery, and they set her in the midst, and said to Him: "Master, this woman was even now taken in adultery. Now Moses in the law commanded us to stone such a one. But what sayest Thou?" And this they said tempting Him, that they might accuse Him. But Jesus, bowing Himself down, wrote with His finger on the ground. When therefore they continued asking Him, He lifted up Himself and said to them: "He that is without sin among you, let him first cast a stone at her." And again stooping down He wrote on the ground. But they hearing this went out one by one, beginning at the eldest. And Jesus alone remained and the woman standing in the midst. Then Jesus, lifting up Himself, said to her: "Woman, where are they that accused thee? Hath no man condemned thee?" Who said: "No man, Lord."

And Jesus said: "Neither will I condemn thee. Go, and now sin no more."

Again therefore Jesus spoke to them, saying: 12. "I am the light of the world. He that followeth Me walketh not in darkness, but shall have the light of life." The Pharisees therefore said to Him: "Thou givest testimony of Thyself; Thy testimony is not true." Jesus answered and said to them: "Although I give testimony of Myself, My testimony is true; for I know whence I came and whither I go; but you know not whence I come or whither I go. You judge according to the flesh; I judge not any man. And if I do judge, My judgment is true, because I am not alone, but I and the Father that sent Me. And in your law it is written that the testimony of two men is true. I am one that give testimony of Myself, and the Father that sent Me giveth testimony of Me." They said therefore to Him: "Where is Thy Father?" Jesus answered: "Neither Me do you know, nor My Father; if you did know Me, perhaps you would know My Father also."

These words Jesus spoke in the Treasury, 20. teaching in the Temple; and no man laid hands on Him, because His hour was not yet come. Again therefore Jesus said to them: "I go, and you shall seek Me, and you shall die in your sin. Whither I go, you cannot come." The Jews therefore said: "Will He kill Himself, because He said, Whither I go, you cannot come?" And He said to them: "You are from beneath, I am from above. You are of this world, I am not of this world. Therefore I said to you that you shall die in your sins. For if you believe not that I am He, you shall die in your sin." They said therefore to Him: "Who art Thou?" Jesus said to them: "The Beginning, Who also speak unto you. Many things I have to speak and to judge of you. But He that sent Me is true, and the things I have heard of Him, these same I speak in the world." And they understood not that He called God His Father.

28. Jesus therefore said to them: "When you shall have lifted up the Son of Man, then shall you know that I am He, and that I do nothing of Myself, but as the Father hath taught Me, these things I speak. And He that sent Me is with Me, and He hath not left Me alone; for I do always the things that please Him."

30. When He spoke these things many believed in Him. Then Jesus said to those Jews who believed Him: "If you continue in My word, you shall be My disciples indeed. And you shall know the truth, and the truth shall make you free." They answered Him: "We are the seed of Abraham, and we have never been slaves to any man; how sayest Thou, You shall be free?"

34. Jesus answered them: "Amen, amen, I say unto you, that whosoever committeth sin is the servant of sin. Now the servant abideth not in the house for ever, but the Son abideth for ever. If therefore the Son shall make you free, you shall be free indeed. I know that you are the children of Abraham, but you seek to kill Me because My word hath no place in you. I speak that which I have seen with My Father, and you do the things which you have seen with your father."

39. They answered and said to Him: "Abraham is our father." Jesus said to them: "If you be the children of Abraham, do the works of Abraham. But now you seek to kill Me, a Man Who hath

spoken the truth to you, which I have heard of God. This, Abraham did not; you do the works of your father."

They said therefore to Him: "We are not born of fornication; we have one Father, even God." Jesus therefore said to them: "If God were your Father, you would indeed love Me. For from God I proceeded and came; for I came, not of Myself, but He sent Me. Why do you not know My speech? Because you cannot hear My word. You are of your father the devil, and the desires of your father you will do. He was a murderer from the beginning, and he stood not in the truth, because truth is not in him. When he speaketh a lie, he speaketh of his own, for he is a liar and the father thereof. But if I say the truth, you believe Me not. Which of you shall convince Me of sin? If I say the truth to you, why do you not believe Me? He that is of God heareth the word of God. Therefore you hear them not, because you are not of God."

The Jews therefore answered and said to Him: "Do not we say well, that Thou art a Samaritan and hast a devil?" Jesus answered: "I have not a devil, but I honour My Father, and you have dishonoured Me. But I seek not My own glory; there is One that seeketh and judgeth. Amen, amen, I say to you, if any man keep My word, he shall not see death for ever." The Jews therefore said: "Now we know that Thou hast a devil. Abraham is dead and the prophets, and Thou sayest: If any man keep My word, he shall not taste death for ever. Art Thou greater than our father Abraham, who is dead, and the prophets who are dead? Whom dost Thou make Thyself?"

Jesus answered: "If I glorify Myself, My glory

is nothing. It is My Father that glorifieth Me, of Whom you say that He is your God. And you have not known Him, but I know Him. And if I shall say that I know Him not, I shall be like to you, a liar. But I do know Him, and do keep His word. Abraham your father rejoiced that he might see My day; he saw it and was glad."

57. The Jews therefore said to Him: "Thou art not yet fifty years old, and hast Thou seen Abraham?" Jesus said to them: "Amen, amen, I say to you, before Abraham was made, I am." They took up stones therefore to cast at Him; but Jesus hid Himself and went out of the Temple.

John 9, 1—41. And Jesus passing by, saw a man who was blind from his birth; and His disciples asked Him: "Rabbi, who hath sinned, this man or his parents, that he should be born blind?" Jesus answered: "Neither hath this man sinned, nor his parents, but that the works of God should be made manifest in him. I must work the works of Him Who sent Me whilst it is day; the night cometh when no man can work. As long as I am in the world, I am the light of the world."

6. When He had said these things, He spat on the ground and made clay of the spittle, and spread the clay upon his eyes, and said to him: "Go, wash in the pool of Siloe," which is interpreted, Sent. He went therefore and washed; and he came seeing. The neighbours therefore, and they who had seen him before that he was a beggar, said: "Is not this he that sat and begged?" Some said: "This is he." But others said: "No, but he is like him." But he said: "I am he." They said therefore to him: "How were thy eyes opened?" He answered: "That Man that is called Jesus made clay, and anointed my eyes,

and said to me: 'Go to the pool of Siloe and wash.' And I went, I washed, and I see." And they said to him: "Where is He?" He saith: "I know not."

They bring him that had been blind to the Pharisees. Now it was the Sabbath when Jesus made the clay and opened his eyes. Again therefore, the Pharisees asked him how he had received his sight. But he said to them: "He put clay upon my eyes and I washed and I see." Some therefore of the Pharisees said: "This Man is not of God, Who keepeth not the Sabbath." But others said: "How can a Man that is a sinner do such miracles?" And there was a division among them. 13.

They say therefore to the blind man again: "What sayest thou of Him that hath opened thy eyes?" And he said: "He is a prophet." The Jews then did not believe concerning him, that he had been blind and had received his sight, until they called the parents of him that had received his sight, and asked them saying: "Is this your son, who you say was born blind? How then doth he now see?" His parents answered them and said: "We know that this is our son, and that he was born blind, but how he now seeth we know not, or who hath opened his eyes we know not; ask himself, he is of age, let him speak for himself." These things his parents said because they feared the Jews; for the Jews had already agreed among themselves, that if any man should confess Him to be Christ, he should be put out of the Synagogue. Therefore did his parents say: "He is of age, ask him." 17.

They therefore called the man again that had been born blind, and said to him: "Give glory to 24.

God; we know that this Man is a sinner." He said therefore to them: "If He be a sinner, I know not; one thing I know, that whereas I was blind, now I see." They said then to him: "What did He to thee? How did He open thy eyes?" He answered them: "I have told you already, and you have heard; why would you hear it again? Will you also become His disciples?" They reviled him therefore and said: "Be thou His disciple, but we are the disciples of Moses. We know that God spoke to Moses, but as to this Man, we know not from whence He is." The man answered and said to them: "Why, herein is a wonderful thing, that you know not from whence He is, and He hath opened my eyes. Now we know that God doth not hear sinners, but if a man be a server of God, and doth His will, him He heareth. From the beginning of the world, it hath not been heard, that any man hath opened the eyes of one born blind. Unless this man were of God, He could not do anything." They answered and said to him: "Thou wast wholly born in sins, and dost thou teach us?" And they cast him out.

35. Jesus heard that they had cast him out, and when He had found him, He said to him: "Dost thou believe in the Son of God?" He answered and said: "Who is He, Lord, that I may believe in Him?" And Jesus said to him: "Thou hast both seen Him, and it is He that talketh with thee." And he said: "I believe, Lord." And falling down he adored Him.

39. And Jesus said: "For judgment I am come into this world, that they who see not may see, and they who see may become blind." And some of the Pharisees, who were with Him, heard, and they said unto Him: "Are we also blind?" Jesus

said to them: "If you were blind, you should not have sin; but now you say: 'We see,' your sin remaineth.

"Amen, amen, I say to you, he that entereth not by the door into the sheepfold, but climbeth up another way, the same is a thief and a robber. But he that entereth in by the door is the shepherd of the sheep. To him the porter openeth, and the sheep hear his voice, and he calleth his own sheep by name, and leadeth them out. And when he hath let out his own sheep, he goeth before them and the sheep follow him, because they know his voice. But a stranger they follow not, but fly from him, because they know not the voice of strangers." John 10, 1—42.

This proverb Jesus spoke to them; but they understood not what He spoke to them. Jesus therefore said to them again: "Amen, amen, I say to you, I am the door of the sheep. All others as many as have come, are thieves and robbers, and the sheep heard them not. I am the door. By Me, if any man enter in, he shall be saved, and he shall go in and go out, and shall find pastures. The thief cometh not but for to steal, and to kill, and to destroy. I am come that they may have life, and may have it more abundantly. 6.

"I am the Good Shepherd; the good shepherd giveth his life for the sheep. But the hireling, and he that is not the shepherd, whose own the sheep are not, seeth the wolf coming, and leaveth the sheep and flieth, and the wolf catcheth and scattereth the sheep. And the hireling flieth because he is a hireling, and he hath no care for the sheep. 11.

"I am the Good Shepherd, and I know Mine, 14.

and Mine know Me. As the Father knoweth Me, and I know the Father; and I lay down My life for My sheep. And other sheep I have that are not of this fold; them also I must bring, and they shall hear My voice, and there shall be one fold and one Shepherd. Therefore doth the Father love Me, because I lay down My life, that I may take it again. No man taketh it away from Me, but I lay it down of Myself, and I have power to lay it down, and I have power to take it up again. This commandment have I received from My Father."

19. A dissension rose again among the Jews for these words; and many of them said: "He hath a devil and is mad. Why hear you Him?" Others said: "These are not the words of one that hath a devil. Can a devil open the eyes of the blind?"[1]

22. And it was the feast of the Dedication of Jerusalem,[2] and it was winter. And Jesus walked in the Temple in Solomon's Porch. The Jews therefore came round about Him, and said to Him: "How long dost Thou hold our souls in suspense? If Thou be the Christ, tell us plainly."

25. Jesus answered them: "I speak to you and you believe not; the works that I do in the name of My Father, they give testimony of Me. But you do not believe because you are not of My sheep. My sheep hear My voice, and I know them, and they follow Me. And I give them life everlasting, and they shall not perish for ever, and no man

---

[1] According to some commentators, our Lord at this point went to live beyond the Jordan, and returned for the feast of the Dedication (verse 22). The foundation for this view lies in the word "again" in verse 40.

[2] December.

shall pluck them out of My hand. That which My Father hath given Me, is greater than all, and no one can snatch them out of the hand of My Father. I and the Father are one."

The Jews then took up stones to stone Him. Jesus answered them: "Many good works I have showed you from My Father; for which of those works do you stone Me?" The Jews answered Him: "For a good work we stone Thee not, but for blasphemy, and because that Thou, being a man, makest Thyself God."

Jesus answered them: "Is it not written in your law, *I said you are gods?* If he called them gods to whom the word was spoken, and the Scripture cannot be broken, do you say of Him Whom the Father hath sanctified and sent into the world: 'Thou blasphemest,' because I said I am the Son of God? If I do not the works of My Father, believe Me not. But if I do, though you will not believe Me, believe the works, that you may know that the Father is in Me, and I in the Father."

They sought therefore to take Him, and He escaped out of their hands. And He went again beyond the Jordan, into that place where John was baptizing first, and there He abode. And many resorted to Him, and they said: "John indeed did no sign, but all things whatsoever John said of this Man were true." And many believed in Him.

Now there was a certain man sick named Lazarus of Bethania, of the town of Mary and of Martha her sister.[1] (And Mary was she that

---

[1] An assumption, based on these words, has gained wide acceptance, that Bethania was the *native place* or *permanent* abode of Martha and Mary, and as a consequence that the

anointed the Lord with ointment, and wiped His feet with her hair, whose brother Lazarus was sick.) His sisters therefore sent to Him, saying: "Lord, behold he whom Thou lovest is sick." And Jesus hearing it said to them: "This sickness is not unto death, but for the glory of God, that the Son of God may be glorified by it." Now Jesus loved Martha and her sister Mary and Lazarus. When He had heard therefore that he was sick, He still remained in the same place two days.

7. Then after that He said to His disciples: "Let us go into Judæa again." The disciples said to Him: "Rabbi, the Jews but now sought to stone Thee, and goest Thou thither again?" Jesus answered: "Are there not twelve hours of the day? If a man walk in the day he stumbleth not, because he seeth the light of this world, but if he walk in the night he stumbleth, because the light is not in him." These things He said, and after that He said to them: "Lazarus our friend sleepeth, but I go that I may awake him out of sleep." His disciples therefore said: "Lord, if he sleep, he shall do well." But Jesus spoke of His death, and they thought He spoke of the repose of sleep. Then therefore Jesus said to

---

"certain town" mentioned by St. Luke (x. 38, p. 120), as inhabited by them, was also Bethania.

Greswell (Diss. xxxii.) complains that the point has never been called in question, or exegetically discussed, and that consequently we find it taken for granted, in most chronologies, that our Lord, in Luke x. 38, above cited, had again approached Jerusalem. Greswell points out, that the same juxtaposition of the prepositions ἀπό and ἐκ occur here, as before in John i. 44, p. 21. Hence he is justified in translating ἀπὸ βηθανίας, ἐκ τῆς κώμης, &c., by "an inhabitant of Bethania [but formerly] from the town of Mary and Martha;" and indeed St. Jerome's translation, *De castello Mariæ*, may be considered as equivalent to this.

them plainly: "Lazarus is dead; and I am glad for your sakes that I was not there, that you may believe. But let us go to him." Thomas, therefore, who is called Didymus, said to his fellow-disciples: "Let us also go, that we may die with Him."

17. Jesus therefore came, and found that he had been four days already in the grave. (Now Bethania was near Jerusalem, about fifteen furlongs off.) And many of the Jews were come to Martha and to Mary to comfort them concerning their brother.

20. Martha, therefore, as soon as she heard that Jesus was come, went to meet Him; but Mary sat at home. Martha therefore said to Jesus: "Lord, if Thou hadst been here my brother had not died; but now also I know that whatsoever Thou wilt ask of God, God will give it to Thee." Jesus said to her: "Thy brother shall rise again." Martha saith to Him: "I know that he shall rise again in the resurrection at the last day." Jesus said to her: "I am the resurrection and the life; he that believeth in Me, although he be dead, shall live, and every one that liveth and believeth in Me, shall not die for ever. Believest thou this?" She saith to Him: "Yea, Lord, I have believed that Thou art Christ, the Son of the living God, Who art come into this world."

28. And when she had said these things, she went and called her sister Mary secretly, saying: "The Master is come, and calleth for thee." She, as soon as she heard this, riseth quickly and cometh to Him. For Jesus was not yet come into the town, but He was still in that place where Martha had met Him. The Jews therefore who were with her in the house and comforted her, when they saw Mary that she rose up speedily and went out,

followed her, saying: "She goeth to the grave to weep there."

32. When therefore Mary was come where Jesus was, seeing Him, she fell down at His feet and saith to Him: "Lord, if Thou hadst been here my brother had not died." Jesus, therefore, when He saw her weeping, and the Jews that were come with her weeping, groaned in the spirit, and troubled Himself and said: "Where have you laid Him?" They say to Him: "Lord, come and see."

36. And Jesus wept. The Jews therefore said: "Behold how He loved him!" But some of them said: "Could not He that opened the eyes of the man born blind, have caused that this man should not die?" Jesus therefore, again groaning in Himself, cometh to the sepulchre. Now it was a cave, and a stone was laid over it.

39. Jesus saith: "Take away the stone." Martha, the sister of him that was dead, saith to Him: "Lord, by this time he stinketh, for he is now of four days." Jesus saith to her: "Did not I say to thee that if thou believe, thou shalt see the glory of God?" They took therefore the stone away. And Jesus lifting up His eyes said: "Father, I give Thee thanks that Thou hast heard Me. And I knew that Thou hearest Me always; but because of the people who stand about have I said it, that they may believe that Thou hast sent Me."

43. When He had said these things, He cried with a loud voice: "Lazarus, come forth." And presently he that had been dead came forth, bound feet and hands with winding bands, and his face was bound about with a napkin. Jesus said to them: "Loose him and let him go."

45. Many therefore of the Jews who were come to

PART IV.   TO THE FOURTH PASCH.   115

Mary and Martha, and had seen the things that Jesus did, believed in Him. But some of them went to the Pharisees, and told them the things that Jesus had done. The chief priests therefore and the Pharisees gathered a council and said: "What do we, for this Man doth many miracles? If we let Him alone so, all men will believe in Him, and the Romans will come and take away our place and nation."

But one of them named Caiaphas, being the 49. High Priest that year, said to them: "You know nothing. Neither do you consider that it is expedient for you that one man should die for the people, and that the whole nation perish not." And this he spoke not of himself, but being the High Priest of that year, he prophesied that Jesus should die for the nation. And not only for the nation, but to gather together in one the children of God that were dispersed.

From that day, therefore, they devised to put 53. Him to death. Wherefore Jesus walked no more openly among the Jews, but He went into a country near the desert, unto a city that is called Ephrem, and there He abode with His disciples.[1]

And it came to pass, when the days of His Luke 9, 51—56. assumption were accomplished, that He steadfastly set His face to go to Jerusalem.[2] And He

---

[1] As at this point in St. John's Gospel, we have indication that a notable interval of time occurred between our Lord retiring to Ephrem, and His arrival in Jerusalem for the last Pasch, we are at liberty to suppose, with Greswell, that after having sojourned at Ephrem for some little time, He passed into Galilee with His disciples, before starting on His last journey, which has now to be recorded.

[2] I follow Greswell in supposing this strong unambiguous statement of St. Luke to indicate the beginning of our Lord's absolutely last journey towards Jerusalem; and that too

sent messengers before His face; and going, they entered into a city of the Samaritans to prepare for Him. And they received Him not, because His face was of one going to Jerusalem. And when His disciples James and John had seen this they said: "Lord, wilt Thou that we command fire to come down from heaven and consume them?" And turning He rebuked them, saying: "You know not of what spirit you are. The Son of Man came not to destroy souls but to save." And they went unto another town.

^{LK}And it came to pass as they walked in the way that a certain man said to Him: "I will follow Thee whithersoever Thou goest." Jesus said to him: "The foxes have holes, and the birds of the air nests, but the Son of Man hath not where to lay His head." But He said to another: "Follow Me." And he said: "Lord, suffer me first to go and to bury my father." And Jesus said to him: "Let the dead bury their dead, but go thou and preach the Kingdom of God." And another said: "I will follow Thee, Lord, but let

Matt. 8, 19—22.
Luke 9, 57—62.

---

although it involves placing the resurrection of Lazarus several weeks prior to the position ordinarily assigned to that event.

Greswell is, however, quite consistent in the view he takes, since, a little later on (Luke x. 38, p. 120), he rejects the theory that the "certain town" in which Martha and Mary entertained our Lord was Bethania, and not rather some town in Galilee. The majority of harmonists, as has been shown in the note to p. 111, do not even discuss the point, but taking for granted that St. Luke means Bethania, are forced to conclude that, even after the above explicit statement, our Lord approached Jerusalem, and departed thence once more, before His final journey.

If the order of events here adopted be correct, the whole journey occupied a period approximately equivalent to our Lent, and accounts for the movements of our Lord between His abode at Ephrem (John xi. 54) and His coming to Jerusalem for the last Pasch (John xi. 55).

me first take my leave of them that are at my house." Jesus said to him: "No man putting his hand to the plough and looking back is fit for the Kingdom of God."

And after these things the Lord appointed also other seventy-two, and He sent them, two and two, before His face into every city and place whither He Himself was to come. Luke 10, 1—12.

And He said to them: "The harvest indeed is great, but the labourers are few. Pray ye therefore the Lord of the harvest, that He send labourers into His harvest. Go! behold I send you as lambs among wolves. Carry neither purse, nor scrip, nor shoes, and salute no man by the way. Into whatsoever house you enter, first say: 'Peace be to this house.' And if the son of peace be there, your peace shall rest upon him, but if not it shall return to you. And in the same house remain eating and drinking such things as they have; for the labourer is worthy of his hire. Remove not from house to house. And into what city soever you enter, and they receive you, eat such things as are set before you. And heal the sick that are therein, and say to them: 'The Kingdom of God is come nigh unto you.' But into whatsoever city you enter, and they receive you not, going forth into the streets thereof, say: 'Even the very dust of your city that cleaveth to us, we wipe off against you. Yet know this, that the Kingdom of God is at hand.' I say to you it shall be more tolerable at that day for Sodom than for that city." 2.

^{MT}Then began He to upbraid the cities wherein were done the most of His miracles, for that they had not done penance. "Wo to thee, Corozain! Wo to thee, Bethsaida! for if in Tyre and Sidon Matt. 11, 20—24. Luke 10, 13—15.

had been wrought the miracles that have been wrought in you, they had long ago done penance in sackcloth and ashes. But I say unto you, it shall be more tolerable for Tyre and Sidon in the Day of Judgment than for you. And thou, Capharnaum, ᴸᴷwhich art exalted unto Heaven; ᴹᵀshalt thou be exalted up to Heaven? thou shalt go down even unto Hell. For if in Sodom had been wrought the miracles that have been wrought in thee, perhaps it had remained unto this day. But I say unto you that it shall be more tolerable for the land of Sodom in the Day of Judgment than for thee.

Luke 10, 16—20.

"He that heareth you heareth Me, and he that despiseth you despiseth Me, and he that despiseth Me, despiseth Him that sent Me."

17. And the seventy-two returned with joy, saying: "Lord, the devils also are subject to us in Thy name." And He said to them: "I saw Satan like lightning falling from Heaven. Behold, I have given you power to tread upon serpents and scorpions, and upon all the power of the enemy, and nothing shall hurt you. But yet rejoice not in this, that spirits are subject to you, but rejoice in this, that your names are written in Heaven."

Matt. 11, 25—27.
Luke 10, 21, 22.

ᴸᴷIn that same hour He rejoiced in the Holy Ghost and said: "I confess to Thee, O Father, Lord of Heaven and earth, because Thou hast hidden these things from the wise and prudent, and hast revealed them to little ones. Yea, Father, for so it hath seemed good in Thy sight. All things are delivered to Me by My Father, and no one knoweth Who the Son is but the Father, and Who the Father is but the Son, and to Whom the Son will reveal Him."

And turning to His disciples He said: "Blessed Luke 10, 23, 24.
are the eyes which see the things which you see.
For I say to you, that many prophets and kings
have desired to see the things that you see, and
have not seen them, and to hear the things which
you hear, and have not heard them.

"Come to Me all you that labour and are Matt. 11, 28—30.
burdened, and I will refresh you. Take up My
yoke upon you, and learn of Me, because I am
meek and humble of heart, and you shall find
rest to your souls; for My yoke is sweet and My
burden light."

And behold a certain lawyer stood up tempting Luke 10, 25—42.
Him and saying: "Master, what must I do to
possess eternal life?" But He said to him: "What
is written in the law? How readest thou?" He
answering said: "*Thou shalt love the Lord thy God
with thy whole heart and with thy whole soul, and
with all thy strength, and with all thy mind, and
thy neighbour as thyself.*" And He said to him:
"Thou hast answered right; this do and thou
shalt live."

But he, willing to justify himself, said to Jesus: 29.
"And who is my neighbour?" And Jesus
answering, said: "A certain man went down from
Jerusalem to Jericho and fell among robbers, who
also stripped him, and having wounded him, went
away, leaving him half dead. And it chanced that
a certain priest went down the same way, and
seeing him, passed by. In like manner also a
Levite, when he was near the place and saw him,
passed by. But a certain Samaritan, being on his
journey, came near him, and seeing him was moved
with compassion. And going up to him he bound
up his wounds, pouring in oil and wine, and setting
him upon his own beast, brought him to an inn

and took care of him. And the next day he took out two pence and gave to the host and said: 'Take care of him, and whatsoever thou shalt spend over and above, I, at my return, will repay thee.' Which of these three, in thy opinion, was neighbour to him that fell among robbers?" But he said: "He that showed mercy to him." And Jesus said to him: "Go, and do thou in like manner."

38. Now it came to pass as they went that He entered into a certain town, and a certain woman named Martha received Him into her house.¹ And she had a sister called Mary, who sitting also at the Lord's feet heard His word. But Martha was busy about much serving; who stood and said: "Lord, hast Thou no care that my sister hath left me alone to serve? Speak to her therefore that she help me." And the Lord answering, said to her: "Martha, Martha, thou art careful, and art troubled about many things. But one thing is necessary. Mary hath chosen the best part, which shall not be taken away from her."

Luke 11, 1—54.

And it came to pass that as He was in a certain place praying, when He ceased, one of His disciples

¹ To strengthen the arguments advanced on pp. 111, 112, in support of the view that the *permanent* home of Martha and Mary was in Galilee (perhaps Magdala), while that of Lazarus was Bethania, near Jerusalem, it may be remarked, first, that the omission of the name of Lazarus is at least noteworthy; secondly, in every other place where Bethania is in question, it is mentioned by name; and lastly, if the Latin tradition be the correct one, that this Mary is one and the same person with Mary Magdalene, we have the positive assertion of the three Synoptists that the latter followed our Lord from Galilee (see Matt. xxvii. 55, 56; Mark xv. 40, 41; Luke xxiii. 49).

Furthermore, the internal evidence afforded by St. Luke in and about this place, does not point to the proximity of our Lord to Jerusalem; a statement which is confirmed by reference to his chapters, xiii. 22, xvii. 11, xviii. 31—35.

said to Him: "Lord, teach us to pray, as John also taught his disciples." And He said to them: "When you pray, say: Father, hallowed be Thy Name; Thy Kingdom come; give us this day our daily bread; and forgive us our sins, for we also forgive every one that is indebted to us; and lead us not into temptation."

And He said to them: "Which of you shall have a friend and shall go to him at midnight, and shall say to him: Friend, lend me three loaves, because a friend of mine has come off his journey to me, and I have not what to set before him; and he from within should answer and say: Trouble me not, the door is now shut, and my children are with me in bed, I cannot rise and give thee. Yet if he shall continue knocking, I say to you although he will not rise and give him because he is his friend, yet because of his importunity he will rise and give him as many as he needeth. And I say to you, Ask, and it shall be given you; seek, and you shall find; knock, and it shall be opened to you. For every one that asketh receiveth, and he that seeketh findeth, and to him that knocketh it shall be opened. And which of you if he ask his father bread, will he give him a stone? or a fish, will he for a fish give him a serpent? or if he shall ask him an egg, will he reach him a scorpion? If you, then, being evil, know how to give good gifts to your children, how much more will your Father from Heaven give the Good Spirit to them that ask Him?"[1]

[1] Much of what, in the following discourses, appears to be mere verbal repetition of St. Matthew's narrative by St. Luke, the majority of commentators are agreed is repetition of doctrine by our Lord Himself, in the different, and even in the same villages and towns, through which He now journeyed for the last time.

14. And He was casting out a devil, and the same was dumb, and when He had cast out the devil the dumb spoke, and the multitudes were in admiration at it, but some of them said: "He casteth out devils by Beelzebub the prince of devils." And others tempting asked of Him a sign from Heaven. But He seeing their thoughts said to them: "Every kingdom divided against itself shall be brought to desolation, and house upon house shall fall. And if Satan also be divided against himself, how shall his kingdom stand? because you say that through Beelzebub I cast out devils. Now if I cast out devils by Beelzebub, by whom do your children cast them out? Therefore they shall be your judges. But if I by the finger of God cast out devils, doubtless the Kingdom of God is come upon you. When a strong man armed keepeth his court, those things are in peace which he possesseth. But if a stronger than he come upon him, and overcome him, he will take away all his armour wherein he trusted, and will distribute his spoils. He that is not with Me is against Me, and he that gathereth not with Me, scattereth.

24. "When the unclean spirit is gone out of a man, he walketh through places without water seeking rest, and not finding, he saith: I will return into my house whence I came out. And when he is come he findeth it swept and garnished. Then he goeth and taketh with him seven other spirits more wicked than himself, and entering in they dwell there. And the last state of that man becomes worse than the first."

27. And it came to pass as He spoke these things, a certain woman from the crowd, lifting up her voice, said to Him: "Blessed is the womb that

bore Thee, and the paps that gave Thee suck."
But He said: "Yea, rather, blessed are they who
hear the word of God and keep it."

And the multitudes running together, He began 29.
to say: "This generation is a wicked generation;
it asketh a sign, and a sign shall not be given it,
but the sign of Jonas the Prophet. For as Jonas
was a sign to the Ninivites, so shall the Son of
Man also be to this generation. The Queen of
the South shall rise in the Judgment with the men
of this generation, and shall condemn them, because she came from the ends of the earth to hear
the wisdom of Solomon, and behold more than
Solomon here! The men of Ninive shall rise in
the Judgment with this generation, and shall condemn it, because they did penance at the preaching
of Jonas, and behold more than Jonas here!

"No man lighteth a candle and putteth it in 33.
a hidden place nor under a bushel, but upon a
candlestick, that they that come in may see the
light. The light of thy body is thy eye; if thy eye
be single, thy whole body will be lightsome, but
if it be evil, thy body also will be darksome. Take
heed therefore that the light which is in thee be
not darkness. If then thy whole body be lightsome, having no part of darkness, the whole shall
be lightsome, and as a bright lamp shall enlighten
thee."

And as He was speaking a certain Pharisee 37.
prayed Him that He would dine with him. And
He going in sat down to eat. And the Pharisee
began to say, thinking within himself, why He was
not washed before dinner. And the Lord said to
him: "Now you Pharisees make clean the outside
of the cup and of the platter, but your inside is
full of rapine and iniquity. Ye fools, did not He

that made that which is without make also that which is within? But yet that which remaineth; give alms, and behold, all things are clean unto you. But wo to you Pharisees, because you tithe mint, and rue, and every herb, and pass over judgment and the charity of God. Now these things you ought to have done, and not to leave the other undone. Wo to you Pharisees, because you love the uppermost seats in the synagogues and salutations in the market-place. Wo to you because you are as sepulchres that appear not, and men that walk over are not aware."

45. And one of the lawyers answering, said to him: "Master, in saying these things Thou reproachest us also." But He said: "Wo to you lawyers also, because you load men with burdens which they cannot bear, and you yourselves touch not the packs with one of your fingers. Wo to you who build the monuments of the prophets, and your fathers killed them. Truly you bear witness that you consent to the doings of your fathers, for they indeed killed them and you build their sepulchres. For this cause also the wisdom of God said: I will send to them prophets and apostles, and some of them they will kill and persecute. That the blood of all the prophets which was shed from the foundation of the world may be required of this generation; from the blood of Abel to the blood of Zacharias, who was slain between the altar and the temple. Yea, I say to you, it shall be required of this generation. Wo to you lawyers, for you have taken away the key of knowledge; you yourselves have not entered in, and those that were entering in you have hindered."

53. And as He was saying these things to them, the Pharisees and the lawyers began vehemently to

urge Him, and to oppress His mouth about many things, lying in wait for Him, and seeking to catch something from His mouth, that they might accuse Him.

And when great multitudes stood about Him, so that they trod one upon another, He began to say to His disciples: "Beware ye of the leaven of the Pharisees, which is hypocrisy. For there is nothing covered which shall not be revealed, nor hidden that shall not be known. For whatsoever things you have spoken in darkness shall be published in the light, and that which you have spoken in the ear in the chambers, shall be preached on the housetops.

"And I say to you, My friends: Be not afraid of them who kill the body, and after that have no more that they can do. But I will show you Whom you shall fear. Fear ye Him, Who after He hath killed, hath power to cast into Hell. Yea, I say to you, fear Him. Are not five sparrows sold for two farthings? and not one of them is forgotten before God. Yea, the very hairs of your head are all numbered. Fear not therefore, you are of more value than many sparrows.

"And I say to you, whosoever shall confess Me before men, him shall the Son of Man also confess before the angels of God. But he that shall deny Me before men shall be denied before the angels of God. And whosoever speaketh a word against the Son of Man, it shall be forgiven him, but to him that shall blaspheme against the Holy Ghost, it shall not be forgiven. And when they shall bring you into the synagogues, and to magistrates and powers, be not solicitous how or what you shall answer, or what you shall say, for the Holy Ghost shall teach you in the same hour what you must say."

13. And one of the multitude said to him: "Master, speak to my brother, that he divide the inheritance with me." But He said to him: "Man, who hath appointed Me judge or divider over you?" And He said to them: "Take heed of all covetousness, for a man's life does not consist in the abundance of things which he possesseth." And He spoke a similitude to them, saying: "The land of a certain rich man brought forth plenty of fruits. And he thought within himself, saying: What shall I do, because I have no room where to bestow my fruits? And he said: This will I do; I will pull down my barns and will build greater, and into them will I gather all things that are grown to me and my goods. And I will say to my soul: Soul, thou hast much goods laid up for many years; take thy rest, eat, drink, make good cheer. But God said to him: Thou fool, this night do they require thy soul of thee, and whose shall those things be which thou hast provided? So is he that layeth up treasure for himself, and is not rich towards God."

22. And He said to His disciples: "Therefore I say to you, be not solicitous for your life what you shall eat, nor for your body what you shall put on. The life is more than the meat and the body is more than the raiment. Consider the ravens, for they sow not, neither do they reap, neither have they storehouse nor barn, and God feedeth them. How much are you more valuable than they? And which of you by taking thought can add to his stature one cubit? If then ye be not able to do so much as the least thing, why are you solicitous for the rest? Consider the lilies, how they grow; they labour not, neither do they spin. But I say to you, not even Solomon in all his glory was clothed like one of these. Now if God clothe in this manner the grass that is to-day in the field, and to-morrow is cast into the oven, how much more you, O ye of little faith?

"And seek not you what you shall eat, or what 29. you shall drink, and be not lifted up on high; for all these things do the nations of the world seek. But your Father knoweth that you have need of these things. But seek ye first the Kingdom of God and His justice, and all these things shall be added unto you. Fear not, little flock, for it hath pleased your Father to give you a Kingdom. Sell what you possess, and give alms. Make to yourselves bags which grow not old, a treasure in Heaven which faileth not, where no thief approacheth nor moth corrupteth. For where your treasure is, there will your heart be also.

"Let your loins be girt and lamps burning in 35. your hands, and you yourselves like to men who wait for their lord when he shall return from the wedding, that when he cometh and knocketh they may open to him immediately. Blessed are those servants whom the lord when he cometh shall find watching. Amen, I say to you, that he will gird himself and make them sit down to meat, and passing will minister unto them. And if he shall come in the second watch, or come in the third watch, and find them so, blessed are those servants. But this know ye, that if the householder did know at what hour the thief would come, he would surely watch, and would not allow his house to be broken open. Be you then also ready, for at what hour you think not the Son of Man will come."

And Peter said to Him: "Lord, dost Thou 41. speak this parable to us, or likewise to all?" And the Lord said: "Who, thinkest thou, is the faithful and wise steward whom his lord setteth over his family to give them their measure of wheat in due season? Blessed is that servant, whom when his lord shall come he shall find so doing. Verily, I say to you, he will set him over all that he possesseth. But if that servant shall say in his heart, My lord is long a-coming, and shall begin to strike the men-servants and the maid-servants, and to eat and to drink and be drunk, the lord of that servant will come in the day that he hopeth not and at the hour that he knoweth not, and shall separate him, and shall appoint him his portion with unbelievers. And that servant who knew the will of his lord and prepared not himself, and did not according to his will, shall be beaten with many stripes. But he that knew not, and did things worthy of stripes, shall be beaten with few stripes. And unto whomsoever much is given, of him much shall be required, and to whom they have committed much, of him they will demand the more.

49. "I am come to cast fire on the earth, and what will I but that it be kindled? And I have a baptism wherewith I am to be baptized, and how am I straitened until it be accomplished. Think ye that I am come to give peace on earth? I tell you no, but separation. For there shall be from henceforth five in one house, divided three against two, and two against three. The father shall be divided against the son, and the son against the father; the mother against the daughter, and the daughter against the mother; the mother-in-law against her daughter-in-law, and the daughter-in-law against her mother-in-law."

54. And He said also to the multitudes: "When you see a cloud rising from the west, presently you

say, A shower is coming, and so it happeneth. And when you see the south wind blow, you say, There will be heat, and it cometh to pass. You hypocrites, you know how to discern the face of the heaven and of the earth, but how is it that you do not discern this time? And why even of yourselves, do you not judge that which is just?

"And when thou goest with thy adversary to the prince, whilst thou art in the way, endeavour to be delivered from him, lest perhaps he draw thee to the judge, and the judge deliver thee to the exacter, and the exacter cast thee into prison. I say to thee, thou shalt not go out thence until thou pay the very last mite." *58.*

And there were present at that very time some that told Him of the Galilæans, whose blood Pilate had mingled with their sacrifices. And He answering said to them: "Think you that these Galilæans were sinners above all the men of Galilee, because they suffered such things? No, I say to you; but unless you shall do penance, you shall all likewise perish. Or those eighteen upon whom the tower fell in Siloe and slew them, think you that they also were debtors above all the men that dwelt in Jerusalem? No, I say to you; but except you do penance, you shall all likewise perish." *Luke 13, 1—35.*

He spoke also this parable: "A certain man had a fig-tree planted in his vineyard, and he came seeking fruit on it and found none. And he said to the dresser of the vineyard: 'Behold for these three years I come seeking fruit on this fig-tree, and I find none; cut it down therefore; why cumbereth it the ground?' But he answering said to him: 'Lord, let it alone this year also, until I dig about it and dung it, and if happily it bear *6.*

fruit; but if not, then after that thou shalt cut it down.'"

10. And He was teaching in their synagogue on their Sabbath. And behold there was a woman who had a spirit of infirmity eighteen years, and she was bowed together, neither could she look upwards at all. Whom, when Jesus saw, He called her unto Him, and said to her: "Woman, thou art delivered from thy infirmity." And He laid His hands upon her, and immediately she was made straight, and glorified God.

14. And the ruler of the synagogue (being angry that Jesus had healed on the Sabbath) answering, said to the multitude: "Six days there are wherein you ought to work. In them therefore come and be healed, and not on the Sabbath-day." And the Lord answering him, said: "Ye hypocrites, doth not every one of you loose his ox or his ass from the manger, and lead them to water? And ought not this daughter of Abraham, whom Satan hath bound, lo, these eighteen years, be loosed from this bond on the Sabbath-day?"

17. And when He said these things all His adversaries were ashamed, and all the people rejoiced for all the things that were gloriously done by Him. He said therefore: "To what is the Kingdom of God like, and whereunto shall I resemble it? It is like a grain of mustard-seed which a man took and cast into his garden, and it grew and became a great tree, and the birds of the air lodged in the branches thereof." And again He said: "Whereunto shall I esteem the Kingdom of God to be like? It is like leaven, which a woman took and hid in three measures of meal, till the whole was leavened."

22. And He went through the cities and towns

teaching, and making His journey to Jerusalem. And a certain man said to Him: "Lord, are they few that are saved?" But He said to them: "Strive to enter by the narrow gate, for many, I say to you, shall seek to enter and shall not be able. But when the Master of the house shall be gone in, and shall shut to the door, you shall begin to stand without and knock at the door, saying: 'Lord, open to us.' And he answering, shall say to you: 'I know you not whence you are.' Then you shall begin to say: 'We have eaten and drunk in Thy presence, and Thou hast taught in our streets.' And He shall say to you: 'I know you not whence you are; depart from Me, all ye workers of iniquity.' There shall be weeping and gnashing of teeth, when you shall see Abraham and Isaac and Jacob and all the prophets, in the Kingdom of God, and you yourselves thrust out. And these shall come from the east and the west, and the north and the south, and shall sit down in the Kingdom of God. And behold, they are last who shall be first, and they are first that shall be last."

The same day there came some of the Pharisees, 31. saying to Him: "Depart and get Thee hence, for Herod hath a mind to kill Thee." And He said to them: "Go and tell that fox, Behold I cast out devils and do cures to-day and to-morrow, and the third day I am consummated. Nevertheless, I must walk to-day, and to-morrow and the day following, because it cannot be that a prophet die out of Jerusalem. Jerusalem, Jerusalem, that killest the prophets, and stonest them that are sent to thee! How often would I have gathered thy children, as the bird doth her brood under her wings, and thou wouldst not! Behold, your house shall be left to you desolate. And I say to you, that you shall not see Me till the time come, when you shall say: 'Blessed is He that cometh in the Name of the Lord.'"

Luke 14, 1—35. And it came to pass, when Jesus went into the house of one of the chief of the Pharisees on the Sabbath-day, to eat bread, that they watched Him. And behold there was a certain man before Him that had the dropsy. And Jesus answering spoke to the lawyers and Pharisees, saying: "Is it lawful to heal on the Sabbath-day?" But they held their peace. But He taking him, healed him, and sent him away. And answering them, He said: "Which of you shall have an ass or an ox fall into a pit, and will not immediately draw him out on the Sabbath-day?" And they could not answer Him to these things.

7. And He spoke a parable also to them that were invited, marking how they chose the first seats at the table, saying to them: "When thou art invited to a wedding, sit not down in the first place, lest perhaps one more honourable than thou be invited by him; and he that invited thee and him, come and say to thee: 'Give this man place;' and then thou begin with shame to take the lowest place. But when thou art invited, go sit down in the lowest place, that when he who invited thee cometh, he may say to thee: 'Friend, go up higher.' Then shalt thou have glory before them who sit at table with thee; because every one that exalteth himself shall be humbled, and he that humbleth himself shall be exalted."

12. And He said to him also that had invited Him: "When thou makest a dinner or a supper, call not thy friends, nor thy brethren, nor thy kinsmen, nor thy neighbours who are rich, lest perhaps they also invite thee again, and a recompense be made to

thee. But when thou makest a feast, call the poor, the maimed, the lame, and the blind; and thou shalt be blessed, because they have not wherewith to make thee recompense, for recompense shall be made thee at the resurrection of the just."

When one of them that sat at table with Him had heard these things, he said to Him: "Blessed is he that shall eat bread in the Kingdom of God." But He said to him: "A certain man made a great supper and invited many. And he sent his servant at the hour of supper to say to them that were invited, that they should come, for now all things are ready. And they began all at once to make excuse. The first said to him: 'I have bought a farm, and I must needs go out and see it; I pray thee, hold me excused.' And another said: 'I have bought five yoke of oxen, and I go to try them; I pray thee, hold me excused.' And another said: 'I have married a wife, and therefore I cannot come.' 15.

"And the servant returning, told these things to his lord. Then the master of the house, being angry, said to his servant: 'Go out quickly into the streets and lanes of the city, and bring in hither the poor and the feeble and the blind and the lame.' 21.

"And the servant said: 'Lord, it is done as thou hast commanded, and yet there is room.' And the lord said to the servant: 'Go out into the highways and hedges, and compel them to come in, that my house may be filled. But I say unto you, that none of those men that were invited shall taste of my supper.'" 22.

And there went great multitudes with Him. And turning He said to them: "If any man come to Me and hate not his father and mother, and wife 25.

and children, and brethren and sisters, yea, and his own life also, he cannot be My disciple. And whosoever doth not carry his cross and come after Me, cannot be My disciple. For which of you having a mind to build a tower, doth not first sit down and reckon the charges which are necessary; whether he hath wherewithal to finish it, lest after he hath laid the foundation and is not able to finish it, all that see it begin to mock him, saying: 'This man began to build, and was not able to finish.' Or what king, about to go to war with another king, doth not first sit down and think whether he be able, with ten thousand, to meet him that with twenty thousand cometh against him; or else, while the other is yet afar off, sending an embassy he desireth conditions of peace. So likewise every one of you that doth not renounce all that he possesseth, cannot be My disciple.

34. "Salt is good. But if the salt shall lose its savour, wherewith shall it be seasoned? It is neither profitable for the land nor for the dung-hill, but shall be cast out. He that hath ears to hear, let him hear."

Luke 15, 1—32. Now the publicans and sinners drew near unto Him to hear Him. And the Pharisees and the Scribes murmured, saying: "This Man receiveth sinners and eateth with them." And He spoke to them this parable, saying: "What man of you that hath an hundred sheep, and if he shall lose one of them, doth he not leave the ninety-nine in the desert, and go after that which was lost until he find it; and when he has found it, lay it upon his shoulders rejoicing; and coming home, call together his friends and neighbours, saying to them: 'Rejoice with me, because I have found my sheep that was lost'? I say to you, that even so there shall be joy in Heaven upon one sinner that doth penance, more than upon ninety-nine just who need not penance.

"Or what woman having ten groats, if she lose 8. one groat, doth not light a candle, and sweep the house, and seek diligently until she find it; and when she has found it, call together her friends and neighbours, saying: 'Rejoice with me, because I have found the groat which I had lost'? So I say to you, there shall be joy before the angels of God upon one sinner doing penance."

And He said: "A certain man had two sons, 11. and the younger of them said to his father: 'Father, give me the portion of substance that falleth to me.' And he divided unto them his substance. And not many days after, the younger son, gathering all together, went abroad into a far country and there wasted his substance, living riotously.

"And after he had spent all, there came a mighty 14. famine in that country, and he began to be in want. And he went and cleaved to one of the citizens of that country; and he sent him into his farm to feed swine. And he would fain have filled his belly with the husks the swine did eat, and no man gave unto him.

"And returning to himself he said: 'How many 17. servants in my father's house abound with bread, and I here perish with hunger! I will arise and will go to my father, and say to him: "Father, I have sinned against Heaven and before thee; I am not now worthy to be called thy son, make me as one of thy hired servants."'

"And rising up he came to his father. And 20. when he was yet a great way off, his father saw him and was moved with compassion, and running to him fell upon his neck and kissed him. And the son said to him: 'Father, I have sinned against Heaven and before thee, I am not now worthy to be called thy son.' And the father said to the servants: 'Bring forth quickly the first robe, and put it on him; and put a ring on his hand, and shoes on his feet; and bring hither the fatted calf and kill it; and let us eat and make merry, because this my son was dead and is come to life again, was lost and is found.' And they began to be merry.

25. "Now his elder son was in the field, and when he drew nigh to the house he heard music and dancing. And he called one of the servants and asked what these things meant. And he said to him: 'Thy brother is come, and thy father hath killed the fatted calf, because he hath received him safe.' And he was angry, and would not go in. His father, therefore, coming out began to entreat him. And he answering, said to his father: 'Behold, for so many years do I serve thee, and I have never transgressed thy commandment, and yet thou hast never given me a kid to make merry with my friends; but as soon as this thy son is come, who hath devoured his substance with harlots, thou hast killed for him the fatted calf.' But he said to him: 'Son, thou art always with me, and all I have is thine. But it was fit we should make merry and be glad, for this thy brother was dead and is come to life again, he was lost and is found.'"

And He said to His disciples: "There was a certain rich man who had a steward, and the same was accused unto him, that he had wasted his goods. And he called him, and he said to him: 'How is it that I hear this of thee? give an account of thy stewardship, for now thou canst be steward no longer.' And the steward said within himself: 'What shall I do, because my lord taketh away from me the stewardship? To dig I am unable, to beg I am ashamed; I know what I will do, that when I shall be removed from the stewardship they may receive me into their houses.' Therefore calling together every one of his lord's debtors, he said to the first: 'How much dost thou owe my lord?' But he said: 'An hundred barrels of oil.' And he said to him: 'Take thy bill and sit down quickly and write, fifty.' Then he said to another: 'And how much dost thou owe?' Who said: 'An hundred quarters of wheat.' He said to him: 'Take thy bill and write, eighty.'

"And the lord commended the unjust steward, forasmuch as he had done wisely, for the children of this world are wiser in their generation than the children of light. And I say to you: Make unto you friends of the mammon of iniquity, that when you shall fail they may receive you into everlasting dwellings. He that is faithful in that which is least is faithful also in that which is greater, and he that is unjust in that which is little is unjust also in that which is greater. If then you have not been faithful in the unjust mammon, who will trust you with that which is the true? And if you have not been faithful in that which is another's, who will give you that which is your own? No servant can serve two masters, for either he will hate the one and love the other, or he will hold to the one and despise the other. You cannot serve God and mammon."

Now the Pharisees who were covetous heard all these things, and they derided Him. And He said to them: "You are they who justify yourselves before men, but God knoweth your hearts, for that which is high to men is an abomination before God. The law and the prophets were until John. From that time the Kingdom of God is preached and every one useth violence towards it. And it is easier for heaven and earth to pass, than one tittle of the law to fall. Every one that putteth away his wife and marrieth another committeth adultery, and he that marrieth her that is put away from her husband committeth adultery.

19. "There was a certain rich man who was clothed in purple and fine linen, and feasted sumptuously every day. And there was a certain beggar named Lazarus who lay at his gate, full of sores, desiring to be fed with the crumbs that fell from the rich man's table, and no one did give him; moreover, the dogs came and licked his sores.

22. "And it came to pass that the beggar died and was carried by angels into Abraham's bosom. And the rich man also died and he was buried in Hell. And lifting up his eyes when he was in torments, he saw Abraham afar off, and Lazarus in his bosom, and he cried and said: 'Father Abraham, have mercy on me, and send Lazarus that he may dip the tip of his finger in water to cool my tongue, for I am tormented in this flame.' And Abraham said to him: 'Son, remember that thou didst receive good things in thy lifetime, and Lazarus evil things, but now he is comforted and thou art tormented. And besides all this, between us and you there is fixed a great chaos, so that they who would pass from hence to you cannot, nor from thence come hither.' And he said: 'Then, Father, I beseech thee that thou wouldst send him to my father's house, for I have five brethren, that he may testify unto them, lest they also come into this place of torments.' And Abraham said to him: 'They have Moses and the prophets, let

them hear them.' But he said: 'No, Father Abraham, but if one went to them from the dead they would do penance.' And he said to him: 'If they hear not Moses and the prophets, neither will they believe if one rise again from the dead.'"

And He said to His disciples: "It is impossible that scandals should not come, but wo to him from whom they come. It were better for him that a mill-stone were hanged about his neck and he be cast into the sea, than that he should scandalize one of these little ones. Luke 17, 1—37.

"Take heed to yourselves. If thy brother sin against thee, reprove him; and if he do penance, forgive him. And if he sin against thee seven times in a day, and seven times in a day be converted unto thee, saying, 'I repent,' forgive him." 3.

And the Apostles said to the Lord: "Lord, increase our faith." And the Lord said: "If you had faith like to a grain of mustard-seed, you might say to the mulberry-tree: 'Be thou rooted up, and be thou transplanted into the sea,' and it would obey you. But which of you having a servant ploughing or feeding cattle, will say to him when he is come from the field: 'Immediately go sit down to meat,' and will not rather say to him: 'Make ready my supper, and gird thyself and serve me, whilst I eat and drink, and afterwards thou shalt eat and drink'? Doth he thank that servant for doing the things which he commanded him? I think not. So you also, when you have done all these things that are commanded you, say: 'We are unprofitable servants; we have done that which we ought to do.'" 5.

And it came to pass as He was going to Jerusalem, He passed through the midst of Samaria and Galilee. And as He entered into a certain town, 11.

there met Him ten men that were lepers, who stood afar off, and lifted their voice, saying: "Jesus, Master, have mercy on us." Whom when He saw, He said: "Go, show yourselves to the priests." And it came to pass as they went, they were made clean. And one of them when he saw that he was made clean, went back, with a loud voice glorifying God. And he fell on his face before His feet, giving thanks, and this was a Samaritan. And Jesus answering, said: "Were not ten made clean, and where are the nine? There is no one found to return and give glory to God but this stranger." And He said to him: "Arise, go thy way, for thy faith hath made thee whole."

20. And being asked by the Pharisees when the Kingdom of God should come, He answered them and said: "The Kingdom of God cometh not with observation; neither shall they say: 'Behold, here! or behold, there!' for lo! the Kingdom of God is within you."

22. And He said to His disciples: "The days will come when you shall desire to see one day of the Son of Man, and you shall not see it. And they shall say to you: 'See here! and see there!' Go ye not after nor follow them, for as the lightning that lighteneth from under heaven, so shall the Son of Man be in His day. But first He must suffer many things, and be rejected by this generation.

26. "And as it came to pass in the days of Noe, so shall it be in the days of the Son of Man. They did eat and drink—they married wives and were given in marriage—until the day that Noe entered the ark, and the Flood came, and destroyed them all. Likewise as it came to pass in the days of Lot; they did eat and drink—they bought and

sold—they planted and built; and in the day that Lot went out of Sodom, it rained fire and brimstone from heaven and destroyed them all.

"Even thus will it be in the day when the Son of Man shall be revealed. In that hour, he that shall be on the housetop and his goods in the house, let him not go down to take them away; and he that shall be in the field let him not return back. Remember Lot's wife. Whosoever shall seek to save his life shall lose it; and whosoever shall lose it shall preserve it. I say to you, in that night there shall be two men in one bed, the one shall be taken, and the other shall be left. Two women shall be grinding together, the one shall be taken and the other shall be left." They answering say to Him: "Where, Lord?" Who said to them: "Wheresoever the body shall be, thither will the eagles also be gathered together." 30.

And He spoke also a parable to them, that we ought always to pray and not to faint, saying: "There was a judge in a certain city, who feared not God, nor regarded man. And there was a certain widow in that city, and she came to him, saying: 'Avenge me of my adversary.' And he would not for a long time. But afterwards he said within himself: 'Although I fear not God, nor regard man, yet because this widow is troublesome to me, I will avenge her, lest continually coming to me she weary me.'" Luke 18, 1—14.

And the Lord said: "Hear what the unjust judge saith! And will not God revenge His elect who cry to Him day and night, and will He have patience in their regard? I say to you that He will quickly revenge them. But yet the Son of Man, when He cometh, shall He find, think you, faith on earth?" 6.

9. And to some who trusted in themselves as just, and despised others, He spoke also this parable: "Two men went up into the Temple to pray, the one a Pharisee, and the other a publican. The Pharisee standing prayed thus with himself: 'O God, I give Thee thanks that I am not like the rest of men, extortioners, unjust, adulterers, as also is this publican. I fast twice in a week, I give tithes of all that I possess.' And the publican, standing afar off, would not so much as lift up his eyes towards heaven, but struck his breast saying: 'O God, be merciful to me a sinner!' I say to you, this man went down to his house justified, rather than the other, because every one that exalteth himself shall be humbled, and he that humbleth himself shall be exalted."

<small>Matt. 19, 1—3.
Mark 10, 1, 2.</small>
^{MT}And it came to pass when Jesus had ended these words, He departed from Galilee and came into the coasts of Judæa beyond Jordan. And great multitudes followed Him, and He healed them there. ^{MK}And as He was accustomed He taught them again.

^{MT}And there came to Him the Pharisees, tempting Him and saying: "Is it lawful for a man to put away his wife for every cause?"

<small>Mark 10, 3—5.</small>
But He answering, saith to them: "What did Moses command you?" Who said: "Moses permitted to write a bill of divorce, and to put her away." To whom Jesus answering, said: "By reason of the hardness of your heart he wrote you that precept.

<small>Matt. 19, 4—6.
Mark 10, 6—9.</small>
^{MT}"Have you not read, that He Who made man from the beginning made them male and female?" And He said: "For this cause shall a man leave father and mother, and shall cleave to his wife, and they two shall be in one flesh. Therefore

now they are not two, but one flesh. What therefore God hath joined together, let no man put asunder."

They said to Him: "Why then did Moses command to give a bill of divorce and to put away?" He said to them: "Because Moses by reason of the hardness of your heart permitted you to put away your wives, but from the beginning it was not so; and I say to you, that whosoever shall put away his wife, except it be for fornication, and shall marry another, committeth adultery, and he that shall marry her that is put away, committeth adultery." Matt. 19, 7—9.

And in the house, again His disciples asked Him concerning the same thing. And He saith to them: "Whosoever shall put away his wife and marry another, committeth adultery against her. And if the wife shall put away her husband and be married to another, she committeth adultery." Mark 10, 10—12.

His disciples say unto Him: "If the case of a man with his wife be so, it is not expedient to marry." Who said to them: "All men take not this word, but they to whom it is given. For there are eunuchs who were born so from their mother's womb, and there are eunuchs who were made so by men, and there are eunuchs who have made themselves eunuchs for the Kingdom of Heaven. He that can take it, let him take it." Matt. 19, 10—12.

^{MT}Then were little children brought to Him, that He should impose hands upon them and pray. ^{MK}And the disciples rebuked them that brought them; whom when Jesus saw, He was much displeased, and saith to them: "Suffer the little children to come unto Me, and forbid them not, for of such is the Kingdom of God. Amen I say to you, whosoever shall not receive the Matt. 19, 13, 14.
Mark 10, 13—15.
Luke 18, 15—17.

Kingdom of God as a little child, shall not enter into it."

^{MK}And embracing them, and laying His hands upon them, He blessed them; ^{MT}and . . . He departed from thence.

^{MK}And when He was gone forth into the way, a certain man running up and kneeling before Him, asked Him: "Good Master, what shall I do that I may receive life everlasting?" And Jesus said to him: "Why callest thou Me good? None is good but one, God. ^{MT}But if thou wilt enter into life keep the Commandments." But he said to Him: "Which?" And Jesus said: "Thou shalt do no murder. Thou shalt not commit adultery. Thou shalt not steal. Thou shalt not bear false witness. Honour thy father and thy mother; and thou shalt love thy neighbour as thyself."

20. The young man saith to Him: "All these have I kept from my youth; what is yet wanting to me?" ^{MK}And Jesus looking on him loved him and said to him: "One thing is wanting unto thee; ^{MT}if thou wilt be perfect, go, ^{LK}sell all whatever thou hast, and give to the poor, and thou shalt have treasure in Heaven, and come, follow Me." ^{MT}And when the young man had heard this word, he went away sad, for he had great possessions.

23. ^{LK}And Jesus seeing him become sad, ^{MK}looking round about, saith to His disciples: "How hardly shall they that have riches enter into the Kingdom of God!" And the disciples were astonished at His words. But Jesus again answering, saith to them: "Children, how hard it is for them that trust in riches to enter into the Kingdom of God! It is easier for a camel to pass through the eye of a needle, than for a rich man to enter into the

Kingdom of God." Who wondered the more, saying among themselves: "Who then can be saved?" And Jesus looking on them, saith: "With men it is impossible, but not with God; for all things are possible with God."

^{MT}Then Peter answering, said to Him: "Behold, we have left all things and have followed Thee; what therefore shall we have?"

27.

And Jesus said to them: "Amen I say to you, that you who have followed Me, in the regeneration, when the Son of Man shall sit on the seat of His majesty, you also shall sit on twelve seats, judging the twelve tribes of Israel.

Matt. 19, 28.

^{MK}"Amen I say to you, there is no man who hath left house, or brethren, or sisters, or father, or mother, or children, or lands, for My sake, and for the Gospel, who shall not receive an hundred times as much now in this time—houses and brethren and sisters and mothers and children and lands, with persecutions; and in the world to come, life everlasting.

Matt. 19, 29.
Mark 10, 29, 30.
Luke 18, 29, 30.

^{MT}"And many that are first shall be last and the last shall be first; [for] the Kingdom of Heaven is like to a householder who went out early in the morning to hire labourers into his vineyard. And having agreed with the labourers for a penny a day he sent them into his vineyard. And going out about the third hour he saw others standing in the market-place idle. And he said to them: 'Go you also into my vineyard, and I will give you what shall be just;' and they went their way. And again he went out about the sixth and the ninth hour, and did in like manner. But about the eleventh hour he went out and found others standing, and he saith to them: 'Why stand you here all the day idle?' They say to him: 'Because

Matt. 19, 30.
Mark 10, 31.
Matt. 20, 1—16.

K

no man hath hired us.' He saith to them: 'Go you also into my vineyard.'

8. "And when evening was come, the lord of the vineyard saith to his steward: 'Call the labourers, and pay them their hire, beginning from the last even to the first.' When therefore they were come that came about the eleventh hour, they received every man a penny. But when the first also came, they thought that they should receive more, and they also received every man a penny. And receiving it, they murmured against the master of the house, saying: 'These last have worked but one hour, and thou hast made them equal to us, that have borne the burden of the day and the heats.' But he answering said to one of them: 'Friend, I do thee no wrong; didst thou not agree with me for a penny? Take what is thine and go thy way; I will also give to this last even as to thee. Or, is it not lawful for me to do what I will? Is thy eye evil because I am good?' So shall the last be first and the first last; for many are called, but few are chosen."

Mark 10, 32.

And they were in the way going up to Jerusalem; and Jesus went before them, and they were astonished, and following Him were afraid.

Matt. 20, 17—19.
Mark 10, 32—34.
Luke 18, 31—33.

^{MK}And taking again the twelve, He began to tell them the things that should befall Him, saying: "Behold we go up to Jerusalem, ^{LK}and all things shall be accomplished which were written by the prophets concerning the Son of Man. For He shall be ^{MK}betrayed to the chief priests, and to the scribes, and ancients; and they shall condemn Him to death, and shall deliver Him to the Gentiles; and they shall mock Him, and spit on Him, and scourge Him, and kill Him; and the third day He shall rise again."

And they understood none of these things, and this word was hid from them, and they understood not the things that were said. ^{Luke 18, 34.}

Then came to Him the mother of the sons of Zebedee, with her sons, ^{MK}James and John, ^{MT}adoring and asking something of Him, ^{MK}saying: "Master, we desire that whatsoever we shall ask, Thou wouldst do it for us." But He said to them: "What would you that I should do for you?" ^{MT}She saith to Him: "Say that these my two sons may sit, the one on Thy right hand, and the other on Thy left, in Thy Kingdom." Jesus answering said: "You know not what you ask. ^{MK}Can you drink of the chalice that I drink of? or be baptized with the baptism wherewith I am baptized?" But they said to Him: "We can." And Jesus saith to them: "You shall indeed drink of the chalice that I drink of; and with the baptism wherewith I am baptized, you shall be baptized. But to sit on My right hand or on My left is not Mine to give to you, but for them for whom it is prepared ^{MT}by My Father." ^{Matt. 20, 20—28. Mark 10, 35—45.}

^{MK}And the ten hearing it, began to be much displeased at James and John. But Jesus calling them, saith to them: "You know that they who seem to rule over the Gentiles, lord it over them, and the great have power over them. But it shall not be so among you, but whosoever will be great, shall be your minister. And whosoever will be first among you shall be the servant of all. For the Son of Man also is not come to be ministered unto, but to minister, and to give His life a redemption for many." ^{41.}

Now it came to pass when He drew nigh to Jericho that a certain blind man sat by the wayside begging. And when he heard the multitude ^{Luke 18, 35—43.}

passing by he asked what this meant. And they told him that Jesus of Nazareth was passing by. And he cried out, saying: "Jesus, Son of David, have mercy on me." And they that went before rebuked him that he should hold his peace, but he cried out much more: "Son of David, have mercy on me." And Jesus standing commanded him to be brought unto Him. And when he was come near, He asked him, saying: "What wilt thou that I do to thee?" But he said: "Lord, that I may see." And Jesus said to him: "Receive thy sight, thy faith hath made thee whole." And immediately he saw and followed Him, glorifying God. And all the people when they saw it gave praise to God.

Luke 19, 1—28. And entering in, He walked through Jericho. And behold there was a man named Zaccheus who was the chief of the publicans, and he was rich. And he sought to see Jesus, Who He was, and he could not for the crowd, because he was low of stature. And running before, he climbed up into a sycamore-tree, that he might see Him, for He was to pass that way. And when Jesus was come to the place, looking up He saw him and said to him: "Zaccheus, make haste and come down, for this day I must abide in thy house." And he made haste and came down, and received Him with joy.

7. And when all saw it, they murmured, saying that He was gone to be a guest with a man that was a sinner. But Zaccheus standing, said to the Lord: "Behold, Lord, the half of my goods I give to the poor, and if I have wronged any man of anything, I restore him four-fold." Jesus said to him: "This day is salvation come to this house, because he also is a son of Abraham. For the

Son of Man is come to seek and to save that which was lost."

As they were hearing these things, He added [11.] and spoke a parable, because He was nigh to Jerusalem, and because they thought that the Kingdom of God should immediately be manifested. He said therefore: "A certain nobleman went into a far country to receive for himself a kingdom, and to return. And calling his ten servants, he gave them ten pounds, and said to them: 'Trade till I come.' But his citizens hated him, and they sent an embassage after him, saying: 'We will not have this man to reign over us.'

"And it came to pass that he returned, having [15.] received the kingdom, and he commanded his servants to be called to whom he had given the money, that he might know how much every man had gained by trading. And the first came, saying: 'Lord, thy pound hath gained ten pounds.' And he said to him: 'Well done, thou good servant; because thou hast been faithful in a little, thou shalt have power over ten cities.' And the second came, saying: 'Lord, thy pound hath gained five pounds.' And he said to him: 'Be thou also over five cities.'

"And another came, saying: 'Lord, behold [20.] here is thy pound, which I have kept laid up in a napkin; for I feared thee, because thou art an austere man; thou takest up what thou didst not lay down, and thou reapest that which thou didst not sow.' He saith to him: 'Out of thy own mouth I judge thee, thou wicked servant. Thou knewest that I was an austere man, taking up what I laid not down, and reaping that which I did not sow, and why then didst thou not give my money into the bank, that at my coming I might have exacted it with usury?' And he said to them that stood by: 'Take the pound away from him, and give it to him that hath ten pounds.' And they said to him: 'Lord, he hath ten pounds.' But I say to you, that to every one that hath shall be given, and he shall abound, and from him that hath not even that which he hath shall be taken from him. But as for those my enemies who would not have me reign over them, bring them hither and kill them before me."

28. And having said these things, He went before, going up to Jerusalem.

Matt. 20, 29—34. Mark 10, 46—52.

^{MK}And as He went out of Jericho with His disciples and a very great multitude, Bartimæus the blind man, the son of Timæus, sat by the wayside begging.[1] Who when he heard that it was Jesus of Nazareth, began to cry out and to say: "Jesus, Son of David, have mercy on me." And many rebuked him, that he might hold his peace; but he cried out a great deal the more: "Son of David, have mercy on me." And Jesus standing still, commanded him to be called. And they call the blind man, saying to him: "Be of better comfort; arise, He calleth thee." Who, casting off his garment, leaped up and came to Him. And Jesus answering, said to him: "What wilt thou that I should do to thee?" And the blind man said to Him: "Rabboni, that I may see." And Jesus saith to him: "Go thy way, thy faith hath made thee whole." And immediately he saw, and followed Him in the way.

John 11, 55, 56.

And the Pasch of the Jews was at hand; and

---

[1] St. Matthew speaks of *two* blind men sitting by the wayside as "they went *out* from Jericho." One of these may, or may not, be the blind man mentioned above by St. Luke as crying out to our Lord "as He drew nigh to Jericho."

PART IV.   TO THE FOURTH PASCH.   151

many from the country went up to Jerusalem before the Pasch to purify themselves. They sought therefore for Jesus, and they discoursed one with another standing in the Temple: "What think you, that He has not come to the festival-day?" And the chief priests and the Pharisees had given a commandment, that if any man knew where He was, he should tell, that they might apprehend Him.

Jesus therefore six days before the Pasch came to Bethania, where Lazarus had been dead, whom Jesus raised to life.   John 12, 1.

^{MK}And when He was in Bethania, in the house of Simon the leper, ... ^{JN}they made Him a supper there, and Martha served; but Lazarus was one of them that were at table with Him.   Matt. 26, 6—13.
Mark 14, 3—9.
John 12, 2—8.

Mary therefore, ^{MT}having an alabaster box, ^{JN}took a pound of ointment of right spikenard of great price, and anointed the feet of Jesus ^{MT}as He was at table, ^{JN}and wiped His feet with her hair, ^{MK}and breaking the alabaster box, she poured it out upon His Head, ^{JN}and the house was filled with the odour of the ointment.

Then one of His disciples, Judas Iscariot, he that was about to betray Him, said: "Why was not this ointment sold for three hundred pence, and given to the poor?" Now he said this, not because he cared for the poor, but because he was a thief, and having the purse, carried the things that were put therein.

^{MT}And the disciples seeing it, had indignation, saying: "To what purpose is this waste? For this might have been sold for much and given to the poor." ^{MK}And they murmured against her.

^{JN}Jesus therefore said: "Let her alone, that she may keep it against the day of My burial. ^{MK}Why

do you molest her? She hath wrought a good work upon Me. For the poor you have always with you, and whensoever you will you may do them good; but Me you have not always. What she had, she hath done; she is come beforehand to anoint My Body for the burial; ^{MT}for she, in pouring this ointment upon My Body, hath done it for My burial. Amen I say to you, wheresoever this Gospel shall be preached in the whole world, that also which she hath done shall be told for a memory of her."

John 12, 9—13.

A great multitude of the Jews knew that He was there, and they came, not for Jesus' sake only, but that they might see Lazarus, whom He had raised from the dead.[1] But the chief priests thought to kill Lazarus also, because many of the Jews, by reason of him, went away and believed in Jesus.

12.

And on the next day a great multitude that was come to the festival-day, when they had heard that Jesus was coming to Jerusalem, took branches of palm-trees, and went forth to meet Him and cried: "Hosanna, blessed is He that cometh in the name of the Lord, the King of Israel."

[John 12, 14.]
[Matt. 21, 1—3.
[Mark 11, 1—3.
[Luke 12, 29-31.

^{MT}And when they drew nigh to Jerusalem and were come ^{LK}to Bethfage and Bethania, unto the mount called Olivet, ^{MT}then Jesus sent two of His disciples, saying to them: "Go ye into the village that is over against you, and immediately you shall find an ass tied, and a colt with her, ^{LK}on which no man ever hath sitten; ^{MT}loose them and

---

[1] This need not be thought at variance with the raising of Lazarus several weeks earlier, if we suppose him, from motives of gratitude or prudence, to have gone with our Lord to Ephrem after his resuscitation (p. 115), and from there to have travelled with Him into and from Galilee, back to Bethania. Confer Greswell, Diss. xxxii.

bring them to Me. And if any man shall say anything to you, say ye that the Lord hath need of them, and forthwith he will let them go."

Now all this was done that it might be fulfilled which was spoken by the prophet, saying: *Tell ye the daughter of Sion: Behold thy King cometh to thee, meek and sitting on an ass, and a colt, the foal of her that is used to the yoke.* Matt. 21, 4, 5.

^{MT}And the disciples going, ^{LK}found the colt standing as He had said unto them, ^{MK}tied before the gate without, in the meeting of two ways, and they loose him. ^{LK}And as they were loosing the colt, the owners thereof said to them: "Why loose you the colt?" ^{MK}Who said to them as Jesus had commanded them: ^{LK}"Because the Lord hath need of him;" ^{MK}and they let him go with them. And they brought the colt to Jesus and they lay their garments upon him, and He sat upon him; ^{JN}as it is written: "Fear not, daughter of Sion; behold thy King cometh sitting on an ass's colt." Matt. 21, 6, 7. Mark 11, 4—7. Luke 19, 32—35.
John 12, 14—16.

These things the disciples did not know at the first; but when Jesus was glorified, then they remembered that these things were written of Him, and that they had done these things to Him.

^{MT}And a very great multitude spread their garments in the way, and others cut boughs from the trees, and strewed them in the way. Matt. 21, 8. Mark 11, 8. Luke 19, 36.

^{JN}The multitude therefore gave testimony, which was with Him when He called Lazarus out of the grave, and raised him from the dead. For which reason also the people came to meet Him, because they heard that He had done this miracle. John 12, 17, 18.

^{LK}And when He was now coming near the descent of Mount Olivet, the whole multitude of His disciples, ^{MK}they that went before and they Matt. 21, 9. Mark 11, 9, 10. Luke 19, 37, 38.

that followed, ᴸᴷbegan with joy to praise God with a loud voice for all the mighty works they had seen, saying: "Blessed be the King Who cometh in the name of the Lord, peace in Heaven, and glory on high! ᴹᵀHosanna to the Son of David! ᴹᴷBlessed be the Kingdom of our father David that cometh, Hosanna in the highest!"

Luke 19, 39—44.

And some of the Pharisees from amongst the multitude said to Him: "Master, rebuke Thy disciples." To whom He said: "I say to you, that if these shall hold their peace, the stones will cry out."

41. And when He drew near, seeing the city, He wept over it, saying: "If thou also hadst known and that, in this thy day, the things that are to thy peace! but now they are hidden from thy eyes. For the days shall come upon thee, and thy enemies shall cast a trench about thee, and compass thee round, and straiten thee on every side, and beat thee flat to the ground and thy children who are in thee; and they shall not leave in thee a stone upon a stone, because thou hast not known the time of thy visitation."

[Mark 11, 11.]
Matt. 21, 10, 11.
Matt. 21, 14-16.

ᴹᵀAnd when He was come into Jerusalem, the whole city was moved, saying: "Who is this?" And the people said: "This is Jesus the Prophet, from Nazareth of Galilee." And there came to Him the blind and the lame in the Temple, and He healed them. And the chief priests and scribes seeing the wonderful things that He did, and the children crying in the Temple, and saying: 'Hosanna to the Son of David,' were moved with indignation, and said to Him: "Hearest Thou what these say?" And Jesus said to them: "Yea, have you never read: *Out of the mouths of infants and sucklings Thou hast perfected praise?*"

The Pharisees therefore said among themselves: "Do you not see that we prevail nothing? Behold the whole world is gone after Him!" John 12, 19—36.

Now there were certain Gentiles among them who came up to adore on the festival-day. These therefore came to Philip, who was of Bethsaida of Galilee, and desired him, saying: "Sir, we would see Jesus." Philip cometh and telleth Andrew. Again Andrew and Philip told Jesus. But Jesus answered them, saying: "The hour is come that the Son of Man shall be glorified. Amen, amen I say to you, unless the grain of wheat, falling into the ground, die, itself remaineth alone. But if it die, it bringeth forth much fruit. He that loveth his life shall lose it, and he that hateth his life in this world, keepeth it unto life eternal. If any man minister to Me, let him follow Me, and where I am there also shall My minister be. If any man minister to Me, him will My Father honour. Now is My Soul troubled. And what shall I say? Father, save Me from this hour? But for this cause I came unto this hour. Father, glorify Thy name."

A voice therefore came from Heaven: "I have both glorified it, and will glorify it again." The multitude therefore that stood and heard, said that it thundered. Others said: "An angel spoke to Him."

Jesus answered: "This voice came not because of Me, but for your sakes. Now is the judgment of the world; now shall the prince of this world be cast out. And I, if I be lifted up from the earth, will draw all things to Myself." (Now this He said, signifying what death He should die.)

The multitude answered Him: "We have heard out of the law that Christ abideth for ever, and how sayest Thou, the Son of Man must be lifted up? Who is this Son of Man?" Jesus therefore said to them: "Yet a little while, the light is among you. Walk whilst you have the light, that the darkness overtake you not; and he that walketh in darkness knoweth not whither he goeth. Whilst you have the light believe in the light, that you may be the children of light." These things Jesus spoke, and He went away and hid Himself from them.

<small>Matt. 21, 17—19.
Mark 11, 11—14.</small>

^{MK}And having viewed all things round about, when now the even-tide was come, He went out to Bethania with the twelve, ^{MT}and remained there.

^{MT}And in the morning, returning into the city ^{MK}from Bethania, He was hungry. And when He had seen afar off a fig-tree having leaves, He came, if perhaps He might find something on it. And when He was come to it He found nothing but leaves, for it was not the time for figs. And answering, He said to it: "May no man hereafter eat fruit of thee any more for ever." And His disciples heard it. ^{MT}And immediately the fig-tree withered away.[1]

<small>Matt. 21, 12, 13.
Mark 11, 15—17.
Luke 19, 45, 46.</small>

^{MK}And they came to Jerusalem; and when He was entered into the Temple ^{MT}of God, ^{MK}He began to cast out them that sold and bought in the Temple, and overthrew the tables of the money-changers and the chairs of them that sold doves. And He suffered not that any man should carry a vessel through the Temple. And He taught, saying to them: "Is it not written: *My house*

---

[1] That is, *began* to wither away on their departure; thus making St. Matthew's next verse (p. 157) refer naturally to the events of the next morning, and correspond exactly with St. Mark's version of the story, as narrated by him, xi. 14, and xi. 20.

shall be called the house of prayer to all nations? but you have made it a den of thieves."

^{MK}Which when the chief priests and the scribes ^{LK}and the rulers of the people, ^{MK}had heard, they sought how they might destroy Him: for they feared Him because the whole multitude was in admiration at His doctrine, ^{LK}and they found not what to do to Him, for all the people were very attentive to hear Him. Mark 11, 18.
Luke 19, 47, 48.

And He was teaching daily in the Temple. Luke 19, 47.

And when evening was come, He went forth out of the city. Mark 11, 19.

^{MK}And when they passed by in the morning, they saw the fig-tree dried up from the roots. ^{MT}And the disciples seeing it, wondered; ^{MK}and Peter remembering, said to Him: "Rabbi, behold the fig-tree which Thou didst curse is withered away." Matt. 21, 20—22.
Mark 11, 20—24.

And Jesus answering, saith to them: "Have the faith of God. ^{MT}Amen I say to you, if you have faith, and stagger not, not only this of the fig-tree shall you do, but ^{MK}whosoever shall say to this mountain: 'Be thou removed and be cast into the sea,' and shall not stagger in his heart, but believe that whatsoever he saith shall be done, it shall be done unto him. Therefore I say unto you, all things whatsoever you ask when ye pray, believe that you shall receive, and they shall come unto you.

"And when you shall stand to pray, forgive, if you have aught against any man, that your Father also Who is in Heaven, may forgive you your sins. But if you will not forgive, neither will your Father that is in Heaven forgive you your sins." Mark 11, 25, 26.

^{MK}And they came again to Jerusalem. And when ^{LK}He was teaching the people in the Temple, Matt. 21, 23—27.
Mark 11, 27—33.
Luke 20, 1—8.

and preaching the Gospel, the chief priests and the scribes with the ancients met together and spoke to Him, saying: "Tell us by what authority dost Thou these things, or who is he that hath given Thee this authority?"

24. ᴹᵀJesus answering, said to them: "I also will ask you one word, which if you shall tell Me, I will also tell you by what authority I do these things. The baptism of John, whence was it? from Heaven or from men?" But they thought within themselves, saying: "If we shall say from Heaven, He will say to us: 'Why then did you not believe him?' But if we shall say from men, we are afraid of the multitude," for all held John as a prophet. And answering Jesus, they said: "We know not." He also said to them: "Neither do I tell you by what authority I do these things.

Matt. 21, 28—32.

"But what think you? A certain man had two sons, and coming to the first, he said: 'Son, go work to-day in my vineyard.' And he answering, said: 'I will not.' But afterwards, being moved with repentance, he went. And coming to the other, he said in like manner. And he answering said: 'I go, sir,' and he went not. Which of the two did the father's will?" They say to Him: "The first." Jesus saith to them: "Amen I say to you, that the publicans and the harlots shall go into the Kingdom of God before you. For John came to you in the way of justice, and you did not believe him; but the publicans and the harlots believed him. But you seeing it, did not even afterwards repent, that you might believe him.

Matt. 21, 33—46.
Mark 12, 1—12.
Luke 20, 9—19.

ᴹᵀ"Hear ye another parable. There was a man, an householder, who planted a vineyard and made a hedge round about it, and dug in it a press, and built a tower, and let it out to husbandmen, and went into a strange country. And when the time of the fruits drew nigh, ᴹᴷhe sent to the husbandmen a servant, to receive of the husbandmen of the fruit of the vineyard. Who having laid hands on him, beat him and sent him away empty.

"And again he sent to them another servant, and him they wounded in the head and used him reproachfully. And again he sent another, and him they killed, and many others, of whom some they beat, and others they killed.

ᴸᴷ"Then the lord of the vineyard said: 'What shall I do?' ᴹᴷHaving therefore yet one son most dear to him, he also sent him unto them last of all, saying: ᴸᴷ'I will send my beloved son; it may be, when they see him, they will reverence him.'

"Whom when the husbandmen saw, they thought within themselves, [and] ᴹᴷsaid one to another: ᴹᵀ'This is the heir; come, let us kill him, and we shall have his inheritance.' And taking him, they cast him forth out of the vineyard and killed him.

"When therefore the lord of the vineyard shall come, what shall he do to these husbandmen? ᴸᴷHe will come and will destroy those husbandmen, and will give the vineyard to others." Which they hearing, said to Him: "God forbid." But He looking on them, said: ᴹᵀ"Have you never read in the Scriptures: *The stone which the builders rejected, the same is become the head of the corner. By the Lord this has been done, and it is wonderful in our eyes.* Therefore I say to you, the Kingdom of God shall be taken from you and shall be given to a nation yielding the fruits thereof. And whosoever shall fall on this stone shall be broken; but on whomsoever it shall fall it shall grind him to powder."

And when the chief priests and Pharisees had

heard His parables, they knew that He spoke of them. And seeking to lay hands on Him they feared the multitudes, because they held Him as a prophet.

Matt. 22, 1—14.

And Jesus answering, spoke again in parables to them, saying: "The Kingdom of Heaven is likened to a King, who made a marriage for his son. And he sent his servants to call them that were invited to the marriage, and they would not come. Again he sent other servants, saying: 'Tell them that were invited, behold I have prepared my dinner; my beeves and fatlings are killed, and all things are ready; come ye to the marriage.' But they neglected and went their ways, one to his farm, and another to his merchandise. And the rest laid hands on his servants, and having treated them contumeliously, put them to death. But when the King had heard of it, he was angry, and sending his armies he destroyed those murderers and burnt their city.

8. "Then saith he to his servants: 'The marriage indeed is ready, but they that were invited were not worthy. Go ye therefore into the highways, and as many as you shall find, call them to the marriage.' And his servants going forth into the ways, gathered together all that they found, both bad and good, and the marriage was filled with guests. And the King went in to see the guests, and he saw there a man who had not on a wedding garment. And he saith to him: 'Friend, how camest thou in hither, not having on a wedding garment?' But he was silent. Then the King said to the waiters: 'Bind his hands and feet, and cast him into the exterior darkness; there shall be weeping and gnashing of teeth.' For many are called, but few are chosen."

PART IV.   TO THE FOURTH PASCH.   161

^{MT}Then the Pharisees going, consulted among themselves how to ensnare Him in His speech. And they sent to Him their disciples with the Herodians, ^{LK}spies who should feign themselves just, that they might take hold of Him in His words, that they might deliver Him up to the authority and power of the governor. And they asked Him, saying: "Master, we know that Thou speakest and teachest rightly, ^{MK}and carest not for any man, for Thou regardest not the person of men, but teachest the way of God in truth. ^{MT}Tell us therefore what dost Thou think? ^{LK}Is it lawful for us to give tribute to Cæsar or not?"

^{MT}But Jesus, knowing their wickedness, said: "Why do you tempt Me, ye hypocrites? Show Me the coin of the tribute;" and they offered Him a penny. And Jesus saith to them: "Whose image and inscription is this?" They say to Him: "Cæsar's." Then He saith to them: "Render therefore to Cæsar the things that are Cæsar's, and to God the things that are God's." ^{LK}And they could not reprehend His word before the people and wondering at His answer they held their peace, ^{MT}and leaving Him, went their ways.

^{MK}And there came to Him ^{MT}that day ^{MK}the Sadducees, who say there is no resurrection, and they asked Him, saying: "Master, Moses wrote unto us that if any man's brother die and leave his wife behind him, and leave no children, his brother shall take his wife and raise up seed to his brother.

"Now there were seven brethren, and the first took a wife, and died leaving no issue. And the second took her, and died, and neither did he leave any issue. And the third in like manner. And the seven all took her in like manner and did not leave issue. Last of all the woman died.

L

"In the resurrection, therefore, when they shall rise again, whose wife shall she be of them? for the seven had her to wife." And Jesus answering saith to them: "Do ye not therefore err because you know not the Scriptures, nor the power of God? For when they shall rise again from the dead, they shall neither marry, nor be married, but are as the angels in Heaven.

ᴸᴷ"The children of this world marry, and are given in marriage, but they that shall be accounted worthy of that world, and of the resurrection from the dead, shall neither be married nor take wives. Neither can they die any more, for they are equal to the angels, and are the children of God, being the children of the resurrection.

ᴹᴷ"And as concerning the dead that they rise again, have you not read in the book of Moses, how in the bush God spoke to him, saying: 'I am the God of Abraham, and the God of Isaac, and the God of Jacob'? He is not the God of the dead, but of the living. You therefore do greatly err."

Matt. 22, 33.
Luke 20, 39, 40.

And the multitude hearing it were in admiration at His doctrine.

And some of the Scribes answering said to Him: "Master, Thou hast said well." And after that they [the Sadducees] durst not ask Him any more questions.

Matt. 22, 34—40.
Mark 12, 28—31.

ᴹᵀBut the Pharisees, hearing that He had silenced the Sadducees, came together. And one of them, a doctor of the law, ᴹᴷthat had heard them reasoning together, and seeing that He had answered them well, asked Him, ᴹᵀtempting Him: "Master, which is the great commandment of the law?" ᴹᴷAnd Jesus answered him: "The first commandment of all is: Hear, O Israel, the Lord thy God is one God; and thou shalt love the Lord thy God with thy whole heart, and with thy whole soul, and with thy whole mind, and with thy whole strength. This is ^{MT}the greatest and ^{MK}the first commandment. And the second is like to it: Thou shalt love thy neighbour as thyself. There is no other commandment greater than these; ^{MT}on these two commandments dependeth the whole law and the prophets."

And the Scribe said to Him: "Well, Master, Thou hast said in truth that there is one God, and there is no other besides Him. And that He should be loved with the whole heart, and with the whole understanding, and with the whole soul, and with the whole strength, and to love one's neighbour as oneself, is a greater thing than all holocausts and sacrifices." And Jesus, seeing that he had answered wisely, said to him: "Thou art not far from the Kingdom of God." And no man after that durst ask Him any question.

Mark 12, 32—34.

^{MT}And the Pharisees being gathered together, Jesus asked them, saying: "What think you of Christ? Whose Son is He?" They say to Him: "David's." He saith to them: "How then doth David in spirit, ^{LK}in the Book of Psalms, ^{MT}call Him Lord? saying ^{MK}by the Holy Ghost: ^{MT}*The Lord said to my Lord: Sit on My right hand, until I make Thy enemies Thy footstool.* If David then called Him Lord, how is He his son?" And no man was able to answer Him a word, neither durst any man from that day forth ask Him any more questions; ^{MK}and a great multitude heard Him gladly.

Matt. 22, 41—46.
Mark 12, 35—37.
Luke 20, 41—44.

^{MT}Then Jesus spoke to the multitudes and to His disciples, saying ^{MK}in His doctrine, ^{LK}and in the hearing of all the people: "The Scribes and Pharisees have sitten on the chair of Moses; all things therefore whatsoever they shall say to you

Matt. 23, 1.
Mark 12, 38.
Luke 20, 45.
Matt. 23, 2—5.

observe and do, but according to their works do ye not; for they say and do not. For they bind heavy and insupportable burdens, and lay them on men's shoulders, but with a finger of their own they will not move them. And all their works they do for to be seen of men; for they make their phylacteries broad and enlarge their fringes.

<small>Matt. 23, 6, 7.
Mark 12, 38—40.
Luke 22, 46, 47.</small>

^{LK}"Beware of the Scribes who desire to walk in long robes, and love salutations in the market-place and the first chairs in the synagogues, and the chief rooms at feasts, ^{MT}and to be called by men Rabbi; ^{LK}who devour the houses of widows, feigning long prayers. These shall receive greater damnation.

<small>Matt. 23, 8—39.</small>

"But be not you called Rabbi, for One is your Master, and all you are brethren. And call none your father upon earth, for One is your Father, Who is in Heaven. Neither be ye called masters, for One is your Master, Christ. He that is the greatest among you shall be your servant, and whosoever shall exalt himself shall be humbled, and he that shall humble himself shall be exalted.

13. "But wo to you, Scribes and Pharisees, hypocrites! because you shut the Kingdom of Heaven against men; for you yourselves do not enter in, and those who are going in you suffer not to enter.

14. "Wo to you, Scribes and Pharisees, hypocrites! because you devour the houses of widows, praying long prayers; for this you shall receive the greater judgment.

15. "Wo to you, Scribes and Pharisees, hypocrites! because you go round about the sea and the land to make one proselyte, and when he is made, you make him the child of Hell two-fold more than yourselves.

16. "Wo to you, blind guides! that say: Whosoever

shall swear by the Temple, it is nothing; but he that shall swear by the gold of the Temple is a debtor. Ye foolish and blind, for whether is greater, the gold, or the Temple that sanctifieth the gold? And whosoever shall swear by the altar it is nothing; but whosoever shall swear by the gift that is upon the altar, is a debtor. Ye blind! for whether is greater, the gift or the altar that sanctifieth the gift? He therefore that sweareth by the altar, sweareth by it and by all things that are upon it. And whosoever shall swear by the Temple, sweareth by it and by Him that dwelleth in it. And he that sweareth by Heaven, sweareth by the throne of God, and by Him that sitteth thereon.

"Wo to you, Scribes and Pharisees! because 23. you tithe mint, and anise, and cummin, and have left the weightier things of the law, judgment and mercy and faith. These things you ought to have done, and not leave those undone. Blind guides, who strain out a gnat and swallow a camel.

"Wo to you, Scribes and Pharisees, hypocrites! 25. because you make clean the outside of the cup and of the dish, but within you are full of rapine and uncleanness. Thou blind Pharisee, first make clean the inside of the cup and of the dish, that the outside may become clean.

"Wo to you, Scribes and Pharisees, hypocrites! 27. because you are like to whited sepulchres, which outwardly appear to men beautiful, but within are full of dead men's bones and of all filthiness. So you also outwardly indeed appear to men just, but inwardly you are full of hypocrisy and iniquity.

"Wo to you, Scribes and Pharisees, hypocrites! 29. that build the sepulchres of the prophets, and adorn the monuments of the just, and say: 'If we had been in the days of our fathers, we would not have been partakers with them in the blood of the prophets.' Wherefore you are witnesses against yourselves, that you are the sons of them that killed the prophets.

32. "Fill ye up then the measure of your fathers. You serpents, generation of vipers, how will you flee from the judgment of Hell? Therefore behold I send to you prophets and wise men and scribes, and some of them you will put to death and crucify, and some you will scourge in your synagogues, and persecute from city to city, that upon you may come all the just blood that hath been shed upon the earth, from the blood of Abel the just, even unto the blood of Zacharias the son of Barachias, whom you killed between the Temple and the altar. Amen, I say to you, all these things shall come upon this generation.

37. "Jerusalem! Jerusalem! thou that killest the prophets, and stonest them that are sent unto thee; how often would I have gathered together thy children, as the hen doth gather her chickens under her wings, and thou wouldst not. Behold your house shall be left to you desolate. For I say to you you shall not see Me henceforth till you say: 'Blessed is He that cometh in the name of the Lord.'"

Mark 12, 41—44.
Luke 21, 1—4.

^MK^And Jesus, sitting over against the treasury, beheld how the people cast money into the treasury, and many that were rich cast in much. And there came a certain poor widow, and she cast in two mites, which make a farthing. And calling His disciples together He saith to them: "Amen, I say to you, this poor widow hath cast in more than all they who have cast into the treasury. For all they did cast in of their abundance, but she of her want cast in all she had, even her whole living."

And in the daytime He was teaching in the Temple, but at night, going out, He abode in the mount that is called Olivet. And all the people came early in the morning to Him in the Temple to hear Him. Luke 21, 37, 38.

And whereas He had done so many miracles before them, they believed not in Him, that the saying of Isaias the Prophet might be fulfilled which he said: *Lord, who hath believed our hearing? and to whom hath the arm of the Lord been revealed?* Therefore they could not believe, because Isaias said again: *He hath blinded their eyes, and hardened their heart, that they should not see with their eyes, nor understand with their heart, and be converted and I should heal them.* These things said Isaias when he saw His glory and spoke of Him. John 12, 37—50.

However, many of the chief men also believed in Him, but because of the Pharisees they did not confess Him, that they might not be cast out of the synagogue. For they loved the glory of men more than the glory of God. 42.

But Jesus cried and said: "He that believeth in Me, doth not believe in Me but in Him that sent Me. And he that seeth Me, seeth Him that sent Me. I am come a light into the world, that whosoever believeth in Me may not remain in darkness. And if any man hear My words and keep them not, I do not judge Him, for I came not to judge the world but to save the world. He that despiseth Me and receiveth not My words, hath one that judgeth Him; the word that I have spoken, the same shall judge him in the last day. For I have not spoken of Myself, but the Father 44.

Who sent Me, He gave Me commandment what I should say, and what I should speak. And I know that His commandment is life everlasting. The things therefore that I speak, even as the Father said unto Me, so do I speak."

^{MK}And as He was going out of the Temple, one of His disciples saith to Him: "Master, behold what manner of stones and what buildings are here." And Jesus answering saith to him: "Seest thou all these great buildings? ^{LK}The days will come in which there shall not be left a stone upon a stone that shall not be thrown down."

^{MK}And as He sat on the Mount of Olivet over against the Temple, Peter and James and John and Andrew asked Him apart: "Tell us, when shall these things be? and what shall be the sign when all these things shall begin to be fulfilled? ^{MT}And what shall be the sign of Thy coming, and of the consummation of the world?"

^{MT}And Jesus answering said to them: "Take heed that no man seduce you. For many will come in My Name saying: 'I am Christ;' ^{MK}and they will deceive many, ^{LK}saying: 'I am He, and the time is at hand;' go ye not after them. And when you shall hear of wars ^{MT}and rumours of wars, ^{LK}and seditions, be not terrified; these things must first come to pass, but the end is not yet."

Then He said to them: "Nation shall rise against nation, and kingdom against kingdom. And there shall be great earthquakes in diverse places, and pestilences and famines and terrors from Heaven, and there shall be great signs; ^{MK}these things are the beginning of sorrows.

^{MK}" But look to yourselves; for ^{LK}before all these things they will lay their hands on you, and perse-

cute you, delivering you up to the synagogues and into prisons, dragging you before kings and governors for My name's sake. And it shall happen unto you for a testimony.

"Then shall they deliver you up to be afflicted, and shall put you to death, and you shall be hated by all nations for My name's sake. And then shall many be scandalized and shall betray one another. And many false prophets shall rise, and shall seduce many. And because iniquity hath abounded, the charity of many shall grow cold. But he that shall persevere to the end, he shall be saved. ^{MT}"And this Gospel of the Kingdom shall be preached in the whole world for a testimony to all nations, and then shall the consummation come. ^{MK}"And when they shall lead you and deliver you up, be not thoughtful beforehand what you shall speak, but whatsoever shall be given you in that hour, that speak ye. For it is not you that speak, but the Holy Ghost. ^{LK}For I will give you a mouth and wisdom, which all your adversaries shall not be able to resist and gainsay. And you shall be betrayed by your parents and brethren and kinsmen and friends, and some of you they will put to death. ^{MK}And the brother shall betray the brother unto death, and the father the son, and children shall rise up against the parents and shall work their death. And you shall be hated by all men for My name's sake, ^{LK}but a hair of your head shall not perish. In your patience you shall possess your souls; ^{MK}but he that shall endure unto the end he shall be saved.

^{MT}"When therefore you shall see the abomination of desolation which was spoken of by Daniel the Prophet, standing in the holy place (he that readeth, let him understand), ^{LK}and when

Matt. 24, 9—13.

Matt. 24, 14.
Mark 13, 10.

Mark 13, 11—13.
Luke 21, 14—19.

Matt. 24, 15—18.
Mark 13, 14—16.
Luke 21, 20, 21.

you shall see Jerusalem compassed about with an army, then know that the desolation thereof is at hand. Then let those who are in Judea flee to the mountains, and those who are in the midst thereof depart out, and those who are in the countries not enter into it; ᴹᵀand he that is on the housetop, let him not come down to take anything out of his house; and he that is in the field, let him not go back to take his coat.

Luke 21, 22.

"For these are the days of vengeance, that all things may be fulfilled that are written.

Matt. 24, 19.
Mark 13, 17.
Luke 21, 23.

ᴸᴷ"But wo to them that are with child, and give suck in those days, for there shall be great distress in the land, and wrath upon this people.

Luke 21, 24.

"And they shall fall by the edge of the sword, and shall be led away captives into all nations; and Jerusalem shall be trodden down by the Gentiles, till the times of the nations be fulfilled.

Matt. 24, 20—25.
Mark 13, 18—23.

ᴹᵀ"But pray that your flight be not in the winter, or on the Sabbath; for there shall be then great tribulation, such as hath not been from the beginning of the world until now, neither shall be. And unless those days had been shortened, no flesh should be saved; but for the sake of the elect those days shall be shortened.

ᴹᵀ"Then if any man shall say to you: 'Lo, here is Christ,' or 'there,' do not believe him. For there shall arise false Christs and false prophets, and shall show great signs and wonders, insomuch as to deceive (if possible) even the elect. Behold I have told it you beforehand.

Matt. 24, 26—28.

"If therefore they shall say to you: 'Behold He is in the desert,' go ye not out; 'Behold He is in the closets,' believe it not. For as lightning cometh out of the east and appeareth even into the west, so shall also the coming of the Son of Man be.

Wheresoever the body shall be, there shall the eagles also be gathered together.

^{MT}"And immediately after the tribulation of those days the sun shall be darkened, and the moon shall not give her light, and the stars shall fall from heaven, and the powers of heaven shall be moved, ^{LK}and upon the earth [shall be] distress of nations, by reason of the confusion of the roaring of the sea and of the waves, men withering away with fear and expectation of what shall come upon the whole world.

^{MT}"And then shall appear the sign of the Son of Man in heaven, and then shall all tribes of the earth mourn, and they shall see the Son of Man coming in the clouds of heaven with much power and majesty. And He shall send His Angels with a trumpet and a great voice; and they shall gather together His elect from the four winds, from the farthest parts of the heavens to the utmost bounds of them.

"But when these things begin to come to pass, look up and lift up your heads, because your redemption is at hand."

^{LK}And He spoke to them a similitude: "See the fig-tree, and all the trees, when they now shoot forth their fruit you know that summer is nigh; so you also when you shall see these things come to pass, know that the Kingdom of God is at hand. ^{MK}Amen, I say to you, that this generation shall not pass away till all these things be done. Heaven and earth shall pass away, but My words shall not pass away.

"And take heed to yourselves lest perhaps your hearts be overcharged with surfeiting and drunkenness and the cares of this life, and that day come upon you suddenly. For as a snare shall it come upon all that sit upon the face of the whole earth. Watch ye therefore, praying at all times that you may be accounted worthy to escape all these things that are to come, and to stand before the Son of Man.

Matt. 24, 36.
Mark 13, 32.

^{MK}"But of that day or hour no man knoweth, neither the angels in Heaven, nor the Son, but the Father ^{MT}alone.

Matt. 24, 37—44.

"And as in the days of Noe so shall also the coming of the Son of Man be. For as in the days before the Flood they were eating and drinking, marrying and giving in marriage, even till that day in which Noe entered into the ark; and they knew not till the Flood came and took them all away; so also shall the coming of the Son of Man be. Then two shall be in the field; one shall be taken and one shall be left. Two women shall be grinding at the mill; one shall be taken, the other shall be left. Watch ye therefore, because you know not what hour your Lord will come. But this know ye, that if the good man of the house knew at what hour the thief would come, he would certainly watch, and would not suffer his house to be broken open. Wherefore be you also ready, because at what hour you know not the Son of Man will come.

Mark 13, 33—37.

"Take ye heed, watch and pray, for ye know not when the time is, even as a man who, going into a far country, left his house and gave authority to his servants over every work, and commanded the porter to watch. Watch ye therefore (for you know not when the lord of the house cometh, at even, or at midnight, or at the cockcrowing, or in the morning); lest coming on a sudden he find you sleeping. And what I say to you I say to all: Watch.

"Who, thinkest thou, is a faithful and wise servant, whom his lord hath appointed over his family, to give them meat in season? Blessed is that servant whom, when his lord shall come, he shall find so doing. Amen, I say to you, he shall place him over all his goods. But if that evil servant shall say in his heart: 'My lord is long a-coming,' and shall begin to strike his fellow-servants, and shall eat and drink with drunkards, the lord of that servant shall come in a day that he hopeth not, and at an hour that he knoweth not, and shall separate him, and appoint his portion with the hypocrites. There shall be weeping and gnashing of teeth. *Matt. 24, 45—51.*

"Then shall the Kingdom of Heaven be like to ten virgins, who, taking their lamps, went out to meet the bridegroom and the bride. And five of them were foolish and five wise. But the five foolish having taken their lamps, did not take oil with them, but the wise took oil in their vessels with the lamps. And the bridegroom tarrying, they all slumbered and slept. *Matt. 25, 1—46.*

"And at midnight there was a cry made: 'Behold the bridegroom cometh, go ye forth to meet him.' Then all those virgins rose and trimmed their lamps. And the foolish said to the wise: 'Give us of your oil, for our lamps are gone out.' The wise answered, saying: 'Lest perhaps there be not enough for us and for you, go ye rather to them that sell, and buy for yourselves.' *6.*

"Now whilst they went to buy, the bridegroom came, and they that were ready went in with him to the marriage, and the door was shut. But at last came also the other virgins, saying: 'Lord, lord, open to us.' But he answering said: 'Amen, I say to you, I know you not.' *10.*

13. "Watch ye therefore, because you know not the day nor the hour. For even as a man going into a far country called his servants and delivered to them his goods. And to one he gave five talents, and to another two, and to another one, to every one according to his proper ability, and immediately he took his journey.

16. "And he that had received the five talents, went his way and traded with the same, and gained other five. And in like manner he that had received the two, gained other two. But he that had received the one, going his way digged into the earth and hid his lord's money.

19. "But after a long time the lord of those servants came and reckoned with them. And he that had received the five talents, coming brought other five talents, saying: 'Lord, thou didst deliver to me five talents, behold I have gained other five over and above.' His lord said to him: 'Well done, good and faithful servant! because thou hast been faithful over a few things, I will place thee over many things, enter thou into the joy of thy lord.' And he also that had received the two talents came and said: 'Lord, thou deliveredst two talents to me, behold I have gained other two.' His lord said to him: 'Well done, good and faithful servant! because thou hast been faithful over a few things I will place thee over many things, enter thou into the joy of thy lord.'

24. "But he that had received the one talent came and said: 'Lord, I know that thou art a hard man; thou reapest where thou hast not sown and gatherest where thou hast not strewed; and being afraid I went and hid thy talent in the earth, behold here thou hast that which is thine.' And his lord answering, said to him: 'Wicked and

slothful servant, thou knewest that I reap where I sow not, and gather where I have not strewed! Thou oughtest therefore to have committed my money to the bankers, and at my coming I should have received my own with usury. Take ye away therefore the talent from him and give it him that hath ten talents. For to every one that hath shall be given, and he shall abound, but from him that hath not, that also which he seemeth to have shall be taken away. And the unprofitable servant cast ye out into the exterior darkness; there shall be weeping and gnashing of teeth.'

"And when the Son of Man shall come in His 31. majesty, and all the Angels with Him, then shall He sit upon the seat of His majesty, and all nations shall be gathered together before Him, and He shall separate them one from another, as the shepherd separateth the sheep from the goats, and He shall set the sheep on His right hand, but the goats on His left.

"Then shall the King say to them that shall be 34. on His right hand: 'Come, ye blessed of My Father, possess you the Kingdom prepared for you from the foundation of the world. For I was hungry, and you gave Me to eat; I was thirsty, and you gave Me to drink; I was a stranger, and you took Me in; naked, and you covered Me; sick, and you visited Me; I was in prison, and you came to Me.'

"Then shall the just answer Him, saying: 37. 'Lord, when did we see Thee hungry, and fed Thee? thirsty, and gave Thee drink? And when did we see Thee a stranger, and took Thee in? or naked, and covered Thee? Or when did we see Thee sick or in prison, and came to Thee?' And the King answering shall say to them: 'Amen,

I say to you, as long as you did it to one of these My least brethren, you did it to Me.'

41. "Then He shall say to them also that shall be on His left hand: 'Depart from Me, you cursed, into everlasting fire, which was prepared for the devil and his angels. For I was hungry and you gave Me not to eat; I was thirsty, and you gave Me not to drink; I was a stranger, and you took Me not in; naked, and you covered Me not; sick and in prison, and you did not visit Me.'

44. "Then they also shall answer Him, saying: 'Lord, when did we see Thee hungry or thirsty or a stranger, or naked or sick or in prison, and did not minister to Thee?' Then He shall answer them, saying: 'Amen, I say to you, as long as you did it not to one of these least, neither did you do it to Me.' And these shall go into everlasting punishment, but the just into life everlasting."

Mark 14, 1.
Luke 22, 1.

^{LK}Now the feast of unleavened bread, which is called the Pasch, was at hand.

Matt. 26, 1, 2.

And it came to pass, when Jesus had ended all these words, He said to His disciples: "You know that after two days shall be the Pasch, and the Son of Man shall be delivered up to be crucified."

Matt. 26, 3—5.
Matt. 26, 14—16.
Mark 14, 1, 2.
Mark 14, 10, 11.
Luke 22, 2—6.

Then were gathered together the chief priests and the ancients of the people into the court of the High Priest, who was called Caiphas, and they consulted together that by subtilty they might apprehend Jesus and put Him to death. But they said: "Not on the festival-day, lest perhaps there should be a tumult among the people."

^{LK}And Satan entered into Judas, who was surnamed Iscariot, one of the Twelve. And he went and discoursed with the chief priests and the magistrates how he might betray Him to them;

^{MT}and [he] said to them: "What will you give me, and I will deliver Him to you?" ^{LK}And they were glad, and covenanted to give him ^{MT}thirty pieces of silver. ^{LK}And he promised. ^{MT}And from henceforth he sought opportunity to betray Him, ^{LK}in the absence of the multitude.

^{JN}Before the festival-day of the Pasch, Jesus, knowing that His hour was come, that He should pass out of this world to the Father, having loved His own who were in the world, He loved them to the end. *John 13, 1.*

^{LK}And the ^{MK}first ^{LK}day of the unleavened bread came, on which it was necessary that the pasch should be killed. And He sent Peter and John, saying: "Go and prepare for us the pasch that we may eat." But they said: "Where wilt Thou that we prepare?" But He said to them: "Behold, as you go into the city there shall meet you a man carrying a pitcher of water; follow him into the house where he entereth in. And you shall say to the good man of the house: 'The Master saith to thee, Where is the guest-chamber, where I may eat the pasch with My disciples?' And he will show you a large dining-room furnished, and there prepare." *Matt. 26, 17—20. Mark 14, 12—17. Luke 22, 7—14.*

^{MK}And the disciples went their way, and came into the city, and they found as He had told them, and they prepared the pasch. And when evening was come, ^{LK}He sat down, and the twelve Apostles with Him.

And He said to them: "With desire I have desired to eat this pasch with you before I suffer. For I say to you, that from this time I will not eat it till it be fulfilled in the Kingdom of God." And having taken the chalice, He gave thanks and *Luke 22, 15—18.*

said: "Take and divide it among you. For I say to you that I will not drink of the fruit of the vine till the Kingdom of God come."

John 13, 2—20. And when supper was done (the devil having now put into the heart of Judas Iscariot, the son of Simon, to betray Him), knowing that the Father had given Him all things into His hands, and that He came from God, and goeth to God, He riseth from supper, and layeth aside His garments, and having taken a towel, girded Himself. After that, He putteth water into a basin, and began to wash the feet of His disciples, and to wipe them with the towel wherewith He was girded.

6. He cometh therefore to Simon Peter, and Peter said to Him: "Lord, dost Thou wash my feet?" Jesus answered and said to him: "What I do thou knowest not now, but thou shalt know hereafter." Peter saith to Him: "Thou shalt never wash my feet." Jesus answered him: "If I wash thee not, thou shalt have no part with Me." Simon Peter saith to Him: "Lord, not only my feet, but also my hands and my head." Jesus saith to him: "He that is washed, needeth not but to wash his feet, but is clean wholly. And you are clean, but not all." For He knew who he was that would betray Him; therefore He said: "You are not all clean."

12. Then, after He had washed their feet and taken His garments, being sat down again, He said to them: "Know you what I have done to you? You call Me Master and Lord, and you say well, for so I am. If then I, being your Lord and Master, have washed your feet, you also ought to wash one another's feet. For I have given you an example, that as I have done to you, so you do also. Amen, amen, I say to you, the servant is not

greater than his lord, neither is the Apostle greater than He that sent him. If you know these things, you shall be blessed if you do them.

"I speak not of you all; I know whom I have chosen. But that the Scripture may be fulfilled: *He that eateth bread with Me shall lift up his heel against Me.* At present I tell you before it come to pass, that when it shall come to pass you may believe that I am He. Amen, amen, I say to you, he that receiveth whomsoever I send, receiveth Me; and he that receiveth Me, receiveth Him that sent Me."

[JN]When Jesus had said these things He was troubled in spirit, [MT]and whilst they were eating He said: "Amen, I say to you, that one of you is about to betray Me."

[JN]The disciples therefore looked one upon another, doubting of whom He spoke; [MT]and they being very much troubled, began every one to say: "Is it I, Lord?" But He answering, said: [LK]"Behold, the hand of him that betrayeth Me, is with Me on the table—[MK]one of the Twelve who dippeth with Me his hand in the dish, [MT]he shall betray Me. The Son of Man indeed goeth, as it is written of Him, but wo to that man by whom the Son of Man shall be betrayed; it were better for him, if that man had not been born."

And Judas that betrayed Him, answering, said: "Is it I, Rabbi?" He saith to him: "Thou hast said it."[1]

Now there was leaning on Jesus' bosom, one of His disciples whom Jesus loved. Simon Peter therefore beckoned to him and said to him: "Who is it of whom He speaketh?" He therefore,

---
[1] The context implies that Judas, who is thought to have been on one side of Jesus, asked about himself in a whisper.

leaning on the breast of Jesus, saith to Him: "Lord, who is it?" Jesus answered: "He it is to whom I shall reach bread dipped." And when He had dipped the bread, He gave it to Judas Iscariot, the son of Simon.

27. And after the morsel, Satan entered into him. And Jesus said to him: "That which thou dost do quickly." Now no man at the table knew to what purpose He said this unto him. For some thought, because Judas had the purse, that Jesus had said to him, "Buy those things which we have need of for the festival-day," or that he should give something to the poor.

30. He therefore having received the morsel, went out immediately. And it was night.

31. When he therefore was gone out, Jesus said: "Now is the Son of Man glorified, and God is glorified in Him. If God be glorified in Him, God also will glorify Him in Himself; and immediately will He glorify Him. Little children, yet a little while I am with you. You shall seek Me, and, as I said to the Jews: 'Whither I go, you cannot come,' so I say to you now. A new commandment I give unto you, that you love one another; as I have loved you that you also love one another. By this shall all men know that you are My disciples, if you have love one for another." Simon Peter saith to Him: "Lord, whither goest Thou?" Jesus answered: "Whither I go thou canst not follow Me now, but thou shalt follow hereafter." Peter saith to Him: "Why cannot I follow Thee now? I will lay down my life for Thee." Jesus answered Him: "Wilt thou lay down thy life for Me? Amen, amen, I say to thee, the cock shall not crow till thou deny Me thrice."

Luke 22, 24—38. And there was also a strife amongst them, which of them should seem to be greater; and He said to them: "The Kings of the Gentiles lord it over them, and they, that have power over them, are called beneficent. But you not so, but he that is the greater among you, let him become as the younger; and he that is the leader as he that serveth. For which is greater, he that sitteth at table or he that serveth? Is not he that sitteth at table? But I am in the midst of you as he that serveth.

"And you are they who have continued with Me in My temptations, and I dispose to you, as My Father hath disposed to Me, a Kingdom, that you may eat and drink at My table in My Kingdom, and may sit upon thrones, judging the twelve tribes of Israel."

And the Lord said: "Simon, Simon, behold Satan hath desired to have you, that he may sift you as wheat, but I have prayed for thee, that thy faith fail not, and thou being once converted confirm thy brethren." Who said to Him: "Lord, I am ready to go with Thee both into prison and to death." And He said: "I say to thee, Peter, the cock shall not crow this day till thou thrice deniest that thou knowest Me."

And He said to them: "When I sent you without purse and scrip and shoes, did you want anything?" But they said: "Nothing." Then said He unto them: "But now he that hath a purse let him take it, and likewise a scrip; and he that hath not, let him sell his coat, and buy a sword. For I say to you, that this that is written must yet be fulfilled in Me: *And with the wicked was He reckoned.* For the things concerning Me have an end." But they said: "Lord, behold here are two swords." And He said to them: "It is enough."

John 14, 1—31. "Let not your heart be troubled. You believe in God, believe also in Me. In My Father's house there are many mansions. If not, I would have told you that I go to prepare a place for you. And if I shall go and prepare a place for you, I will come again, and will take you to Myself, that where I am you also may be. And whither I go you know, and the way you know."

5. Thomas saith to Him: "Lord, we know not whither Thou goest, and how can we know the way?"

6. Jesus saith to him: "I am the Way, and the Truth, and the Life. No man cometh to the Father but by Me. If you had known Me, you would without doubt have known My Father also, and from henceforth you shall know Him, and you have seen Him."

8. Philip saith to Him: "Lord, show us the Father, and it is enough for us."

9. Jesus saith to him: "So long a time have I been with you, and have you not known Me? Philip, he that seeth Me, seeth the Father also. How sayest thou: 'Show us the Father'? Do you not believe that I am in the Father, and the Father in Me? The words that I speak to you, I speak not of Myself. But the Father Who abideth in Me, He doth the works. Believe you not that I am in

12. the Father, and the Father in Me? Otherwise believe for the very works' sake.

"Amen, amen, I say to you, he that believeth in Me, the works that I do, he also shall do, and greater than these shall he do, because I go to the Father. And whatsoever you shall ask the Father in My name, that will I do, that the Father may be glorified in the Son. If you shall ask Me anything in My name, that I will do. If you love Me, keep My commandments.

"And I will ask the Father, and He shall give 16. you another Paraclete, that He may abide with you for ever, the Spirit of Truth, Whom the world cannot receive, because it seeth Him not, nor knoweth Him; but you shall know Him, for He shall abide with you, and shall be in you. I will not leave you orphans; I will come to you. Yet a little while, and the world seeth Me no more; but you see Me, because I live, and you shall live. In that day you shall know that I am in My Father, and you in Me, and I in you. He that hath My commandments, and keepeth them, he it is that loveth Me. And he that loveth Me shall be loved of My Father, and I will love him, and will manifest Myself to him."

Judas saith to Him, not the Iscariot: "Lord, 22. how is it that Thou wilt manifest Thyself to us, and not to the world?"

Jesus answered and said to him: "If any one 23. love Me, he will keep My word, and My Father will love him, and We will come to him, and will make Our abode with him. He that loveth Me not, keepeth not My words. And the word which you have heard is not Mine, but the Father's Who sent Me. These things have I spoken to you, abiding with you. But the Paraclete, the Holy Ghost, Whom the Father will send in My name, He will teach you all things, and bring all things to your mind whatsoever I shall have said to you.

"Peace I leave with you, My peace I give unto 27. you; not as the world giveth do I give unto you. Let not your heart be troubled, nor let it be afraid. You have heard that I said to you: 'I go away, and I come unto you. If you loved Me, you would indeed be glad because I go to the Father; for the Father is greater than I. And now I have told you before it come to pass, that when it shall come to pass, you may believe. I will not now speak many things with you. For the prince of this world cometh, and in Me he hath not anything. But that the world may know that I love the Father, and as the Father hath given Me commandment, so do I. Arise, let us go hence."ʰ

Matt. 26, 26—28.
Mark 14, 22—24.
Luke 22, 19, 20.

ᴹᴵAnd whilst they were at supper, Jesus took bread, and blessed and broke and gave to His disciples, and said:¹ "Take ye and eat, this is My Body ᴸᴷwhich is given for you. Do this for a commemoration of Me."

In like manner ᴹᵗtaking the chalice, He gave thanks and gave to them, saying: "Drink ye all of this. For this is My Blood of the New Testament, which shall be shed for many unto the remission of sins.

Matt. 26, 29.
Mark 14, 25.

ᴹᵀ"And I say to you, I will not drink from henceforth of this fruit of the vine, until that day when I shall drink it with you new, in the Kingdom of My Father.

ohn 15, 1—27.

"I am the true vine, and My Father is the husbandman. Every branch in Me that beareth not fruit He will take away; and every one that beareth fruit, He will purge it, that it may bring forth more fruit. Now you are clean, by reason of the word which I have spoken to you. Abide in Me, and I in you. As the branch cannot bear fruit of itself, unless it abide in the vine, so neither can you, unless you abide in Me. I am the vine, you are the branches; he that abideth in Me, and

---

¹ Compare Father Coleridge (*Passiontide*, vol. ii.). He sees in these words, a change to another room for that part of the supper, during which our Lord intended to institute the Blessed Sacrament. The final departure from the Cenacle, he considers, is that recorded by the same Evangelist (chap. xviii. 1).

I in him, the same beareth much fruit, for without Me you can do nothing. If any one abide not in Me, he shall be cast forth as a branch and shall wither; and they shall gather him up, and cast him into the fire, and he burneth. If you abide in Me, and My words abide in you, you shall ask whatever you will, and it shall be done unto you. In this is My Father glorified, that you bring forth very much fruit, and become My disciples.

"As the Father hath loved Me, I also have loved you. Abide in My love. If you keep My commandments you shall abide in My love; as I also have kept My Father's commandments, and do abide in His love. These things I have spoken to you that My joy may be in you, and your joy may be filled.

"This is My commandment, that you love one another, as I have loved you. Greater love than this no man hath, that a man lay down his life for his friends. You are My friends, if you do the things that I command you. I will not now call you servants, for the servant knoweth not what his lord doth. But I have called you friends; because all things whatsoever I have heard of My Father I have made known to you. You have not chosen Me, but I have chosen you, and have appointed you, that you should go and should bring forth fruit; and your fruit should remain; that whatsoever you shall ask of the Father in My name He shall give it you.

"These things I command you, that you love one another. If the world hate you, know ye that it hath hated Me before you. If you had been of the world, the world would love its own; but because you are not of the world, but I have chosen you out of the world, therefore the world hateth you. Remember My word that I said to you: 'The servant is not greater than his master.' If they have persecuted Me, they will also persecute you. If they have kept My word, they will keep yours also. But all these things they will do to you for My name's sake, because they know not Him that sent Me. If I had not come and spoken to them, they would not have sin; but now they have no excuse for their sin. He that hateth Me, hateth My Father also. If I had not done among them the works that no other man hath done, they would not have sin; but now they have both seen and hated, both Me and My Father. But that the word may be fulfilled which is written in their law: *They hated Me without cause.*

26. "But when the Paraclete cometh Whom I will send you from the Father, the Spirit of Truth Who proceedeth from the Father, He shall give testimony of Me. And you shall give testimony, because you are with Me from the beginning.

John 16, 1—33.

"These things have I spoken to you, that you may not be scandalized. They will put you out of the synagogues, yea, the hour cometh, that whosoever killeth you, will think that he doth a service to God. And these things will they do to you, because they have not known the Father nor Me. But these things I have told you, that when the hour shall come you may remember that I told you of them.

5. "But I told you not these things from the beginning, because I was with you. And now I go to Him that sent Me, and none of you asketh Me: 'Whither goest Thou?' But because I have spoken these things to you, sorrow hath filled your heart. But I tell you the truth: it is expedient to you that I go; for if I go not, the Paraclete will not

come to you; but if I go, I will send Him to you. And when He is come, He will convince the world of sin, and of justice, and of judgment. Of sin: because they believed not in Me. And of justice: because I go to the Father; and you shall see Me no longer. And of judgment: because the prince of this world is already judged.

"I have yet many things to say to you; but you cannot bear them now. But when He, the Spirit of Truth, is come, He will teach you all truth. For He shall not speak of Himself; but what things soever He shall hear, He shall speak; and the things that are to come He shall show you. He shall glorify Me, because He shall receive of Mine, and shall show it to you. All things whatsoever the Father hath are Mine. Therefore I said, that He shall receive of Mine, and show it to you. A little while, and now you shall not see Me; and again a little while, and you shall see Me, because I go to the Father."

Then some of His disciples said one to another: "What is this that He saith to us: 'A little while and you shall not see Me: and again a little while, and you shall see Me;' and: 'because I go to the Father'?" They said therefore: "What is this that He saith: 'A little while'? We know not what He speaketh."

And Jesus knew that they had a mind to ask Him, and He said to them: "Of this do you inquire among yourselves, because I said: 'A little while and you shall not see Me, and again a little while, and you shall see Me.' Amen, amen, I say to you, that you shall lament and weep, but the world shall rejoice; and you shall be made sorrowful, but your sorrow shall be turned into joy. A woman when she is in labour, hath sorrow, because her

hour is come; but when she hath brought forth
the child, she remembereth no more the anguish,
for joy that a man is born into the world. So
also you now indeed have sorrow, but I will see
you again, and your heart shall rejoice; and your
joy no man shall take from you. And in that day
you shall not ask Me anything. Amen, amen, I
say to you, if you ask the Father anything in My
name, He will give it you. Hitherto you have not
asked anything in My name. Ask, and you shall
receive, that your joy may be full.

25. "These things I have spoken to you in proverbs.
The hour cometh when I will no more speak to
you in proverbs, but I will show you plainly of the
Father. In that day you shall ask in My name,
and I say not to you that I will ask the Father for
you; for the Father Himself loveth you, because
you have loved Me, and have believed that I came
out from God. I came forth from the Father, and
am come into the world; again I leave the world,
and I go to the Father."

29. His disciples say to Him: "Behold now Thou
speakest plainly and speakest no proverb. Now
we know that Thou knowest all things, and that
Thou needest not that any man should ask Thee.
By this we believe that Thou camest forth from
God."

32. Jesus answered them: "Do you now believe?
Behold the hour cometh, and it is now come, that
you shall be scattered, every man to his own, and
shall leave Me alone; and yet I am not alone,
because the Father is with Me. These things I
have spoken to you, that in Me you may have
peace. In the world you shall have distress; but
have confidence, I have overcome the world."

John 17, 1—26. These things Jesus spoke, and lifting up His

eyes to heaven, He said: "Father, the hour is come, glorify Thy Son, that Thy Son may glorify Thee. As Thou hast given Him power over all flesh, that He may give eternal life to all whom Thou hast given Him. Now this is eternal life, that they may know Thee, the only true God, and Jesus Christ Whom Thou hast sent. I have glorified Thee on the earth, I have finished the work which Thou gavest Me to do; and now glorify Thou Me, O Father, with Thyself, with the glory which I had, before the world was, with Thee.

"I have manifested Thy name to the men whom Thou hast given Me out of the world. Thine they were and to Me Thou gavest them, and they have kept Thy word. Now they have known that all things which Thou hast given Me are from Thee; because the words which Thou gavest Me, I have given to them, and they have received them, and have known in very deed, that I came out from Thee, and they have believed that Thou didst send Me. I pray for them; I pray not for the world, but for them whom Thou hast given Me, because they are Thine, and all My things are Thine, and Thine are Mine, and I am glorified in them.

"And now I am not in the world, and these are in the world, and I come to Thee. Holy Father, keep them in Thy name, whom Thou hast given Me, that they may be one, as We also are. While I was with them, I kept them in Thy name. Those whom Thou gavest Me have I kept, and none of them is lost, but the son of perdition, that the Scripture may be fulfilled. And now I come to Thee, and these things I speak in the world, that they may have My joy filled in themselves. I have given them Thy word; and the world hath hated them, because they are not of the world, as I also

am not of the world. I pray not that Thou shouldst take them out of the world, but that Thou shouldst keep them from evil. They are not of the world, as I also am not of the world. Sanctify them in truth; Thy word is truth. As Thou hast sent Me into the world, I also have sent them into the world; and for them do I sanctify Myself, that
20. they also may be sanctified in truth.

"And not for them only do I pray, but for them also who through their word shall believe in Me; that they all may be one, as Thou Father in Me and I in Thee, that they also may be one in Us; that the world may believe that Thou hast sent Me. And the glory which Thou hast given Me, I have given to them, that they may be one, as We also are one. I in them, and Thou in Me, that they may be made perfect in one, and the world may know that Thou hast sent Me, and hast loved them, as Thou hast also loved Me.

24. "Father, I will that where I am, they also whom Thou hast given Me, may be with Me, that they may see My glory which Thou hast given Me, because Thou hast loved Me before the creation of the world. Just Father, the world hath not known Thee, but I have known Thee, and these have known that Thou hast sent Me; and I have made known Thy name to them, and will make it known, that the love, wherewith Thou hast loved Me, may be in them, and I in them.

PART V.

PASSION AND DEATH.

^{JN}WHEN Jesus had said these things, ^{MT}a hymn being said, ^{JN}He went forth with His disciples, ^{LK}according to His custom, to the Mount of Olives, ^{JN}over the brook Cedron, where there was a garden . . . (Matt. 26, 30. Mark 14, 26. Luke 22, 39. John 18, 1.)

^{MK}And Jesus saith to them: "You will all be scandalized in My regard this night. For it is written: *I will strike the Shepherd, and the sheep shall be dispersed.* But after I shall be risen again, I will go before you into Galilee." But Peter saith to Him: "Although all shall be scandalized in Thee, yet not I." (Matt. 26, 31—35. Mark 14, 27—31.)

And Jesus saith to Him: "Amen, I say to thee, to-day, even in this night, before the cock crow twice, thou shalt deny Me thrice." But he spoke the more vehemently: "Although I should die together with Thee, I will not deny Thee." And in like manner also said they all.

^{MT}Then Jesus came with them to a country place, which is called Gethsemani; and He said to His disciples: "Sit you here, till I go yonder and pray." ^{MK}And He taketh Peter and James and John with Him, and He began to fear and to be heavy. And He saith to them: "My Soul is sorrowful even unto death; stay you here and watch." (Matt. 26, 36—44. Mark 14, 32—40. Luke 22, 40—42. Luke 22, 45, 46.)

^{LK}And He was withdrawn away from them a stone's cast; and kneeling down, ^{MK}He fell flat on the ground, and He prayed that if it might be, the hour might pass from Him. And He said: "Abba, Father, all things are possible to Thee; remove this chalice from Me; but not what I will, but what Thou wilt."

^{MT}And He cometh to His disciples and findeth them asleep. And He said to Peter: "What! couldst thou not watch one hour with Me? Watch ye and pray that ye enter not into temptation. The spirit indeed is willing, but the flesh weak."

Again He went the second time and prayed, saying: "O My Father, if this chalice cannot pass away unless I drink it, Thy will be done." And He cometh again, and findeth them asleep, for their eyes were heavy. And leaving them He went away again, and He prayed the third time, saying the same words.

Luke xxii, 43, 44. And there appeared to Him an Angel from Heaven strengthening Him. And being in an agony, He prayed the longer. And His sweat became as drops of blood trickling down upon the ground.

Matt. xxvi, 45, 46.
Mark xiv, 41, 42. ^{MT}Then He cometh to His disciples ^{MK}the third time, and saith to them: "Sleep ye now and take rest.

"It is enough, the hour is come; behold the Son of Man shall be betrayed into the hands of sinners. Rise up, let us go. Behold, he that will betray Me is at hand."

John 18, 2. And Judas also, who betrayed Him, knew the place, because Jesus had often resorted thither together with His disciples.

Matt. xxvi, 47.
Mark xiv, 43.
Luke xxii, 47.
John 18, 3. ^{JN}Judas therefore, having received a band of soldiers and servants from the Chief Priests and

the Pharisees, cometh thither with lanterns and torches and weapons; ^{LK}and he . . . went before them and drew near to Jesus to kiss Him.

^{MK}[For he] had given them a sign, saying: "Whomsoever I shall kiss, that is He; lay hold on Him and lead Him away carefully." Matt. 26, 48, 49.
Mark 14, 44, 45

And when he was come, immediately going up to Him, he saith: "Hail! Rabbi," and he kissed Him.

^{MT}And Jesus said to him: "Friend, whereto art thou come? ^{LK}Judas, dost thou betray the Son of Man with a kiss?" Matt. 26, 50.
Luke 22, 48.

Jesus therefore, knowing all things that should come upon Him, went forward and said to them: "Whom seek ye?" They answered Him: "Jesus of Nazareth." Jesus saith to them: "I am He." John 18, 4—9.

And Judas also who betrayed Him, stood with them. As soon then as He had said to them: "I am He," they went backward, and fell to the ground. Again therefore He asked them: "Whom seek ye?" And they said: "Jesus of Nazareth." Jesus answered: "I have told you that I am He; if therefore you seek Me, let these go their way;" that the word might be fulfilled which He said: Of them whom Thou hast given Me, I have not lost any one.

^{MT}Then they came up and laid hands upon Him and held Him. Matt. 26, 50.
Mark 14, 46.

And they that were about Him, seeing what would follow, said to Him: "Lord, shall we strike with the sword?" Luke 22, 49.

^{JN}Then Simon Peter, having a sword, drew it, and struck the servant of the High Priest, and cut off his right ear. And the name of the servant was Malchus. Matt. 26, 51.
Mark 14, 47.
Luke 22, 50.
John 18, 10.

Luke 22, 51.

But Jesus answering said: "Suffer ye thus far." And when He had touched his ear He healed him.

Matt. 26, 52.
John 18, 11.

MTThen Jesus said to Peter: "Put up again thy sword into its place.

Matt. 26, 52—54.

"For all that take the sword shall perish with the sword. Thinkest thou that I cannot ask My Father, and He will give Me presently more than twelve legions of angels? How then shall the Scripture be fulfilled: that so it must be done?

John 18, 11.

"The chalice which My Father hath given Me, shall I not drink it?"

Matt. 26, 55, 56.
Mark 14, 48, 49.
Luke 22, 51—53.

LKAnd Jesus said to the Chief Priests and Magistrates of the Temple, and the ancients that were come unto Him: "Are you come out as it were against a thief, with swords and clubs, MTto apprehend Me? I sat daily with you teaching in the Temple, and you laid not hands on Me; LKbut this is your hour and the power of darkness." MTNow all this was done, that the Scriptures of the prophets might be fulfilled.

Matt. 26, 56.
Mark 14, 50.

MKThen His disciples leaving Him, all fled away.

Mark 14, 51, 52.

·And a certain young man followed Him, having a linen cloth cast about his naked body, and they laid hold on him. But he, casting off the linen cloth, fled from them naked.

Matt. 26, 57.
Mark 14, 53.
Luke 22, 54.
John 18, 12, 13.

JNThen the band and the tribune and the servants of the Jews took Jesus and bound Him. And they led Him away to Annas first, for he was father-in-law to Caiphas, who was High Priest of that year.

John 18, 14.

Now Caiphas was he, who had given the counsel to the Jews, that it was expedient that one man should die for the people.

Matt. 26, 58.
Mark 14, 54.
Luke 22, 54.
John 18, 15.

JNAnd Simon Peter followed Jesus MTafar off, JNand so did another disciple.

And that disciple was known to the High Priest, and went in with Jesus into the court of the High Priest. But Peter stood at the door without. The other disciple, therefore, who was known to the High Priest, went out and spoke to the porteress, and brought in Peter. And the maid that was porteress saith to Peter: "Art not thou also one of this Man's disciples?" He saith: "I am not." John 18, 15—17.

Now the servants and officers stood at a fire of coals, because it was cold, and warmed themselves; and with them was Peter also standing and warming himself. Matt. 26, 58. Mark 14, 54. Luke 22, 55. John 18, 18.

^{MT}And there came to him a servant-maid ^{MK}of the High Priest; and when she had seen Peter warming himself, ^{LK}and had earnestly beheld him, she said: "^{MK}Thou also was with Jesus of Nazareth, ^{MT}the Galilæan." But he denied before them all, saying: ^{LK}"Woman, I know Him not: ^{MK}I neither know nor understand what thou sayest."[1] Matt. 26, 69, 70. Mark 14, 66—68. Luke 22, 55—57.

And he went forth before the court, and the cock crew. Mark 14, 68.

The High Priest then asked Jesus of His disciples and of His doctrine. Jesus answered him: "I have spoken openly to the world; I have always taught in the Synagogue and in the Temple, whither all the Jews resort, and in secret I have spoken nothing. Why askest thou Me? Ask John 18, 19—24.

---

[1] The principle which underlies the treatment of this and the other two denials of St. Peter, is, according to Fouard, Alford, and others, the only one by which the positive statements contained in the accounts of the four inspired writers, can be reconciled one with another. These commentators maintain that, while the *occasions* of the denials were three-fold and distinct, the interrogations and denials on each of the three occasions may have been numerous, and certainly were something more than three simple questions and answers.

them who have heard what I have spoken unto them; behold, they know what things I have said."

And when He had said these things, one of the servants standing by, gave Jesus a blow, saying: "Answerest Thou the High Priest so?" Jesus answered him: "If I have spoken evil, give testimony of the evil; but if well, why strikest thou Me?"

And Annas sent him bound to Caiphas, the High Priest.

<small>Matt. 26, 57, 58.
Mark 14, 53, 54.
Luke 22, 54.</small>

ᴹᴷAnd all the priests and the scribes and the ancients were assembled together. And Peter followed Him ... even into the court of the High Priest.

<small>Matt. 26, 71, 72.
Mark 14, 69, 70.
Luke 22, 58.
John 18, 25.</small>

ᴹᵀAnd as he went out of the gate, another maid saw him, and she saith to ᴹᴷthe standers-by: ᴹᵀ"This man also was with Jesus of Nazareth." And again he denied with an oath, that: "I know not the Man."

ᴸᴷAnd ... another seeing him, ᴶᴺstanding and warming himself ... said therefore to him: "Art not thou also one of His disciples?" He denied it, and said: ᴸᴷ"O man, I am not."

<small>Matt. 26, 59—66.
Mark 14, 55—64.</small>

ᴹᵀNow the Chief Priests and the whole Council sought false witness against Jesus, that they might put Him to death; and they found not, whereas many false witnesses had come in; ᴹᴷand their evidence did not agree. ᴹᵀAnd last of all there came in two false witnesses, ᴹᴷsaying: "We heard Him say: 'I will destroy this Temple, made with hands, and within three days, I will build another not made with hands.'" And their witness did not agree.

And the High Priest, rising up in the midst, asked Jesus saying: "Answerest Thou nothing to the things that are laid to Thy charge by these men?" But He held His peace, and answered nothing.

^{MT}And the High Priest said to Him: "I adjure Thee, by the living God, that Thou tell us, if Thou be the Christ, the Son of God." Jesus saith to him: "Thou hast said it. Nevertheless I say to you, hereafter you shall see the Son of Man sitting on the right hand of the power of God, and coming in the clouds of heaven."

Then the High Priest rent his garments, saying: "He hath blasphemed, what further need have we of witnesses? Behold, now you have heard the blasphemy, what think you?" But they answering said: "He is guilty of death."

^{LK}And after the space as it were of one hour[1] ^{JN}one of the servants of the High Priest, a kinsman to him whose ear Peter cut off, saith to him: "Did not I see thee in the garden with Him?" Again therefore Peter denied.

Matt. 26, 73, 74.
Mark 14, 70—72.
Luke 22, 59, 60.
John 18, 26, 27.

^{MK}And . . . they came, that stood by, and said again to Peter: "Surely thou art one of them, for thou art also a Galilæan, ^{MT}even thy speech doth discover thee." Then he began to curse and swear, ^{MK}saying: "I know not this Man of Whom you speak." And immediately the cock crew again.

^{LK}And the Lord turning looked on Peter. ^{MK}And Peter remembered the word that Jesus had said unto him: "Before the cock crow twice, thou shalt thrice deny Me."^{MT} And going forth, he wept bitterly.

Matt. 26, 75.
Mark 14, 72.
Luke 22, 61, 62.

^{LK}And the men that held Him, mocked Him and struck Him. ^{MT}Then did they spit on His face and buffeted Him. ^{LK}And they blindfolded Him, and smote His face ^{MT}with the palms of their

Matt. 26, 67, 68.
Mark 14, 65.
Luke 22, 63—65.

---

[1] *i.e.* Since Peter's last denial.

hands, saying: "Prophesy unto us, O Christ! who is he that struck Thee?" ^{LK}And blaspheming, many other things they said against Him.

^{MT}And when morning was come, all the Chief Priests and ancients of the people took council against Jesus that they might put Him to death. ^{LK}And they brought Him into their council, saying: "If Thou be the Christ, tell us." And He saith to them: "If I shall tell you, you will not believe Me, and if I shall also ask you, you will not answer Me, nor let Me go. But hereafter the Son of Man shall be sitting on the right hand of the power of God."

Then said they all: "Art Thou then the Son of God?" Who said: "You say that I am." And they said: "What need we any farther testimony? For we ourselves have heard it from His own mouth."

^{LK}And the whole multitude of them rising up, ^{MK}bound Jesus and led Him away, ^{MT}and delivered Him to Pontius Pilate the Governor.

Then Judas, who betrayed Him, seeing that He was condemned, repenting himself, brought back the thirty pieces of silver to the Chief Priests and ancients, saying: "I have sinned in betraying innocent blood." But they said: "What is that to us? Look thou to it." And casting down the pieces of silver in the Temple, he departed, and went and hanged himself with a halter.

But the Chief Priests having taken the pieces of silver, said: "It is not lawful to put them into the Corbona, because it is the price of blood." And after they had consulted together, they bought with them the potter's field, to be a burying-place for strangers. Wherefore that field was called Haceldama, that is, The Field of Blood, even to this day. Then was fulfilled that which was spoken by Jeremias the Prophet, saying: *And they took the thirty pieces of silver, the price of Him that was prized, whom they prized of the children of Israel. And they gave them unto the potter's field as the Lord appointed to me.*

Then they led Jesus from Caiaphas to the Governor's hall; and it was morning. And they went not into the hall, that they might not be defiled, but that they might eat the Pasch. Pilate therefore went out to them, and said: "What accusation bring you against this Man?" John 18, 28—32.

They answered and said to him: "If He were not a malefactor, we would not have delivered Him up to thee." Pilate therefore said: "Take Him you, and judge Him according to your law." The Jews therefore said to him: "It is not lawful for us to put any man to death;" that the word of Jesus might be fulfilled, which He said, signifying what death He should die.

And they began to accuse Him, saying: "We have found this Man perverting our nation, and forbidding to give tribute to Cæsar, and saying, that He is Christ the King." Luke 23, 2.

^(JN)Pilate therefore went into the hall again, and called Jesus, and said to Him: "Art Thou the King of the Jews?" Jesus answered: "Sayest thou this thing of thyself, or have others told it thee of Me?" Pilate answered: "Am I a Jew? Thy own nation and the Chief Priests have delivered Thee up to me. What hast Thou done?" Matt. 27, 11.
Mark 15, 2.
Luke 23, 3.
John 18, 33-38.

Jesus answered: "My Kingdom is not of this world. If My Kingdom were of this world, My servants would certainly strive, that I should not be delivered to the Jews; but now My Kingdom is not from thence."

Pilate therefore said to Him: "Art Thou a King then?" Jesus answered: "Thou sayest that I am a King. For this was I born, and for this came I into the world, that I should give testimony to the truth; every one that is of the truth heareth My voice." Pilate saith to Him: "What is truth?"

And when he had said this, he went forth again to the Jews, and saith to them: "I find no cause in Him."

Matt. 27, 12—14.
Mark 15, 3—5.
^{MK}And the Chief Priests accused Him in many things. ^{MT}And when He was accused by the Chief Priests and ancients He answered nothing. Then Pilate saith to Him: "Dost Thou not hear how great testimonies they allege against Thee?" And He answered him to never a word, so that the Governor wondered exceedingly.

Luke 23, 4—16.
And Pilate said to the Chief Priests and to the multitude: "I find no cause in this Man." But they were the more earnest, saying: "He stirreth up the people, teaching throughout all Judea, beginning from Galilee to this place."

But Pilate, hearing Galilee, asked if the Man were of Galilee. And when he understood that He was of Herod's jurisdiction, he sent Him away to Herod, who was also himself at Jerusalem in those days.

8. And Herod, seeing Jesus, was very glad, for he was desirous of a long time to see Him, because he had heard many things of Him, and he hoped to see some sign wrought by Him. And he questioned Him in many words. But He answered him nothing.

And the Chief Priests and the Scribes stood by earnestly accusing Him. And Herod with his army set Him at nought, and mocked Him, putting on Him a white garment, and sent Him back to Pilate.

And Herod and Pilate were made friends together that same day, for before they were enemies one to another.

And Pilate calling together the Chief Priests and the magistrates and the people, said to them: "You have presented unto me this Man as one that perverteth the people, and behold I, having examined Him before you, find no cause in this Man, in those things wherein you accuse Him; no, nor Herod neither; for I sent you to him, and behold nothing worthy of death is done to Him. I will chastise Him, therefore, and release Him."

^{MT}Now upon the solemn day, the Governor was accustomed ^{LK}of necessity ^{MT}to release to the people one prisoner, whom they would. And he had then a notorious prisoner that was called Barabbas, ^{MK}who was put in prison with some seditious men, who in the sedition had committed murder.

And when the multitude was come up, they began to desire that he would do as he had ever done unto them. ^{MT}They therefore being gathered together, Pilate said: "Whom will you that I release to you, Barabbas, or Jesus, that is called Christ?"

^{MK}For he knew that the Chief Priests had delivered Him up out of envy.

And as he was sitting in the place of judgment, his wife sent to him, saying: "Have thou nothing to do with that just Man, for I have suffered many things this day in a dream because of Him."

^{MT}But the Chief Priests and ancients persuaded the people, that they should ask Barabbas, and make Jesus away. And the Governor answering,

said to them: "Whether will you of the two to be released unto you?"

^{LK}But the whole multitude together cried out, saying: "Away with this Man, and release unto us Barabbas." ^{JN}And Barabbas was a robber.

^{LK}And Pilate again spoke to them, desiring to release Jesus: ^{MK}"What will you then that I do to the King of the Jews—^{MT}Jesus, that is called Christ?"

^{LK}But they cried again, saying: "Crucify Him, crucify Him." ^{MK}And Pilate ^{LK}said to them the third time: "Why, what evil hath this Man done? I find no cause of death in Him; I will chastise Him, therefore, and let Him go." But they were instant with loud voices, requiring that He might be crucified, and their voices prevailed.

And Pilate, seeing that he prevailed nothing, but that rather a tumult was made, taking water, washed his hands before the people, saying: "I am innocent of the Blood of this just Man; look you to it." And the whole people answering said: "His Blood be upon us and upon our children."

^{MK}So Pilate, being willing to satisfy the people, ^{LK}gave sentence that it should be as they required. And he released unto them ^{MT}Barabbas—^{LK}him who for murder and sedition had been cast into prison, whom they had desired; but Jesus, ^{MK}when he had scourged Him, ^{LK}he delivered up to their will, ^{MK}to be crucified.

^{MT}Then the soldiers of the Governor, taking Jesus into the hall, gathered together unto Him the whole band, and, stripping Him, ^{MK}they clothe Him with purple. ^{MT}And platting a crown of thorns, they put it upon His head, and a reed in His right hand. And bowing the knee before Him, ^{MK}they began to salute Him, ^{MT}[and] they

mocked Him, saying: "Hail! King of the Jews."
And spitting upon Him, they took the reed and
struck His head.

Pilate therefore went forth again, and saith to John 19, 4—16.
them: "Behold, I bring Him forth unto you, that
you may know that I find no cause in Him."
(Jesus therefore came forth, bearing the crown of
thorns and the purple garment). And he saith to
them: "Behold the Man!"

When the Chief Priests, therefore, and the
servants had seen Him, they cried out, saying:
"Crucify Him! crucify Him!" Pilate saith to
them: "Take Him you, and crucify Him, for I
find no cause in Him."

The Jews answered him: "We have a law, and
according to the law He ought to die, because He
made Himself the Son of God." When Pilate
therefore had heard this saying, he feared the
more. And he entered into the hall again, and
he said to Jesus: "Whence art Thou?" But
Jesus gave him no answer.

Pilate therefore saith to Him: "Speakest Thou
not to me? Knowest Thou not that I have power
to crucify Thee, and I have power to release
Thee?" Jesus answered: "Thou shouldst not
have any power against Me, unless it were given
thee from above. Therefore, he that hath delivered
Me to thee hath the greater sin."

And from henceforth Pilate sought to release
Him. But the Jews cried out, saying: "If thou
release this Man, thou art not Cæsar's friend; for
whosoever maketh himself a king, speaketh against
Cæsar."

Now when Pilate had heard these words, he
brought Jesus forth and sat down in the judgment-
seat, in the place that is called Lithostrotos, and

in Hebrew Gabbatha. And it was the parasceve of the Pasch, about the sixth hour.

And he saith to the Jews: "Behold your King!" But they cried out: "Away with Him! away with Him! crucify Him!" Pilate saith to them: "Shall I crucify your King?" The Chief Priests answered: "We have no King but Cæsar."

Then, therefore, he delivered Him to them for to be crucified. ᴶᴺAnd they took Jesus, ᴹᴷand after they had mocked Him, they took off the purple from him, and put His own garments on Him, and they led Him out to crucify Him.

And bearing His own Cross He went forth.

And there were also two other malefactors led with Him to be put to death.

ᴸᴷAnd as they led Him away, they laid hold on one Simon of Cyrene coming from the country, ᴹᴷthe father of Alexander and of Rufus; ᴸᴷand they laid the Cross on him to carry after Jesus.

And there followed Him a great multitude of people and of women, who bewailed and lamented Him. But Jesus turning to them, said: "Daughters of Jerusalem, weep not over Me, but weep for yourselves and for your children. For behold, the days shall come wherein they will say: Blessed are the barren, and the wombs that have not borne, and the paps that have not given suck. Then shall they begin to say to the mountains: Fall upon us; and to the hills: Cover us. For if in the greenwood they do these things, what shall be done in the dry?"

ᴹᴷAnd they bring Him into the place called Golgotha, which being interpreted, is the place of Calvary.

ᴹᴷAnd they gave Him to drink wine, mingled

with myrrh. ^{MT}And when He had tasted He would not drink.

And it was the third hour. Mark 15, 25.

^{MK}And they crucified Him ... and with Him they crucified ^{LK}the robbers, one on the right hand, and the other on the left, ^{JN}and Jesus in the midst. Matt. 27, 38.
Mark 15, 25—27.
Luke 23, 33.
John 19, 18.

And the Scripture was fulfilled which saith: *And with the wicked He was reputed.* Mark 15, 28.

And Jesus said: "Father, forgive them, for they know not what they do." Luke 23, 34.

^{JN}And Pilate wrote a title also—^{MK}the inscription of His cause—^{JN}and he put it upon the Cross, ^{MT}over His head. ^{JN}And the writing was: Jesus of Nazareth, King of the Jews. This title, therefore, many of the Jews did read, because the place where Jesus was crucified was nigh to the city, and it was written in Hebrew, in Greek, and in Latin. Matt. 27, 37.
Mark 15, 26.
Luke 23, 38.
John 19, 19-22.

Then the Chief Priests of the Jews said to Pilate: "Write not, The King of the Jews, but that: He said, I am the King of the Jews." Pilate answered: "What I have written, I have written."

^{JN}The soldiers, therefore, when they had crucified Him, took His garments (and they made four parts, to every soldier a part), and also His coat. Now the coat was without seam, woven from the top throughout. They said then one to another: "Let us not cut it, but let us cast lots for it whose it shall be; ^{MT}that it might be fulfilled which was spoken of by the Prophet, saying: *They divided My garments among them, and upon My vesture they cast lots.* Matt. 27, 35.
Mark 15, 24.
Luke 23, 34.
John 19, 23, 24.

And the soldiers indeed did these things. John 19, 24.

And they sat and watched Him. Matt. 27, 36.

And the people stood beholding. Luke 23, 35.

^{MT}And they that passed by blasphemed Him, Matt. 27, 39, 40.
Mark 15, 29, 30.

wagging their heads and saying: "Vah! Thou that destroyest the Temple of God, and in three days dost rebuild it, save Thy own self. If Thou be the Son of God, come down from the Cross."

Matt. 27, 41—43.
Mark 15, 31, 32.
Luke 23, 35.

^{MT}In like manner also the Chief Priests, with the scribes and ancients, mocking, said ^{MK}one to another: "He saved others, Himself He cannot save. Let Christ the King of Israel come down now from the Cross, that we may see and believe. ^{MT}He trusted in God, let Him now deliver Him if He will have Him, for He said: I am the Son of God."

Luke 23, 36, 37.

And the soldiers also mocked Him, coming to Him and offering Him vinegar, and saying: "If Thou be the King of the Jews, save Thyself."

Matt. 27, 44.
Mark 15, 32.

^{MT}And the self-same thing the thieves also, that were crucified with Him, reproached Him with.

. . . . .

Luke 23, 39—43.

And one of those robbers who were hanged, blasphemed Him, saying: "If Thou be Christ, save Thyself and us." But the other answering, rebuked him, saying: "Neither dost thou fear God, seeing thou art under the same condemnation? And we indeed justly, for we receive the due reward of our deeds, but this Man hath done no evil."

And he said to Jesus: "Lord, remember me when Thou shalt come into Thy Kingdom." And Jesus said to him: "Amen, I say to thee, this day thou shalt be with Me in Paradise."

John 19, 25—27.

Now there stood by the Cross of Jesus, His Mother, and His Mother's sister Mary of Cleophas, and Mary Magdalene. When Jesus, therefore, had seen His Mother, and the disciple standing whom He loved, He saith to His Mother: "Woman, behold thy son." After that He saith to the disciple: "Behold thy Mother." And from that hour the disciple took her to his own.

^{LK}And it was almost the sixth hour; ^{MK}and when the sixth hour was come, ^{LK}there was darkness over the whole earth until the ninth hour; and the sun was darkened. *Matt. 27, 45. Mark 15, 33. Luke 23, 44, 45.*

^{MK}And at the ninth hour Jesus cried out with a loud voice, saying: "Eloi! Eloi! lamma sabacthani?" Which is, being interpreted: My God! My God! why hast Thou forsaken Me? And some of the standers-by hearing, said: "Behold, He calleth Elias." *Matt. 27, 46, 47. Mark 15, 34, 35.*

Afterwards Jesus, knowing that all things were now accomplished, that the Scripture might be fulfilled, said: "I thirst." *John 19, 28.*

^{JN}Now there was a vessel set there full of vinegar; ^{MT}and immediately one of them running, took a sponge and filled it with vinegar, ^{MK}and putting it upon a reed, ^{JN}put it to His mouth, ^{MT}and gave Him to drink. *Matt. 27, 48. Mark 15, 36. John 19, 29.*

^{MT}And the others said: "Let be, let us see whether Elias will come to deliver Him." *Matt. 27, 49. Mark 15, 36.*

Jesus, therefore, when He had taken the vinegar, said: "It is consummated." *John 19, 30.*

^{MT}And Jesus again crying with a loud voice, said: *Matt. 27, 50. Mark 15, 37. Luke 23, 46.*

"Father, into Thy hands I commend My spirit." *Luke 23, 46.*

^{LK}And saying this, ^{JN}and bowing His head, He gave up the ghost. *Matt. 27, 50. Mark 15, 37. Luke 23, 46. John 19, 30.*

^{MT}And behold the veil of the Temple was rent in two from the top even to the bottom. *Matt. 27, 51. Mark 15, 38. Luke 23, 45.*

And the earth quaked, and the rocks were rent, and the graves were opened, and many bodies of the saints that had slept, arose, and coming out of the tombs after His Resurrection, came into the holy city and appeared to many. *Matt. 27, 51—53.*

Matt. 27, 54—56.
Mark 15, 39—41.
Luke 23, 47—49.

^{MK}And the Centurion who stood over against Him, seeing, that crying out in this manner He had given up the ghost, said: "Indeed this Man was the Son of God." ^{MT}And they that were with him watching Jesus, having seen the earthquake and the things that were done, were sore afraid, saying: "Indeed this was the Son of God." ^{LK}And all the multitude of them that were come together to that sight, and saw the things that were done, returned striking their breasts.

And all His acquaintance, and the women that had followed Him from Galilee, ^{MT}ministering unto Him, ^{LK}stood afar off beholding these things; ^{MK}among whom was Mary Magdalene; and Mary the mother of James the Less and of Joseph; and Salome, ^{MT}the mother of the sons of Zebedee, ^{MK}who also, when He was in Galilee, followed Him, and ministered to Him; and many other women that came up with Him to Jerusalem.

John 19, 31—37.

Then the Jews (because it was the parasceve), that the bodies might not remain upon the Cross on the Sabbath-day (for that was a great Sabbath-day), besought Pilate that their legs might be broken, and that they might be taken away.

The soldiers therefore came, and they broke the legs of the first, and of the other that was crucified with Him. But after they were come to Jesus, when they saw that He was already dead, they did not break His legs, but one of the soldiers with a spear opened His side, and immediately there came out blood and water. And he that saw it hath given testimony, and his testimony is true; and he knoweth that he saith true, that you also may believe. For these things were done that the Scripture might be fulfilled: *You shall not break a bone of Him.* And again another Scrip-

PART V.   PASSION AND DEATH.   209

ture saith: *They shall look on Him Whom they pierced.*

^{JN}And after these things, ^{MK}when evening was now come, ^{MT}there came a certain rich man of Arimathea, ^{LK}a city of Judea, ^{MT}named Joseph, ^{LK}who was a councillor, a good and a just man; (the same had not consented to their counsel and doings) ... who also himself looked for the Kingdom of God. This man ^{MK}came and went in boldly to Pilate and begged the body of Jesus ^{JN}(because he was a disciple of Jesus, but secretly for fear of the Jews). Matt. 27, 57, 58.
Mark 15, 42, 43.
Luke 23, 50—52.
John 19, 38.

But Pilate wondered that He should be already dead; and sending for the Centurion, he asked him if He were already dead. Mark 15, 44.

^{MK}And when he had understood it by the Centurion, ^{MT}Pilate commanded that the body should be delivered ^{MK}to Joseph. Matt. 27, 58.
Mark 15, 45.
John 19, 38.

He came, therefore ... and Nicodemus also came, he who at first came to Jesus by night, bringing a mixture of myrrh and aloes, about a hundred pounds. John 19, 38, 39.

^{MK}And Joseph, bringing fine linen, and taking Him down, wrapped Him up in the fine linen, ^{JN}with the spices, as the manner of the Jews is to bury. Now there was in the place where He was crucified, a garden; ^{MT}and Joseph, taking the body ... laid it in his own new monument, which he had hewed out in a rock ^{JN}in the garden—a new sepulchre wherein no man yet had been laid. ^{MT}And he rolled a great stone to the door of the monument and went his way. Matt. 27, 59, 60.
Mark 15, 46.
Luke 23, 53.
John 19, 40, 41.

'And it was the day of the Parasceve, and the Sabbath drew on. Luke 23, 54.

There, therefore, because of the Parasceve of the Jews, they laid Jesus, because the sepulchre was nigh at hand. John 19, 42.

O

Matt. 32, 61.
Mark 15, 47.

^{MK}And Mary Magdalene and Mary the mother of Joseph, ^{MT}sitting over against the sepulchre beheld where He was laid.

Luke 23, 55, 56.

And the [other] women that were come with Him from Galilee, following after, saw the sepulchre, and how His body was laid; and returning, they prepared spices and ointments;[1] and on the Sabbath-day they rested according to the commandment.

Matt. 27, 62—66.

And the next day which followed the day of preparation, the Chief Priests and the Pharisees came together to Pilate, saying: "Sir, we have remembered that that seducer said, while He was yet alive: 'After three days I will rise again.' Command, therefore, the sepulchre to be guarded until the third day, lest perhaps His disciples come, and steal Him away, and say to the people: 'He is risen from the dead;' and the last error shall be worse than the first."

Pilate said to them: "You have a guard; go, guard it as you know." And they departing made the sepulchre sure, sealing the stone, and setting guards.

[1] Note here, in anticipation of the story of the Resurrection, how St. Luke's party of women "prepared spices and ointments" on the Friday; not so the party mentioned by the other three Evangelists and headed by St. Mary Magdalene, who, as St. Mark (xvi. 1) informs us, bought them "when the Sabbath was past."

PART VI.

THE RESURRECTION AND ASCENSION; THE DESCENT OF THE HOLY GHOST.

[NOTE.—The better to understand the very brief Gospel narrative, the reader is asked to glance first at the Table of Contents, Part VI.]

AND in the end of the Sabbath, when it began to dawn towards the first day of the week, came Mary Magdalene and the other Mary [from Bethania to Jerusalem] to see the sepulchre.[1]   Matt. 28, 1.

And when the Sabbath was past, [they] and Salome bought sweet spices, that coming they might anoint Jesus. . . .   Mark 16 1—9.

But He rising early, the first day of the week, appeared first to Mary Magdalene, out of whom

---

[1] The above interpretation of St. Matthew's meaning is an attempt to bring into harmony two contending views; the one that the holy women "came to see the sepulchre" on the evening of Holy Saturday, and also *again* on Easter Sunday morning; the other, that St. Matthew's words imply one visit only.

The theory of two visits is upheld by Dr. Westcott (in *John; Speaker's Commentary*), and by Father Coleridge (*Vita Vitæ Nostræ*). These commentators base their opinion on the fact, which no one can contravene, that the Jewish day, and therefore the Sabbath, began and ended at sunset. Hence they contend, the phrase *in the end of the Sabbath*, means at or near sunset of our Saturday. Nor is this contention in the least affected by

He had cast seven devils. [His appearing was after this manner.]

Matt. 28, 2—4.

Behold there was a great earthquake; for an angel of the Lord descended from Heaven, and coming, rolled back the stone and sat upon it. And his countenance was as lightning and his raiment as snow. And for fear of him, the guards were struck with terror and became as dead men.

> the use of the qualifying clause, *when it began to dawn towards the first day of the week*, since the Greek and the Latin word used in St. Matthew to denote this dawning, is the same as occurs in St. Luke xxiii. 54, where, speaking of this very Sabbath, he says: *the Sabbath drew on*, literally *was dawning*, at a time when the body of our Lord had just been taken down from the Cross; that is, about sunset on Friday evening.
>
> Those who maintain the alternative view, of the one visit in the morning, contend that, in the first place, there is no tradition in the Church of a preliminary visit, and secondly, that the internal evidence afforded by St. Matthew's account of the Resurrection is not in harmony with such a supposition. Hence they apply the phrase *end of the Sabbath*, either to the whole night preceding the dawning of a new day (Sunday), or they say the Evangelist is speaking of the natural day beginning at midnight, and not at all of the Jewish day.
>
> The reading adopted in the text harmonizes these two views. It supposes, first, that Magdalene is the sister of Martha and Lazarus; secondly, that she went out to them at Bethania after the Crucifixion; thirdly, that she spent the Sabbath there; and lastly, that she started thence with her companion Mary, the mother of James, about sunset, so as to be in Jerusalem in time to buy spices before the bazaars closed for the night. Salome, the mother of St. John, who is said to have had a house in Jerusalem, was, we may infer from St. Mark (xvi. 1), sought out by the two friends, and the three in company made the necessary purchases. The important process of preparing the spices may or may not have occupied much time, but all was in readiness for as early a start in the morning as possible, indeed, according to St. John (xx. 1), "when it was yet dark."
>
> Bearing in mind that Bethania was close on two miles to the east, while Calvary was on the west of the city, the reader will see that our interpretation of St. Matthew's meaning does less violence to the sequence of his story than the interpolation of a second visit.

PART VI. THE DESCENT OF THE HOLY GHOST.

And very early in the morning, the first day of the week, they [the above women] came to the sepulchre, the sun being now risen. And they say to one another: "Who shall roll us back the stone from the door of the sepulchre?" And looking, they saw the stone rolled back. For it was very great. Mark 16, 2 · 4. [John 20, 1].

She [Magdalene] ran, therefore, and cometh to Simon Peter, and to the other disciple whom Jesus loved, and saith to them: "They have taken away the Lord out of the sepulchre, and we know not where they have laid Him." John 20, 2.

And entering into the sepulchre, they [the other two women] saw a young man sitting at the right side clothed with a white robe, and they were astonished. Mark 16, 5.

MKWho said to them: "Be not affrighted, you seek Jesus of Nazareth, Who was crucified; MTHe is not here, for He is risen as He said. Come, and see the place where the Lord was laid; and going quickly, MKtell His disciples and Peter, MTthat He is risen; and behold, He will go before you into Galilee, there you shall see Him, MKas He told you. MTLo! I have foretold it to you." Matt. 28, 5—8. Mark 16, 6—8.

MKBut they going out, fled from the sepulchre; for a trembling and fear had seized them; and they said nothing to any man, for they were afraid. MTAnd they went . . . quickly . . . with fear and great joy, running to tell His disciples.

LKBut [meantime] Peter, rising up, JNwent out, and that other disciple; and they came to the sepulchre. And they both ran together; and that other disciple did outrun Peter, and came first to the sepulchre; when he stooped down, he saw the linen cloths lying, but yet he went not in. Then Luke 24, 12] John 20, 3—10.

cometh Simon Peter following him, and went into the sepulchre, ^{LK}and stooping down he saw the linen cloths laid by themselves; ^{JN}and the napkin that had been about His head, not lying with the linen cloths, but apart, wrapped up into one place. Then that other disciple also went in, who came first to the sepulchre, and he saw and believed; for as yet they knew not the Scripture, that He must rise again from the dead. The disciples, therefore, departed again to their home, ^{LK}and went away wondering [each] in himself at that which had come to pass.

John 20, 11—17.

But Mary stood at the sepulchre without, weeping. Now as she was weeping, she stooped down, and looked into the sepulchre; and she saw two angels in white, sitting, one at the head, and one at the feet, where the body of Jesus had been laid. They say to her: "Woman, why weepest thou?" She saith to them: "Because they have taken away my Lord, and I know not where they have laid Him."

14. When she had thus said, she turned herself back, and saw Jesus standing; and she knew not that it was Jesus. Jesus saith to her: "Woman, why weepest thou? Whom seekest thou?" She, thinking that it was the gardener, saith to him: "Sir, if thou hast taken Him hence, tell me where thou hast laid Him, and I will take Him away."

16. Jesus saith to her: "Mary." She turning, saith to Him: "Rabboni" (which is to say: Master). Jesus saith to her: "Do not touch Me; for I am not yet ascended to My Father; but go to My brethren, and say to them: 'I ascend to My Father, and to your Father, to My God, and to your God.'"

Mark 16, 10.
John 20, 18.

^{JN}And Mary Magdalene ^{MK}went and told them

PART VI. THE DESCENT OF THE HOLY GHOST.

that had been with Him, who were mourning and weeping, ᴶᴺand telleth the disciples: "I have seen the Lord, and these things He said to me." ᴹᴷAnd they hearing that He was alive and had been seen by her, did not believe. *Mark 16, 11.*

And behold Jesus met them [also, the other two women], saying: "All hail." But they came up and took hold of His feet, and adored Him. Then Jesus said to them: "Fear not, go tell My brethren that they go into Galilee, there they shall see Me." *Matt. 28, 9, 10.*

Who when they were departed, behold some of the guards came into the city, and told the Chief Priests all things that had been done. And they being assembled together with the ancients, taking counsel, gave a great sum of money to the soldiers, saying: "Say you: His disciples came by night, and stole Him away when we were asleep. And if the Governor shall hear of this, we will persuade him and secure you." *Matt. 28, 11—15.*

So they taking the money, did as they were taught. And this word was spread abroad among the Jews even unto this day.

And [also] on the first day of the week, very early in the morning, they [St. Luke's party of women]¹ came to the sepulchre, bringing the spices which they had prepared, and they found the stone rolled back from the sepulchre. And going in, they found not the body of the Lord Jesus. And it came to pass, as they were astonished in their minds at this, behold two men stood by them in shining apparel. And as they were afraid and bowed down their countenance towards the ground, they said unto them: "Why seek you the living with the dead? *Luke 24, 1—11.*

¹ See note to page 210.

He is not here, but He is risen. Remember how He spoke unto you, when He was yet in Galilee, saying: 'The Son of Man must be delivered into the hands of sinful men, and be crucified; and the third day rise again.'" And they remembered His words. And going back from the sepulchre, they told all these things to the eleven and to all the rest.

And it was Mary Magdalene, and Joanna and Mary of James and the other women that were with them, who told these things to the Apostles. And these words seemed to them as idle tales; and they did not believe them.

[Mark 16, 12, 13.]
[Luke 24, 13—35.]

^{MK}After that He appeared in another shape to two of them walking as they were going into the country, ^{LK} to a town which was sixty furlongs from Jerusalem, named Emmaus. And they talked together of all these things which had happened. And it came to pass that, while they talked and reasoned with themselves, Jesus Himself also drawing near went with them; but their eyes were held that they should not know Him.

17. And He said to them: "What are these discourses, that you hold one with another as you walk, and are sad?" And the one of them whose name was Cleophas, answering, said to Him: "Art Thou only a stranger in Jerusalem, and hast not known the things that have been done there in these days?"

19. To whom He said: "What things?" And they said: "Concerning Jesus of Nazareth, Who was a Prophet, mighty in work and word before God and all the people; and how our Chief Priests and Princes delivered Him to be condemned to death, and crucified Him. But we hoped that it was He

that should have redeemed Israel; and now besides all this, to-day is the third day since these things were done. Yea, and certain women also of our company affrighted us, who before it was light were at the sepulchre, and not finding His body, came, saying that they had also seen a vision of angels, who say that He is alive. And some of our people went to the sepulchre, and found it so as the women had said, but Him they found not."

Then He said to them: "O foolish, and slow of [25.] heart to believe in all things which the prophets have spoken. Ought not Christ to have suffered these things, and so to enter into His glory?" And, beginning at Moses and all the prophets, He expounded to them in all the Scriptures the things that were concerning Him.

And they drew nigh to the town whither they [28.] were going; and He made as though He would go farther, but they constrained Him, saying: "Stay with us, because it is towards evening, and the day is now far spent." And He went in with them.

And it came to pass, while He was at table with [30.] them, He took bread, and blessed, and brake, and gave to them. And their eyes were opened, and they knew Him; and He vanished out of their sight. And they said one to the other: "Was not our heart burning within us, whilst He spoke in the way, and opened to us the Scriptures?"

And rising up the same hour, they went back to [33.] Jerusalem; and they found the eleven gathered together, and those that were with them, saying: "The Lord has risen indeed, and hath appeared to Simon." And they told what things were done in the way, and how they knew Him in the breaking of bread; [MK]neither did they believe them.

[JN]Now when it was late that same day, the first Luke 24, 36, 37. John 20, 19.

day of the week, and the doors were shut, where the disciples were gathered together for fear of the Jews, Jesus came and stood in the midst, and said to them: "Peace be to you, ᴸᴷit is I, fear not." But they, being troubled and affrighted, supposed that they saw a spirit.

_{Luke 24, 38, 39.} And He said to them: "Why are you troubled, and why do thoughts arise in your hearts? See My hands and feet, that it is I myself; handle and see; for a spirit hath not flesh and bones as you _{Luke 24, 40.} see Me to have." ᴸᴷAnd when He had said this, _{John 20, 20.} He showed them His hands and feet, ᴶᴺand His side. The disciples therefore were glad, when they saw the Lord.

_{Luke 24, 41—43.} But while they yet believed not, and wondered for joy, He said: "Have you here anything to eat?" And they offered Him a piece of broiled fish and a honeycomb. And when He had eaten before them, taking the remains He gave it to them.

_{John 20, 21—23.} He said therefore to them again: "Peace be to you. As the Father hath sent Me, I also send you." When He had said this, He breathed on them; and He said to them: "Receive ye the Holy Ghost; whose sins you shall forgive, they are forgiven them; and whose sins you shall retain, they are retained."

_{Luke 24, 44—48.} And He said to them: "These are the words which I spoke to you while I was yet with you: that all things must needs be fulfilled which are written in the law of Moses, and in the prophets, and in the Psalms, concerning Me."

Then He opened their understanding, that they might understand the Scriptures. And He said to them: "Thus it is written, and thus it behoved Christ to suffer, and to rise again from the dead the third day; and that penance and remission of sins should be preached in His name unto all nations, beginning at Jerusalem. And you are witnesses of these things."

Now Thomas, one of the twelve, who is called Didymus, was not with them when Jesus came. The other disciples therefore said to him: "We have seen the Lord." But he said to them: "Except I shall see in His hands the print of the nails, and put my finger into the place of the nails, and put my hand into His side, I will not believe." John 20, 24—31.

And after eight days, again His disciples were within, and Thomas with them. Jesus cometh, the doors being shut, and stood in the midst and said: "Peace be to you." Then He said to Thomas: "Put in thy finger hither, and see My hands; and bring hither thy hand, and put it into My side, and be not faithless but believing." Thomas answered and said to Him: "My Lord and my God." Jesus saith to him: "Because thou hast seen Me, Thomas, thou hast believed; blessed are they that have not seen, and have believed."

Many other signs also did Jesus in the sight of His disciples, which are not written in this book. But these are written that you may believe that Jesus is the Christ, the Son of God, and that, believing, you may have life in His name.

After this, Jesus showed Himself again to the disciples at the Sea of Tiberias[1] And He showed Himself after this manner. There were together Simon Peter, and Thomas who is called Didymus, and Nathanael who was of Cana in Galilee, and the sons of Zebedee, and two others of His disciples. John 21, 1—25.

---

[1] In Galilee, Mt. 28, 16.

Simon Peter saith to them: "I go a-fishing." They say to him: "We also come with thee." And they went forth and entered into the ship, and that night they caught nothing.

4. But when the morning was come, Jesus stood on the shore; yet the disciples knew not that it was Jesus. Jesus therefore said to them: "Children, have you any meat?" They answered Him: "No." He saith to them: "Cast the net on the right side of the ship, and you shall find." They cast therefore; and now they were not able to draw it for the multitude of fishes.

7. That disciple therefore whom Jesus loved, said to Peter: "It is the Lord." Simon Peter, when he heard that it was the Lord, girt his coat about him (for he was naked), and cast himself into the sea. But the other disciples came in the ship (for they were not far from the land, but as it were two hundred cubits), dragging the net with fishes.

9. And as soon as they came to land, they saw hot coals lying, and a fish laid thereon, and bread. Jesus saith to them: "Bring hither of the fishes which you have now caught. Simon Peter went up, and drew the net to land full of great fishes, one hundred and fifty-three; and although there were so many, the net was not broken. Jesus saith to them: "Come and dine." And none of them who were at meat durst ask Him: Who art Thou? knowing that it was the Lord. And Jesus cometh and taketh bread, and giveth them; and fish in like manner.

14. This is now the third time that Jesus was manifested to His disciples after He was risen from the dead.

When therefore they had dined, Jesus saith to Simon Peter: "Simon, son of John, lovest thou

Me more than these?" He saith to Him: "Yea, Lord, Thou knowest that I love Thee." He said to him: "Feed My lambs."

He saith to him again: "Simon, son of John, lovest thou Me?" He saith to Him: "Yea, Lord, Thou knowest that I love Thee." He saith to him: "Feed My lambs."

He said to him the third time: "Simon, son of John, lovest thou Me?" Peter was grieved because He had said to him the third time: Lovest thou Me? and he said to Him: "Lord, Thou knowest all things; Thou knowest that I love Thee." He saith to Him: "Feed My sheep.

"Amen, amen, I say to thee, when thou wast 18. younger thou didst gird thyself, and didst walk where thou wouldst. But when thou shalt be old, thou shalt stretch forth thy hand, and another shall gird thee, and lead thee whither thou wouldst not." And this He said signifying by what death he should glorify God. And when He had said this, He saith to him: "Follow Me."

Peter, turning about, saw that disciple whom 20. Jesus loved following, who also leaned on His breast at supper and said: Lord, who is he that shall betray Thee? Him therefore, when Peter had seen, he saith to Jesus: "Lord, and what shall this man do?" Jesus saith to him: "So I will have him to remain till I come, what is it to thee? follow thou Me."

This saying, therefore, went abroad among the 23. brethren, that that disciple should not die; and Jesus did not say to him, he should not die, but: So I will have him to remain till I come, what is it to thee? This is that disciple who giveth testimony of these things, and hath written these things; and we know that his testimony is true. But there are also many other things which Jesus did, which, if they were written every one, the world itself, I think, would not be able to contain the books that should be written—^{AT}of all things which Jesus began to do and to teach, until the day on which, giving commandment by the Holy Ghost to the Apostles whom He had chosen, He was taken up. To whom also He showed Himself alive after His Passion by many proofs, for forty days appearing to them, and speaking to them of the Kingdom of God.

Acts 1, 1—3.

And the eleven disciples went ... unto the mountain [in Galilee] where Jesus had appointed them.

Matt. 28, 16.

Then was He seen by more than five hundred brethren at once, of whom many remain until this present, and some are fallen asleep.

1 Cor. 15, 6.

And seeing Him they adored; but some doubted. And Jesus coming spoke to them, saying: "All power is given to Me in Heaven and in earth. Going, therefore, teach ye all nations, baptizing them in the name of the Father, and of the Son, and of the Holy Ghost. Teaching them to observe all things, whatsoever I have commanded you; and behold I am with you all days even to the consummation of the world."

Matt. 28, 17—20.

After that, He was seen by James.

1 Cor. 15, 7.

^{MK}At length[1] He appeared to the eleven as they were at table; and He upbraided them with their incredulity and hardness of heart, because they did not believe them who had seen Him, after He was risen again.

[Mark 16, 14.
1 Cor. 15, 7.]

^{AT}And eating together with them, He commanded them, that they should not depart from Jerusalem,

[Luke 24, 49.
Acts 1, 4, 5.]

---

[1] Literally : lastly.

but should wait for the promise of the Father, which "you have heard," saith He, "by My mouth; for John indeed baptized with water, but you shall be baptized with the Holy Ghost, not many days hence."

And He led them out as far as Bethania. Luke 24, 50.

They therefore who were come together, asked Him, saying: "Lord, wilt Thou at this time restore again the Kingdom to Israel?" But He said to them: "It is not for you to know the times or moments, which the Father has put in His own power; but you shall receive the power of the Holy Ghost coming upon you, and you shall be witnesses unto Me in Jerusalem, and in all Judea, and Samaria, and even to the uttermost part of the earth." Acts 1, 6—8.

And He said to them: "Go ye into the whole world and preach the Gospel to every creature. He that believeth and is baptized, shall be saved; but he that believeth not, shall be condemned. And these signs shall follow them that believe: In My name they shall cast out devils; they shall speak with new tongues; they shall take up serpents; and if they shall drink any deadly thing it shall not hurt them; they shall lay hands upon the sick, and they shall recover." Mark 16, 15—18.

^{MK}And the Lord Jesus, after He had spoken to them, ^{LK}lifting up His hands He blessed them. And it came to pass whilst He blessed them He departed from them; ^{AT}and . . . while they looked on, He was raised up, and a cloud received Him out of their sight; ^{LK}and [He] was carried up to Heaven, ^{MK}and sitteth on the right hand of God. Mark 16, 19.
Luke 24, 50, 51.
Acts 1, 9.

And while they were beholding Him going up to heaven, behold two men stood by them in white garments, who also said: "Ye men of Galilee, Acts 1, 10, 11.

why stand you looking up to Heaven? This Jesus Who is taken up from you into Heaven, shall so come as you have seen Him going into Heaven."

[Luke 24, 52.]
[Acts 1, 12—26.]

ᴸᴷAnd they adoring, went back into Jerusalem with great joy, ᴬᵀfrom the mount which is called Olivet, which is nigh Jerusalem, within a Sabbath-day's journey. And when they were come in, they went up into an upper room, where abode Peter and John, James and Andrew, Philip and Thomas, Bartholomew and Matthew, James of Alpheus and Simon Zelotes, and Jude the brother of James. All these were persevering with one mind in prayer with the women, and Mary the Mother of Jesus, and with His brethren.

15. In those days Peter rising up in the midst of the brethren said (now the number of persons together was about one hundred and twenty): "Men brethren, the Scripture must needs be fulfilled which the Holy Ghost spoke before by the mouth of David concerning Judas, who was the leader of them that apprehended Jesus; who was numbered with us, and had obtained part of this ministry. And he indeed hath possessed a field of the reward of iniquity, and being hanged, burst asunder in the midst, and all his bowels gushed out. And it became known to all the inhabitants of Jerusalem, so that the same field was called in their tongue: Haceldama, that is to say: The field of blood. For it is written in the Book of Psalms: *Let their habitation become desolate, and let there be none to dwell therein; and his bishopric let another take.*

21. "Wherefore of these men who have companied with us, all the time that the Lord Jesus came in and went out among us, beginning from the Baptism of John, until the day wherein He was

PART VI. THE DESCENT OF THE HOLY GHOST.

taken up from us, one of these must be made a witness with us of His Resurrection."

And they appointed two, Joseph, called Barsabas, who was surnamed Justus, and Mathias. And praying they said: "Thou Lord, Who knowest the hearts of all men, show whether of these two Thou hast chosen to take the place of this ministry and apostleship, from which Judas hath by transgression fallen, that he might go to his own place."

And they gave them lots, and the lot fell upon Mathias, and he was numbered with the eleven Apostles.

And they were always in the Temple, praising and blessing God. Amen.

And when the days of the Pentecost were accomplished, they were all together in one place. And suddenly there came a sound from heaven, as of a mighty wind coming, and it filled the whole house where they were sitting. And there appeared to them parted tongues as it were of fire, and it sat upon every one of them; and they were all filled with the Holy Ghost.

And they began to speak with divers tongues, according as the Holy Ghost gave them to speak.

Now there were dwelling at Jerusalem, Jews, devout men out of every nation under heaven. And when this was noised abroad, the multitude came together, and were confounded in mind because that every man heard them speak in his own tongue. And they were all amazed and wondered, saying: "Behold are not all these that speak, Galileans? And how have we heard every man our own tongue wherein we were born: Parthians, and Medes, and Elamites, and inhabitants of Mesopotamia, Judea and Cappadocia, Pontus and Asia, Phrygia and Pamphilia, Egypt and the parts of Lybia about Cyrene, and strangers of Rome; Jews, also, and proselytes, Cretes and Arabians, we have heard them speak in our own tongues the wonderful works of God." And they were all astonished, and wondered, saying one to another: "What meaneth this?" But others mocking, said: "These men are full of new wine."

But Peter standing up with the eleven, lifted up his voice, and spoke to them: "Ye men of Judea, and all you that dwell in Jerusalem, be this known to you, and with your ears receive my words; for these are not drunk as you suppose, seeing it is but the third hour of the day; but this is that which was spoken of by the Prophet Joel: *And it shall come to pass, in the last days (saith the Lord), I will pour out of My Spirit upon all flesh; and your sons and daughters shall prophesy, and your young men shall see visions, and your old men shall dream dreams. And upon My servants, indeed, and upon My handmaids will I pour out in those days of My Spirit, and they shall prophesy. And I will show wonders in the heaven above, and signs on the earth beneath, blood and fire, and vapour of smoke. The sun shall be turned into darkness, and the moon into blood, before the great and manifest day of the Lord come. And it shall come to pass that whosoever shall call upon the name of the Lord, shall be saved.*

"Ye men of Israel hear these words: Jesus of Nazareth, a man approved of God among you, by miracles and wonders and signs, which God did by Him in the midst of you as you also know; this same being delivered up by the determinate counsel and foreknowledge of God, you by the hands of wicked men have crucified and slain.

Whom God ·hath raised up, having loosed the sorrows of Hell, as it was impossible that He should be holden by it. For David saith concerning Him: *I foresaw the Lord before My face, because He is at My right hand that I may not be moved. For this My heart hath been glad and My tongue hath rejoiced; moreover My flesh also shall rest in hope; because Thou wilt not leave My Soul in Hell, nor suffer Thy Holy One to see corruption. Thou hast made known to Me the ways of life. Thou shalt make Me full of joy with Thy countenance.*

"Ye men, brethren, let me freely speak to you of the Patriarch David, that he died and was buried, and his sepulchre is with us to this present day. Whereas, therefore, he was a prophet and knew that God had sworn to him with an oath, that out of the fruit of his loins one should sit upon his throne; foreseeing this, he spoke of the Resurrection of Christ: for neither was He left in Hell, neither did His flesh see corruption.

"This Jesus hath God raised again, whereof all we are witnesses. Being exalted, therefore, by the right hand of God, and having received of the Father the promise of the Holy Ghost, He hath poured forth this which you see and hear. For David ascended not into Heaven, but he himself said: *The Lord said to my Lord, sit Thou at my right hand, until I make Thy enemies Thy footstool.* Therefore let all the house of Israel know most certainly that God hath made both Lord and Christ, this same Jesus Whom you have crucified."

Now when they had heard these things, they had compunction in their heart, and said to Peter and to the rest of the Apostles: "What shall we do, men and brethren?" But Peter said to them:

"Do penance and be baptized every one of you in the name of Jesus Christ, for the remission of your sins; and you shall receive the gift of the Holy Ghost. For the promise is to you and to your children, and to all that are afar off, whomsoever the Lord our God shall call."

40. And with very many other words did he testify and exhort them, saying: "Save yourselves from this perverse generation." They therefore that received his words were baptized; and there were added in that day about three thousand souls. And they were persevering in the doctrine of the Apostles, and in the communication of the breaking of bread, and in prayers. And fear came upon every soul. Many wonders also and signs were done by the Apostles in Jerusalem, and there was great fear in all. And all they that had believed were together and had all things in common; their possessions and goods they sold, and divided them to all, according as every one had need.

46. And continuing daily with one accord in the Temple, and breaking bread from house to house, they took their meat with gladness and simplicity of heart; praising God and having favour with all the people. And the Lord increased daily together such as should be saved.

Mark 16, 20. And they [the Apostles and disciples] going forth preached everywhere, the Lord working withal and confirming the word with signs that followed.

INDEX.

ST. MATTHEW.

CH.	VV.	PAGE	CH.	VV.	PAGE	CH.	VV.	PAGE
i.	1-25	6	ix.	9-13	45	xiii.	1-9	62
ii.	1-23	12		14-17	45		10-17	63
iii.	1-3	15		18-21	69		18-23	64
	4-6	16		22	70		24-30	64
	7-10	16		23-26	71		31,32	65
	11	17		27-34	71		33	66
	12	17		35	72		34,35	66
	13	17		36-38	72		36-53	66
	14,15	17	x.	1	72		54-58	72
	16,17	17		2-8	73	xiv.	1,2	76
iv.	1,2	19		9-11	73		3-12	76
	3-11	19		12,13	73		13	77
	11	20		14	73		13-21	78
	12	27		15-42	73		22-36	80
	13-16	32	xi.	1	75	xv.	1	84
	17-22	32		2-11	57		2-11	85
	23	34		12-15	58		12-14	86
	24,25	34		16-19	58		15-28	86
v.	1-48	35		20-24	117		29-31	87
vi.	1-34	38		25-27	118		32-39	88
vii.	1-29	40		28-30	119	xvi.	1-10	88
viii.	1	42	xii.	1-4	48		11,12	89
	2-4	43		5-7	48		13-16	90
	5-10	55		8-13	48		17-19	90
	11-13	56		14	51		20,21	90
	14-17	33		15,16	51		22,23	91
	18	67		17-21	52		24-28	91
	19-22	116		22,23	60	xvii.	1-3	91
	23-27	67		24-26	60		4-8	92
	28	68		27,28	60		9	92
	29	68		29	60		10-13	92
	30-34	68		30	60		14-16	93
ix.	1	69		31,32	61		17	94
	2	44		33-45	61		18	94
	2-8	44		46-50	62		19	94

p*

CH.	VV.	PAGE	CH.	VV.	PAGE	CH.	VV.	PAGE
xvii.	20	94	xxiv.	1-8	168	xxvii.	1	198
	21,22	94		9-13	169		2	198
	23-26	95		14	169		3-10	198
xviii.	1,2	95		15-18	169		11	199
	3,4	95		19	170		12-14	200
	5	96		20-25	170		15-17	201
	6	96		26-28	170		18	201
	7	96		29-31	171		19	201
	8,9	96		32-35	171		20,21	201
	10-35	97		36	172		22,23	202
xix.	1-3	142		37-44	172		24,25	202
	4-6	142		45-51	173		26	202
	7-9	143	xxv.	1-46	173		27-30	202
	10-12	143	xxvi.	1,2	176		31	204
	13,14	143		3-5	176		32	204
	15	144		6-13	151		33	204
	16-27	144		14-16	176		34	204
	28	145		17-20	177		35	205
	29	145		21-24	179		36	205
	30	145		25	179		37	205
xx.	1-16	145		26-28	184		38	205
	17-19	146		29	184		39,40	205
	20-28	147		30	191		41-43	206
	29-34	150		31-35	191		44	206
xxi.	1-3	152		36-44	191		45	207
	4,5	153		45,46	192		46,47	207
	6,7	153		47	192		48	207
	8	153		48,49	193		49	207
	9	153		50	193		50	207
	10,11	154		50	193		50	207
	12,13	156		51	193		51	207
	14-16	154		52	194		51-53	207
	17-19	156		52-54	194		54-56	208
	20-22	157		55,56	194		57,58	209
	23-27	157		56	194		58	209
	28-32	158		57	194		59,60	209
	33-46	158		57,58	196		61	209
xxii.	1-14	160		58	194		62-66	210
	15-32	161		58	195	xxviii.	1	211
	33	162		59-66	196		2-4	212
	34-40	162		67,68	197		5-8	213
	41-46	163		69,70	195		9,10	215
xxiii.	1	163		71,72	196		11-15	215
	2-5	163		73,74	197		16	222
	6,7	164		75	197		17-20	222
	8-39	164						

ST. MARK.

CH.	VV.	PAGE	CH.	VV.	PAGE	CH.	VV.	PAGE
i.	1	3	v.	1-3	68	ix.	29	94
	2-4	15		4,5	68		30,31	94
	5,6	16		6,7	68		32	95
	7,8	17		8-10	68		32-35	95
	9	17		11-17	68		36	96
	10,11	17		18-20	69		37-39	96
	12,13	19		21	69		40	96
	13	20		22-28	69		41	96
	14	27		29-33	70		42-47	96
	14-20	32		34	70		48-49	97
	21-28	33		35-38	70	x.	1,2	142
	29-34	33		39-43	71		3-5	142
	35-38	34	vi.	1-6	72		6-9	142
	39	34		7	72		10-12	143
	40-44	43		8-10	73		13-15	143
	45	43		11	73		16	144
ii.	1,2	44		12,13	75		17-28	144
	3	44		14	76		29,30	145
	4	44		15,16	76		31	145
	5-12	44		17-29	76		32	146
	13	45		30-44	78		32-34	146
	14-17	45		45-56	80		35-45	147
	18-22	45	vii.	1	84		46-52	150
	23-26	48		2-4	84	xi.	1-3	152
	27	48		5-16	85		4-7	153
	28	48		17-30	86		8	153
iii.	1-5	48		31-37	87		9,10	153
	6	51	viii.	1-10	88		11	154
	7	51		11-21	88		11-14	156
	7-12	51		22-26	89		15-17	156
	13-19	52		27-29	90		18	157
	20,21	56		30-32	90		19	157
	22-26	60		32,33	91		20-24	157
	27	60		34-39	91		25,26	157
	28,29	61	ix.	1-3	91		27-33	157
	30	61		4-7	92	xii.	1-12	158
	31-35	62		8	92		13-27	161
iv.	1-9	62		9	92		28-31	162
	10-12	63		10-12	92		32-34	163
	13	63		13-15	93		35-37	163
	14-20	64		16-19	93		38	163
	21-25	64		19	93		38-40	164
	26-29	65		20-23	93		41-44	166
	30-32	65		24-26	94	xiii.	1-9	168
	33,34	66		27	94		10	169
	35-40	67		28	94		11-13	169

CH.	VV.	PAGE	CH.	VV.	PAGE	CH.	VV.	PAGE
xiii.	14-16	169	xiv.	54	195	xv.	29,30	205
	17	170		55-64	196		31,32	206
	18-23	170		65	197		32	206
	24-27	171		66-68	195		33	207
	28-31	171		68	195		34,35	207
	32	172		69,70	196		36	207
	33-37	172		70-72	197		36	207
xiv.	1	176		72	197		37	207
	1,2	176	xv.	1	198		37	207
	3-9	151		1	198		38	207
	10,11	176		2	199		39-41	208
	12-17	177		3-5	200		42,43	209
	18-21	177		6-9	201		44	209
	22-24	184		10	201		45	209
	25	184		11	201		46	209
	26	191		12-14	202		47	210
	27-31	191		15	202	xvi.	1	211
	32-40	191		16-19	202		2-4	213
	41,42	192		20	204		5	213
	43	192		21	204		6-8	213
	44,45	193		22	204		9	213
	46	193		23	204		10	214
	47	193		24	205		11	215
	48,49	194		25	205		12,13	216
	50	194		25	205		14	222
	51,52	194		26	205		15-18	223
	53	194		27	205		19	223
	53,54	196		28	205		20	228
	54	194							

ST. LUKE.

CH.	VV.	PAGE	CH.	VV.	PAGE	CH.	VV.	PAGE
i.	1-4	2	iii.	21,22	17	v.	18	44
	5-56	3		23-38	18		19	44
	57-80	8	iv.	1,2	19		20-26	44
ii.	1-39	9		3-13	19		27-32	45
	40-52	14		14	30		33-39	45
iii.	1,2	15		14-30	31	vi.	1-4	48
	3-6	15		31-37	33		5-10	48
	7-9	16		38-41	33		11	51
	10-15	16		42,43	34		12-16	52
	16	17		44	34		17-49	53
	17	17	v.	1-12	42	vii.	1-9	55
	18	17		12-14	43		10	56
	19,20	27		15,16	43		11-18	56
	21	17		17	44		19-28	57

INDEX.

CH.	VV.	PAGE	CH.	VV.	PAGE	CH.	VV.	PAGE
vii.	29,30	58	x.	23,24	119	xxii.	39	191
	31-35	58		25-42	119		40-42	191
	36-50	58	xi.	1-54	120		43,44	192
viii.	1-3	60	xii.	1-59	125		45,46	191
	4-8	62	xiii.	1-35	129		47	192
	9,10	63	xiv.	1-35	132		48	193
	11-15	64	xv.	1-32	134		49	193
	16-18	64	xvi.	1-31	136		50	193
	19-21	62	xvii.	1-37	139		51	194
	22-25	67	xviii.	1-14	141		52,53	194
	26,27	68		15-17	143		54	194
	28	68		18-28	144		54	194
	29	68		29,30	145		54	196
	29-31	68		31-33	146		55	195
	32-37	68		34	147		55-57	195
	38,39	69		35-43	147		58	196
	40	69	xix.	1-28	148		59,60	197
	41-44	69		29-31	152		61,62	197
	44-47	70		32-35	153		63-65	197
	48	70		36	153		66-71	198
	49,50	70		37,38	153	xxiii.	1	198
	51-56	71		39-44	154		2	199
ix.	1,2	72		45,46	156		3	199
	3,4	73		47	157		4-16	200
	5	73		47,48	157		17	201
	6	75	xx.	1-8	157		18	201
	7,8	76		9-19	158		19	201
	8,9	76		20-38	161		20-23	202
	10-17	78		39,40	162		24,25	202
	18-20	90		41-44	163		26	204
	21,22	90		45	163		27-31	204
	23-27	91		46,47	164		32	204
	28-30	91	xxi.	1-4	166		33	204
	31,32	92		5-13	168		33	205
	33-36	92		14-19	169		34	205
	36	92		20,21	169		34	205
	37	93		22	170		35	205
	38-41	93		23	170		35	206
	42	93		24	170		36,37	206
	43	94		25-27	171		38	205
	44	94		28	171		39-43	206
	44,45	94		29-33	171		44,45	207
	46-48	95		34-36	171		45	207
	48	96		37,38	167		46	207
	48-50	96	xxii.	1	176		46	207
	51-56	115		2-6	176		46	207
	57-62	116		7-14	177		47-49	208
x.	1-12	117		15-18	177		50-52	209
	13-15	117		19,20	184		53	209
	16-20	118		21-23	179		54	209
	21,22	118		24-38	180		55,56	210

CH.	VV.	PAGE	CH.	VV.	PAGE	CH.	VV.	PAGE
xxiv.	1-11	215	xxiv.	40	218	xxiv.	50	223
	12	213		41-43	218		50,51	223
	13-35	216		44-48	218		52	224
	36,37	217		49	222		53	226
	38,39	218						

ST. JOHN.

CH.	VV.	PAGE	CH.	VV.	PAGE	CH.	VV.	PAGE
i.	1-14	1	xiii.	1	177	xix.	4-16	203
	15-18	17		2-20	178		16	204
	19-51	20		21,22	179		17	204
ii.	1-12	22		23-38	179		17	204
	13-25	24	xiv.	1-31	182		18	205
iii.	1-36	25	xv.	1-27	184		19-22	205
iv.	1-3	27	xvi.	1-33	186		23,24	205
	4-42	27	xvii.	1-26	188		24	205
	43-54	30	xviii.	1	191		25-27	206
v.	1-15	47		2	192		28	207
	16-47	49		3	192		29	207
vi.	1-13	78		4-9	193		30	207
	14-21	80		10	193		30	207
	22-72	81		11	194		31-37	208
vii.	1	94		11	194		38	209
	2-53	99		12,13	194		38	209
viii.	1-59	102		14	194		38,39	209
ix.	1-41	106		15	194		40,41	209
x.	1-42	109		15-17	195		42	209
xi.	1-54	111		18	195	xx.	1	213
	55,56	150		19-24	195		2	213
xii.	1	151		25	196		3-10	213
	2-8	151		26,27	197		11-17	214
	9-13	152		28-32	199		18	214
	14	152		33-38	199		19	217
	14-16	153		39	201		20	218
	17,18	153		40	201		21-23	218
	19-36	155	xix.	1	202		24-31	219
	37-50	167		2,3	202	xxi.	1-25	219

QUARTERLY SERIES.

1, 4. **The Life and Letters of St. Francis Xavier.**
By the Rev. H. J. Coleridge, S.J. Two vols. 10s. 6d.

2. **The Life of St. Jane Frances Fremyot de Chantal.** By Emily Bowles. 5s.

3. **The History of the Sacred Passion.** By Father Luis de la Palma, S.J. Translated from the Spanish. 5s.

6. **The Life of Dona Luisa de Carvajal.** By Lady Georgiana Fullerton. Second Edition, 3s. 6d.

7. **The Life of St. John Berchmans.** By the Rev. F. Goldie, S.J. 6s.

13. **The Story of St. Stanislaus Kostka.** Third and enlarged Edition. 4s. 6d.

15. **The Chronicle of St. Antony of Padua.** "The Eldest Son of St. Francis." Edited by the Rev. H. J. Coleridge, S.J. In Four Books. 5s. 6d.

18. **An English Carmelite.** The Life of Catherine Burton, Mother Mary Xaveria of the Angels, of the English Teresian Convent at Antwerp. Collected from her own writings, and other sources, by Father Thomas Hunter, S.J. 6s.

22. **The Suppression of the Society of Jesus** in the Portuguese Dominions. From documents hitherto unpublished. By the Rev. Alfred Weld, S.J. 7s. 6d.

23. **The Christian Reformed in Mind and Manners.** By Benedict Rogacci, S.J. The Translation edited by the Rev. H. J. Coleridge, S.J. 7s. 6d.

24. **The Sufferings of the Church in Brittany** during the Great Revolution. By Edward Healy Thompson. 6s. 6d.

25. **The Life of Margaret Mostyn** (Mother Margaret of Jesus), Religious of the Reformed Order of Our Blessed Lady of Mount Carmel (1625-1679). By the Very Rev. Edmund Bedingfield. 6s.

26. **The Life of Henrietta D'Osseville** (in Religion, Mother Ste. Marie), Foundress of the Institute of the Faithful Virgin. Arranged and Edited by the Rev. J. G. MacLeod, S.J. 5s. 6d.

30. **The Life of St. Thomas of Hereford.** By Father L'Estrange, S.J. 6s.

32. **The Life of King Alfred the Great.** By the Rev. A. G. Knight, S.J. 6s.

34, 58, 67. **The Life and Letters of St. Teresa.** Three Vols. By the Rev. H. J. Coleridge, S.J. 7s. 6d. each.

35, 52. **The Life of Mary Ward.** By Mary Catherine Elizabeth Chambers, of the Institute of the Blessed Virgin. Edited by the Rev. H. J. Coleridge, S.J. Two Vols. 15s.

39. **Pious Affections towards God and the Saints.** Meditations for Every Day in the Year, and for the principal Festivals. From the Latin of the Ven. Nicolas Lancicius, S.J. 7s. 6d.

40. **The Life of the Ven. Claude de la Colombiere.** Abridged from the French Life by Eugene Sequin, S.J. 5s.

41, 42. **The Life and Teaching of Jesus Christ** in Meditations for Every Day in the Year. By Father Nicolas Avancino, S.J. Two vols. 10s. 6d.

43. **The Life of Lady Falkland.** By Lady G. Fullerton. 5s.

47. **Gaston de Segur.** A Biography. Condensed from the French Memoir by the Marquis de Segur, by F. J. M. A. Partridge. 3s. 6d.

48. **The Tribunal of Conscience.** By Father Gaspar Druzbicki, S.J. 3s. 6d.

50. **Of Adoration in Spirit and Truth.** By Father J. Eusebius Nieremberg. With a Preface by the Rev. P. Gallwey, S.J. 6s. 6d.

56. **During the Persecution.** Autobiography of Father John Gerard, S.J. Translated from the original Latin by the Rev. G. R. Kingdon, S.J. 5s.

59. **The Hours of the Passion.** Taken from the "Life of Christ" by Ludolph the Saxon. 7s. 6d.

62. **The Life of Jane Dormer, Duchess of Feria.** By Henry Clifford. Transcribed from the Ancient Manuscript by the late Canon E. E. Estcourt, and edited by the Rev. Joseph Stevenson, S.J. 5s.

65. **The Life of St. Bridget of Sweden.** By F. J. M. A. Partridge. 6s.

66. **The Teachings and Counsels of St. Francis Xavier.** From his Letters. 5s.

70. **The Life of St. Alonso Rodriguez.** By the Rev. Francis Goldie, S.J. 7s. 6d.

71. **Chapters on the Parables.** By the Rev. H. J. Coleridge, S.J. 7s. 6d.

73. **Letters of St. Augustine.** Selected and Translated by Mary H. Allies. 6s. 6d.

74. **A Martyr from the Quarter-Deck.** Alexis Clerc, S.J. By The Lady Herbert. 5s.

75. **Acts of English Martyrs**, hitherto unpublished. By the Rev. John H. Pollen, S.J. With a Preface by the Rev. John Morris, S.J. 7s. 6d.

77. **The Life of St. Francis di Geronimo**, of the Society of Jesus. By A. M. Clarke. 6s.

79, 80. **Aquinas Ethicus; or, the Moral Teaching** of St. Thomas. By the Rev. Joseph Rickaby, S.J. 2 vols. 12s.

81. **The Spirit of St. Ignatius, Founder of the** Society of Jesus. Translated from the French of the Rev. Father Xavier de Franciosi, of the same Society. 6s.

82. **Jesus, the All-Beautiful.** A Devotional Treatise on the Character and Actions of our Lord. By the Author of *The Voice of the Sacred Heart* and *The Heart of Jesus of Nazareth.* Edited by the Rev. J. G. MacLeod, S.J. Second Edition. 6s. 6d.

83. **Saturday Dedicated to Mary.** From the Italian of Father Cabrini, S.J. With Preface and Introduction by the Rev. R. F. Clarke, S.J. 6s.

84. **The Life of Augustus Henry Law,** Priest of the Society of Jesus. By Ellis Schreiber. 6s.

85. **The Life of the Venerable Joseph Benedict Cottolengo,** Founder of the Little House of Providence in Turin. Compiled from the Italian Life of Don P. Gastaldi, by a Priest of the Society of Jesus. 4s. 6d.

86. **The Lights in Prayer** of the Ven. Louis de la Puente, the Ven. Claude de la Colombière, and the Rev. Father Paul Segneri. 5s.

87. **Two Ancient Treatises on Purgatory.** A Remembrance for the Living to Pray for the Dead, by Father James Mumford, S.J. And Purgatory Surveyed, by Father Richard Thimelby, S.J. With Introduction and an Appendix on the Heroic Act, by Father John Morris, S.J. 5s.

88. **Life of St. Francis Borgia.** By A. M. Clarke, author of the *Life of St. Francis di Geronimo.* The first Life of the Saint written in English. 6s. 6d.

89. **The Life of Blessed Antony Baldinucci.** By Father Francis Goldie, S.J. 6s.

90. **Distinguished Irishmen of the Sixteenth Century.** By the Rev. Edmund Hogan, S.J. 6s.

91. **Journals kept during Times of Retreat by** Father John Morris, S.J. Selected and Edited by Father J. H. Pollen, S.J. 6s.

92. **The Life of the Reverend Mother Mary of St. Euphrasia Pelletier,** First Superior General of the Congregation of Our Lady of Charity of the Good Shepherd of Angers. By A. M. Clarke. With Preface by His Eminence Cardinal Vaughan, Archbishop of Westminster. With Portrait. 6s.

WORKS ON THE LIFE OF OUR LORD.

BY THE REV. H. J. COLERIDGE, S.J.

Published in the Quarterly Series.

INTRODUCTORY VOLUMES.

19, 20. **The Life of our Life.** Introduction and Harmony of the Gospels, new edition, with the Introduction re-written. Two vols. 15s.

36. **The Works and Words of our Saviour,** gathered from the Four Gospels. 7s. 6d.

46. **The Story of the Gospels.** Harmonized for Meditation. 7s. 6d.

THE HOLY INFANCY.

49. **The Preparation of the Incarnation.** New Edition. 7s. 6d.

53. **The Nine Months.** The Life of our Lord in the Womb. 7s. 6d.

54. **The Thirty Years.** Our Lord's Infancy and Early Life. New Edition. 7s. 6d.

THE PUBLIC LIFE OF OUR LORD.

12. **The Ministry of St. John Baptist.** 6s. 6d.

14. **The Preaching of the Beatitudes.** New Edition. 6s. 6d.

17. **The Sermon on the Mount.** To the end of the Lord's Prayer. 6s. 6d.

27. **The Sermon on the Mount.** From the end of the Lord's Prayer. 6s. 6d.

31. The Training of the Apostles. Part I. 6s. 6d.
37. The Training of the Apostles. Part II. 6s. 6d.
45. The Training of the Apostles. Part III. 6s. 6d.
51. The Training of the Apostles. Part IV. 6s. 6d.
57. The Preaching of the Cross. Part I. 6s. 6d.
63. The Preaching of the Cross. Part II. 6s.
64. The Preaching of the Cross. Part III. 6s.

HOLY WEEK.

68. **Passiontide.** Part I. 6s. 6d.
72. **Passiontide.** Part II. 6s. 6d.
76. **Passiontide.** Part III. 6s. 6d.
78. The Passage of our Lord to the Father. 7s. 6d. Conclusion of *The Life of our Life*.

---

38. The Return of the King. Discourses on the Latter Days. By the Rev. H. J. Coleridge, S.J. Second Edition. 7s. 6d.
44. The Baptism of the King. Considerations on the Sacred Passion. By the Rev. H. J. Coleridge, S.J. 7s. 6d.
55. The Mother of the King. Mary during the Life of our Lord. By the Rev. H. J. Coleridge, S.J. 7s. 6d.
60. The Mother of the Church. Mary during the first Apostolic Age. By the Rev. H. J. Coleridge, S.J. 6s.
The Prisoners of the King. Thoughts on the Catholic Doctrine of Purgatory. By the Rev. H. J. Coleridge, S.J. New Edition. 4s.
The Seven Words of Mary. By the Rev. H. J. Coleridge, S.J. 2s.

BY THE LATE REV. JOHN MORRIS, S.J.

The Life and Martyrdom of St. Thomas Becket. Second and Enlarged Edition. In one vol. large post 8vo, 12s. 6d. Or in two volumes, 13s.

Catholic England in Modern Times. Royal 8vo, cloth, 1s. 6d. net.

Two Missionaries under Elizabeth. A Confessor and an Apostate. Demy 8vo, cloth. 14s.

The Catholics of York under Elizabeth. Demy 8vo, cloth. 14s.

The Life of Father John Gerard, S.J. Third Edition, re-written and enlarged, 14s.

The Letter-Books of Sir Amias Poulet, Keeper of Mary Queen of Scots. 3s. 6d.

The Venerable Sir Adrian Fortescue, Knight of the Bath, Knight of St. John, Martyr. With Portrait and Autograph. 1s. 6d.

Canterbury: Our old Metropolis. 9d.

The Tombs of the Archbishops in Canterbury Cathedral. 1s. 6d.

Canterbury. A Guide for Catholics. With Plans. 1d.

The Heroic Act of Charity in behalf of the Souls in Purgatory. 1d.

Instructions for Novices in Daily Duties, Meditation, Vocation. Cloth, post free, 2s. net.; or in three separate parts, paper wrapper, 6d. net, by post, 7d.

HISTORICAL PAPERS.

EDITED BY THE LATE REV. JOHN MORRIS, S.J.

1. **The Spanish Inquisition.** By the Rev. Sydney F. Smith, S.J. 1d.
2. **The False Decretals.** By the Rev. Richard F. Clarke, S.J. 1d.
3. **Cranmer and Anne Boleyn.** By the Rev. Joseph Stevenson, S.J. 2d.

4. **The Pallium.** By the Rev. Herbert Thurston, S.J. 2d.
5. **The Immuring of Nuns.** By the Rev. Herbert Thurston, S.J. 1d.
6. **The Huguenots.** By the Rev. William Loughnan, S.J. 1d.
7. **How "the Church of England washed her Face."** By the Rev. Sydney F. Smith, S.J. 1d.
8. **St. Bartholomew's Day, 1572.** By the Rev. William Loughnan, S.J. 1d.
9. **The Rood of Boxley,** or How a Lie Grows. By the Rev. T. E. Bridgett, C.SS.R. 3d.
10. **The First Experiment in Civil and Religious Liberty.** By James Carmont. 1d.
11. **Was St. Aidan an Anglican?** By the Rev. Sydney F. Smith, S.J. 1d.
12. **The Gordon Riots.** By Lionel Johnson, B.A. 1d.
13. **The Great Schism of the West.** By the Rev. Sydney F. Smith, S.J. 2d.
14. **Rome's Witness against Anglican Orders.** By the Rev. Sydney F. Smith, S.J. 2d.

EDITED BY THE REV. SYDNEY F. SMITH, S.J.

15. **The Book of Common Prayer and the Mass.** By the Rev. R. C. Laing. 1d.
16. **Religious Instruction in England during the Fourteenth and Fifteenth Centuries.** By Dom Francis Aidan Gasquet, O.S.B. 2d.
17. **England's Title: Our Lady's Dowry: Its History and Meaning.** By the Rev. T. E. Bridgett, C.SS.R. 1d.

The above numbers in three volumes, bound in cloth, 1s. each.

18. **Dr. Littledale's Theory of the Disappearance** of the Papacy. By the Rev. Sydney F. Smith, S.J. 2d.
19. **Dean Farrar on the Observance of Good Friday.** By the Rev. Herbert Thurston, S.J. 1d.
20. **Savonarola and the Reformation.** By the Very Rev. J. Proctor, O.P. 3d.

English Manuals of Catholic Theology.

OUTLINES OF DOGMATIC THEOLOGY.

BY

SYLVESTER JOSEPH HUNTER, S.J.

Three Volumes.   Price 6s. 6d. each.

TREATISES.

VOL. I.—TREATISE	I.	The Christian Revelation.
,,	II.	The Channel of Doctrine.
,,	III.	Holy Scripture.
,,	IV.	The Church.
,,	V.	The Roman Pontiff.
,,	VI.	Faith.
VOL. II.—TREATISE	VII.	The One God.
,,	VIII.	The Blessed Trinity.
,,	IX.	The Creation. The Angels.
,,	X.	Man Created and Fallen.
,,	XI.	The Incarnation.
,,	XII.	The Blessed Virgin.
VOL. III.—TREATISE	XIII.	Actual Grace.
,,	XIV.	Justification.
,,	XV.	The Sacraments in General.
,,	XVI.	Baptism.
,,	XVII.	Confirmation.
,,	XVIII.	The Holy Eucharist.
,,	XIX.	Penance.
,,	XX.	Extreme Unction.
,,	XXI.	Orders.
,,	XXII.	Matrimony.
,,	XXIII.	The Four Last Things.

Opinions of the Press on "Outlines of Dogmatic Theology."

"The second volume of Father Hunter's *Outlines of Dogmatic Theology* has just reached us, and we hasten to lay before our readers some of the impressions which a necessarily hasty perusal of a lengthy closely-reasoned book of nearly six hundred pages has made upon us. To our thinking the learned author has succeeded admirably in his praiseworthy purpose of putting before the English-speaking public, Catholic and otherwise, the outlines, at least, of those scientific treatises of dogmatic theology whose more detailed and fuller study is the proper duty of the ecclesiastical student.... Many interesting pieces of information about the tenets of the numerous non-Catholic sects around us are to be found up and down this volume; information which we ought to have at hand, but which it is difficult to procure.... The student will find it a very valuable companion to the lengthier works in common use in our seminaries; even the ordinary reader, anxious to gain a fuller knowledge of 'the faith once delivered to the saints,' will be charmed by the easy style and logical sequence of the treatises and chapters, which open out a vista of those magnificent truths which have for eighteen centuries employed the prayerful studies of generations of learned men, and which will be for all eternity a wonder ever new when faith has given place to vision.... The book is a learned, valuable, and frankly honest introduction to the noblest and most necessary of sciences."—*The Tablet*, August 31, 1895.

"Father Hunter's work is of distinct advantage, and should be widely read. His exposition is all that could be desired—lucid and cogent. Keeping close to the principles of St. Thomas Aquinas, the Rev. author does not refuse to glance at modern errors, which gives his book a decided value. The opening treatise of the volume before us [vol. ii.]—that on "The One God"—introduces such difficult matters as the *scientia-media*, free-will, the problem of evil, and is, therefore, one of a character to test the powers of a writer. Father Hunter's account of them leaves nothing to be desired. We wish the work a wide circulation, alike among Catholics and non-Catholics."—*Freeman's Journal*, August 16, 1895.

"The style of Father Hunter is remarkably clear; his diction has a legal accuracy, and is entirely free from any technicalities of foreign turns. This instances a distinct development of the English language as now handled by Catholic writers, who make it rich in Catholic phraseology without detracting from its purity. And, apart from the phraseology, this work enriches the literature itself with a new edition of what has been so long denied to it, the classic statement of truths, which it is the one thing necessary to know and to embody in thought and life."—*American Ecclesiastical Review*, April, 1895.

"It is the desire of the Church that all who have the opportunity should study her theology. She by no means desires to confine this useful and interesting pursuit of truth to those whose official duty it is, or will be, to teach the truths of faith. Father Hunter, in publishing his present work, has endeavoured to place in the hands of all a suitable means of carrying into effect this wish of the Catholic Church.... The general order of the work is admirable. The style is for the most part sufficiently attractive for subjects of the nature discussed in the volume. The arguments are nearly always cogent. Hence its utility, especially in countries where Protestantism is the principal error to be avoided, cannot be doubted."—*Irish Ecclesiastical Record*, March, 1895.

ENGLISH MANUALS OF CATHOLIC PHILOSOPHY.

(STONYHURST SERIES.)

EDITED BY RICHARD F. CLARKE, S.J.

Extract from a Letter of His Holiness the Pope to the Bishop of Salford, on the Philosophical Course at Stonyhurst.

"You will easily understand, Venerable Brother, the pleasure We felt in what you reported to Us about the College of Stonyhurst in your diocese, namely, that by the efforts of the Superiors of this College, an excellent course of the exact sciences has been successfully set on foot, by establishing professorships, and by publishing in the vernacular for their students text-books of Philosophy, following the principles of St. Thomas Aquinas. On this work We earnestly congratulate the Superiors and teachers of the College, and by letter We wish affectionately to express Our good-will towards them."

---

1. **Logic.** By RICHARD F. CLARKE, S.J., formerly Fellow and Tutor of St. John's College, Oxford. Second Edition. Price 5s.

2. **First Principles of Knowledge.** By JOHN RICKABY, S.J., late Professor of Logic and General Metaphysics at St. Mary's Hall, Stonyhurst. Second Edition. Price 5s.

3. **Moral Philosophy (Ethics and Natural Law).** By JOSEPH RICKABY, S.J., M.A. Lond.; late Professor of Ethics at St. Mary's Hall, Stonyhurst. Third Edition. Price 5s.

4. **Natural Theology.** By BERNARD BOEDDER, S.J., Professor of Natural Theology at St. Mary's Hall, Stonyhurst. Price 6s. 6d.

5. **Psychology.** By MICHAEL MAHER, S.J., M.A. Lond.; Professor of Mental Philosophy at Stonyhurst. Second Edition. Price 6s. 6d.

6. **General Metaphysics.** By JOHN RICKABY, S.J. Second Edition. Price 5s.

Supplementary Volume.

Political Economy. By C. S. DEVAS, Esq., M.A., Examiner in Political Economy in the Royal University of Ireland. Price 6s. 6d.

Opinions of the Press on "Manuals of Catholic Philosophy."

LOGIC.

"An excellent text-book of Aristotelian logic, interesting, vivid, sometimes almost racy in its illustrations, while from first to last it never, so far as we have noticed, diverges from Aristotelian orthodoxy."—*Guardian.*

FIRST PRINCIPLES OF KNOWLEDGE.

"It is a hopeful sign of the times that a Catholic professor should freely enter the lists of debate in opposition to acknowledged masters of recent philosophy. The Jesuit Father is no respecter of persons."—*Journal of Education.*

MORAL PHILOSOPHY.

"The style of the book is bright and easy, and the English (as we need not say) extremely good. . . . The manual will be welcome on all sides as a sound, original, and fairly complete English treatise on the groundwork of morality."—*Dublin Review.*

"Father Rickaby, with his Aristotelian and scholastic training, is always definite and clear, distrustful of sentiment, with an answer ready for every assailant."—*Mind*, No. 54.

NATURAL THEOLOGY.

"This volume considerably increases the debt which English-speaking Catholics owe to the Jesuit Fathers who have brought out the 'Stonyhurst Series' of philosophical manuals. It is really a treatise *de Deo* dealing with the proofs of the existence of God, the Divine attributes, and the relation of God to the world—in plain intelligible English, and adapted to the difficulties raised in our own country at the present day. The author is evidently well acquainted with Mill, Spencer, Huxley, and other contemporary writers; they are quoted freely and clearly answered."—*Dublin Review*, October, 1891.

PSYCHOLOGY.

"Father Maher's joining of old with new in his *Psychology* is very skilful; and sometimes the highly systematized character of the scholastic doctrine gives him a certain advantage in the face of modern psychological classifications with their more tentative character. . . . The historical and controversial parts all through the volume are in general very carefully and well managed."—*Mind.*

"This work cannot be too highly recommended."—*The Tablet*, November 1, 1890.

GENERAL METAPHYSICS.

"It will be seen, then, that we deny the merit of profundity to Father Rickaby's work; it will, however, do more good than harm; it is full of a learning rare and curious in England, and is tempered by an English common sense and a real acquaintance with English thought."—*Athenæum*, April 18, 1891.

POLITICAL ECONOMY.

"A concise but extraordinarily comprehensive text-book, with plenty of human interest, attractive—if now and then rather slight—illustrations from real life—and last, but not least, a clear, and on the whole a correct, exposition of the elements of economic science."—*Speaker.*

www.ingramcontent.com/pod-product-compliance
Lightning Source LLC
Chambersburg PA
CBHW031352230426
43670CB00006B/512